THE WRITER'S SURVIVAL GUIDE

THE WRITER'S SURVIVAL GUIDE

by
Jean Rosenbaum, M.D. & Veryl Rosenbaum, Psa.

Writer's
Digest
Books

Cincinnati, Ohio

Library of Congress Cataloging in Publication Data

Rosenbaum, Jean
    The writer's survival guide.
    Includes index.
    1. Authorship—Psychological aspects.
I. Rosenbaum, Veryl. II. Title.
PN151.R67   808'.025'019   82-2072
ISBN 0-89879-056-5   AACR2

Book design by Barron Krody.

To our cherished friends,
Lucille and Todd Webb,
for their artistic example
and decades of creative support.

Contents

slow you down . . . take the active role . . . Discovering what causes your work to be returned . . . False notions about rejections . . . Normal reactions to rejection . . . Channeling anger and releasing frustration . . . A practical plan for cleaning up your act.

Chapter Four
Your Psychohistory: An Aid to Creativity 67

Constructing your personal psychohistory . . . Understanding your unconscious tape recording . . . Revealing hidden memories . . . Unlocking repressed feelings . . . Freeing up creative energies . . . How to borrow from your past and strengthen your writing.

Chapter Five
Guilt and the Creative Process 89

Why writers must learn to deal with guilt . . . The single most insidious time waster . . . How the unconscious affects your writing . . . Understanding and overcoming the negative forces that cause guilt . . . Guilt triggers, buried and obvious . . . Reshaping the super-ego for greater creativity.

Chapter Six
Psychological Blocks Against Creativity 107

The price of creativity . . . How to deal with loneliness, depression, anxiety and anger . . . Solving emotional conflicts increases creative energies . . . When to seek a psychotherapist and how to shop for one . . . A simple tool for preventing and overcoming writer's block . . . Alcohol, drugs and the writer.

Chapter Seven
Developing a Productive Lifestyle 151

How to plan and set in motion a lifestyle for optimum creativity

. . . Overcoming self-indulgent habits . . . Identifying and avoiding superficial commitments . . . Controlling your environment and creating an effective writing atmosphere . . . How to stay healthy, creative, and sane.

Chapter Eight
Developing an Emotional Support System

Buffer the isolation of your craft . . . Making healthy and happy people connections . . . Balancing creative pursuits with personal contentment . . . How having friends of both sexes can enhance your creativity . . . Avoiding people who are threatened by creativity . . . Dealing with jealousy . . . How to handle an envious friend or mate.

Chapter Nine
You Are in Business

You're in business . . . Overcoming the "artistic" myth . . . Developing realistic expectations . . . How to be assertive . . . How to present yourself professionally . . . Transference, what it is, and how it can subtly undermine editorial relationships.

Chapter Ten
The Special Problems of Success

How will you deal with success? . . . Examining your fantasies . . . Will success cause writer's block? . . . Handling the reactions of others . . . Using success to increase creativity and grow as a person . . . Should you answer all your fan mail? . . . Learning the art of celebration.

Chapter Eleven
The Psychology of Media Promotion

How to be charming and informative when dealing with the media . . . Overcoming shyness . . . An inside look at television and radio . . . How to give enjoyable and entertaining interviews . . . Training for the tour . . . What to expect from

publishers and publicity people . . . Staying sane on tour . . .
The writer as performer.

Chapter Twelve

Introduction

BEING A WRITER—whether part time or full time—means you must handle unique problems. You must learn to cope with a variety of internal and external stresses that interfere with creativity.

How do you forge optimistically on when the mail brings four rejections? What can you do to allay those nagging doubts about your talents? How can you juggle a job and a family and still find time to ponder ideas and write? Can you keep believing in yourself as a writer despite paralyzing procrastination or a total blackout of ideas? How do you cope with the surprise of success?

This book answers these questions and discusses many other maladies that plague writers, offering you a guide to survival in a profession fraught with insecurity.

We (your authors) are practicing psychoanalysts and active freelance writers. Over a combined forty years of practice we have discovered solutions to many of the problems you undoubtedly have faced and most likely will face as a writer. For instance, we have found that by gaining insight into yourself and the unconscious motivations of your personality, you can free up psychological energies that can be used to increase your creativity.

It is our hope and our aim to help make your life as a writer more enjoyable and satisfying by showing how you can deal effectively with the highs and lows that are part and parcel of your chosen craft.

This book is for you, the writer, to help you as you pursue one of the most lonely, difficult, demanding, and ultimately rewarding of professions.

Chapter One

The Creative Personality

CHOOSING TO BE a writer sets you apart from the general population. While others work with the security of a regular paycheck, you are usually self-employed, without financial guarantees. On the positive side, you are the recorder, predictor, and visionary of your society, able to stimulate thought, entertain, influence opinion, reveal beauty, expose ugliness—touch your audience's heart and mind through the power of words. The writer's life is often lonely and discouraging, but anyone who accepts the calling harbors a secret pride in his membership in the family of writers.

Beginner or veteran, we all share distinct traits that push us in the direction of original writing.

Declaring Your Creativity

The recurring desire to communicate thoughts and feelings with words on paper classifies you as a creative person.

Do you feel uncomfortable about accepting creativity as a part of your personality? Even established authors often mumble modestly and squirm uneasily when called upon to discuss their creative gifts.

The creative mystique needs to be replaced with an understanding of what it means to be creative. You are a creative writer if you think of original ideas or fresh approaches to concepts and feel compelled to express yourself by transforming your thoughts into language.

Being creative is not magical, though feeling the hum of creative energy working inside your mind *can* transcend most human experiences. The work involved in transferring that persistent murmur into individual expression quickly removes any mystical notions about creativity.

Creative writers can't count on inspiration from the elusive muse. They must dedicate themselves to improving their craft, and must commit themselves to expending a great deal of energy in order to achieve success, probably with little outside encouragement.

In order to feel comfortable about defining yourself as creative, you must have a genuine love of writing and a degree of confidence that you can succeed. Modesty is irrelevant if you are creative. But creativity doesn't automatically mean superiority, either; affirming your creativity doesn't mean you're jumping onto an elitist platform. What you do with your gift will determine its ultimate value.

Some talented people shy away from the "creative" label because they know that artistic commitment involves a personal responsibility to produce. If you hide behind the safety of, "I'm not really *very* creative," then you can avoid the obligations of an active artist. But you will also never experience the stimulating challenge of your gift or enjoy the pleasure of competing in the business side of writing.

Perhaps you're an experienced writer, or possibly you have not yet experienced and discovered your vehicle of expression—fiction, poetry, editorials, inspirational or informative nonfiction, plays, cartoons, screenplays, speeches, or fillers. Whichever avenue you explore, or have chosen, your confidence and productivity will grow when you use the psychological aids set forth in the following chapters.

The Family of Writers

Writers belong to a very special family of artists, related to each other by their unique talents. Welcome to the family, where there's always room for one more obsessed observer, keenly watching and recording.

Getting Started

"I have an idea for a novel about the fears of a young person about to leave home. I'm shy about taking the giant step from idea to writing it down. It's too early to tell people I'm a writer, isn't it?" says Janet, a college sophomore. "Don't you need writing credentials before an editor will read your work?"

Even the most successful writers began their careers with apprehensions, but they forged ahead through the thicket of fears and anxieties and started to write. Your first efforts may never see print, but they will have launched you as a writer, creating work that reflects your unique perceptions.

If you, like Janet, feel uncomfortable about announcing artistic intentions, don't tell anyone until you have finished a project. Completed material will give you the confidence to call yourself a writer.

When you identify yourself as a writer, you'll meet people who will dole out respect only if you're published. Even then, there are nonwriting snobs who inquire in a disbelieving tone about the name of the magazine or book publisher before they accept you as worthwhile. They may discount your work if the publisher is not well known. Some people judge a writer inconsequential if he directs his talents to nonfiction, while others think poetry is a waste of time. You can't count on noncreative people who don't understand the complexities of writing to make you feel good about your decision to be a writer. You don't have to defend or explain your career, what you write about, or why you continue in the face of rejection. Your sense of career identity must come from within, and from your accomplishments—the opinions of others—good, bad, or indifferent—are really irrelevant.

People who talk down to you or make you feel defensive are threatened by the mysteries of the written word and by the courage it takes to become a freelancer.

A novice poet received a letter from an editor harshly rejecting her submission and suggesting that she stop sending out such inferior work and leave poetry to serious artists. The author was momentarily crushed and deflated. She was sure that her poetry was well written. Instead of yielding to this minor critic, she continued to write and submit her works to literary magazines. To date she has published over five hundred poems and has received several prizes. "That editor may well have forced me to prove that I was not just the dabbler she insinuated. I was just twenty, but I had a strong enough belief in my talents to put aside her negative judgment."

Take the first step. Begin to write, and then write some more. Keep writing until you are satisfied enough with your efforts to participate in the business side of writing—submissions to the marketplace. Creativity does not exempt you from handling business details, contrary to the head-in-the-clouds attitude of artists of every stripe.

The documented "acceptance" known as publication is not a prerequisite to belonging to the vast and multitalented writers' family. Your writing efforts and willingness to compete are your credentials.

Of course, in order to achieve what most of us consider writing success—publication—a beginner must study and become proficient with practical writing tools and the conventions of his profession, such as submission requirements. A firm grasp of the mechanics is necessary to any trade. Those acquired skills speak for themselves when a writer queries an editor with a carefully constructed, well-researched letter or presents a cleanly typed, error-free manuscript. Editors are not interested in your age, education, race, or creed. What they want is demonstrated excellence of craft and they will eagerly accept and acknowledge any material that measures up to their standards.

The Fear of Writing

Mr. Matthews, a creative writing instructor we took a course from, urged us to write something every day. "Write and continue to write until the act itself becomes a part of your daily routine. Don't think of writing as alien and full of roadblocks. If you write every day, you'll incorporate it as a valuable, learned skill, just like learning to walk and talk eventually become natural. You stumbled a lot when you were developing verbal and motor aptitudes and should expect the same starts and stops as a writer.

"Do not imagine a stern critic leaning over your shoulder, scowling and scoffing at your efforts. Get in touch with that driving force for personal expression common to creative people and use it to propel you to keep trying."

Mr. Matthews offered encouragement, criticism, and advice to his aspiring students as we filled reams of paper with amateurish poems, plays, and stories. His goal was to get students comfortable with the *act* of writing. He knew that many beginning writers had an actual fear of putting words on paper. He thought they stymied themselves by assuming that rough drafts required perfection.

"First write down your thoughts and feelings, then we'll worry about refinements. Getting the ideas down is the most important thing at the start—the particular combination of words you first use is not sacred. Specific word combinations can become extremely valuable once you rewrite them to crystal clarity. Even then, they are subject to change and improvement."

Adopting this view of one's first drafts breaks down the unfounded fear of writing. Your identity as a writer will deepen and solidify in proportion to the amount of words you produce. Your self-image will strengthen, doubts will be reduced, and your psychic energies will flow into your creative storehouse.

A Personality Profile

Who are the members of this family of writers? We come in all shapes, sizes, ages, races, temperaments, backgrounds, and social classes.

Writers share several personality characteristics that set them apart from the general population. In fact, these traits are largely the reason some people routinely label writers eccentric, weird, and just plain crazy. However, these are also the characteristics that make writers a very special and favored breed.

Modes of Expression

Can you express yourself more effectively in writing than speaking?

The quiet and unhurried process of writing is very different from spontaneous speaking. Before you write down the words that become a story, a progression of ideas, imaginative rumination (plot, characters, style), and a sifting of options about action takes place. While writing, you can stop to consider precise wording to add spice and clarity to the subject. You can observe and judge the first draft, avoiding the evaluation of others.

Some fortunate authors are at ease with both verbal and written forms of communication, but most feel more at home expressing their ideas in writing.

The price of success often includes promoting your product. You can't stand up and say, "Read my book." Instead you have to explain why the reader should spend his money to learn what you have to say. "I'd rather type than talk," reports Reuben, a writer of self-help books. "In reality, writing advice books or articles means you must learn to speak confidently about your subject. I try to sidestep giving a lecture and ask audiences to hand me questions, which I can answer in short spurts. I've forced myself to look relaxed and to talk casually. I can achieve this state by rereading my book very carefully before I give a talk or appear on television."

Some writers say they prefer writing to talking because they think faster than they speak and end up spluttering and stuttering. Others complain that people expect them to have an extensive vocabulary and perfect grammar and feel they are on stage.

In actuality, you don't have to prove your skill with words every time you speak just because you're a writer. You only have to prove your skill when you write a query letter, work on an assignment, or submit a completed manuscript.

The Watchers

Do you constantly notice and remember people's mannerisms, voice patterns, facial contours, and reactions?

Writers are watchers, silently making notes on everything, even in the most mundane circumstances.

For example, many people consider passing through airports an unpleasant interlude of travel. But writers rarely "pass through" any event. A crowded terminal becomes a feast to the writer's eye, affording endless opportunities to note peculiarities of dress, speech, and behavior. A writer is unable to resist eavesdropping on strangers' conversations. Alert and sensitive, the ever-curious writer stores away and records the drama of human interaction. The writer waits impatiently for takeoffs and arrivals, just like other passengers. But the author moves beyond personal inconvenience, mentally preserving the scene for a future story.

Writers observe, scan, and make notes while others glide through experiences with no special awareness of the moment's texture. This trait is often so automatic that authors assume everyone is reading the scene.

A good exercise to practice sketches of a variety of people can be done in airports, bus depots, or train stations. Write down quick descriptions of the physical characteristics of passengers, their behavior and attitudes. You'll learn to note the amazing differences among people and become adept at distinguishing characters by describing their personal styles.

"I wrote a prize-winning short story in the baggage claim at a large airport," said Marilyn, film critic and short story writer. "It was about the stone-faced attendant who, with machinelike precision, processed the irate passengers' complaints of lost luggage. The group of strangers was united by anxiety and anger against the woman, adding a psychological edge to my story, which told about a nun, a reporter, and a gangster thrown together in an airport because of lost luggage, and how they reacted to the uncaring attendant and each other. I was so busy scribbling my ideas that I almost missed my turn to hassle the bored airline representative."

The Probers

Do you tend to question pronouncements by authority figures? Most writers are questioners, probing beyond superficiality. You probably aren't content to receive information passively. One of the main reasons writers are compelled to communicate is to stimulate thought or express different viewpoints. Writers are interested in authenticity—they cannot accept statements at face value just because a person with authority speaks.

"My writing career started during the Vietnam era," recounts Jamie, a poet. "Until then I only worried about finishing school and earning a living, never in my twenty-six years thinking I was creative.

"Enraged by the horrors of that war, I started writing poetry that showed my distrust and disgust for politicians and the military. The act of writing released my pent-up fury, but I wanted to reach others so I submitted to poetry magazines. A surge of anti-war little mags began at that time. Letters from fellow poets further expanded my awareness and sparked creative ideas.

"My latent creativity needed a cause to wake it up. Current-events apathy came to an end for me during those years. Now when I hear politicians making bland, double-talk statements, hiding information to fool the public, it propels me to my typewriter to bang out more social commentary poetry."

Sheila, an investigative reporter, recounts that her parents encouraged their offspring to dissect and discuss daily world events. "They believed it was lazy to accept information like a sponge. I became interested in journalism during high school largely because my parents talked so much about finding out the facts: My mother's motto was, 'If you don't ask questions, you'll soon stop thinking.' "

Your inquiring bent can improve and give depth to your writing. When typing a fact or opinion, mentally assume a skeptical reader's position, demanding adequate clarification, and become the first critic to read your statement.

The Different Ones

Did you feel different from your peers when you were growing up?

Everyone experiences feeling peculiar and alone at some point or other during the developmental years because individual growth is so variable. For example, children who begin puberty before their friends feel out of place until their peers catch up. But children born with special gifts almost always feel a distinct and ongoing separation between themselves and others, even though they may not be able to precisely define that difference.

Those who are destined to become writers begin wondering about the hows and whys of the world long before normal children. When gifted youngsters share their ideas with playmates, they are often met with blank stares or flat-out rejections. In order to fit in, creative children may cover up their divergent thoughts and pretend to be like everyone else, while at the same time feeling like aliens. Many artists have told us that they didn't meet other creative people until their teens, whereupon they enjoyed a great sense of relief and camaraderie to be with others who felt the need to express themselves with original works.

"When I was five, my head was filled with a marvelous fantasy world, occupied by miniature people who lived on a tiny planet," remembers Jonathan, a mystery writer. "I talked about my fantasy characters as if they were real. My playmates wanted proof of my minuscule people and planet, and wouldn't believe they existed. I became frustrated because they couldn't use their imaginations. My reserved parents talked only when giving orders or to discuss 'reality.' They were confounded when I began intense and excited descriptions of my specal world.

"I felt out of place with my stodgy parents and bored with my friends. Luckily, my sister was enthralled with my fantasies. She would listen intently, always eager for more details. I loved her adoration and belief in my stories.

"Today, sitting at my writing desk, I imagine her bright, glowing face cajoling me for the next installment. The vision spurs me on when I'm stuck for intriguing twists in a mystery.

"I was 'different' but, until high school, was unable to think of that distinction in a positive way. An English teacher assigned us to write personal sketches about childhood memories. When she read the story of my tiny kingdom, she used it as an example of creative children's fantasies. She could have placed a crown upon my giddy head, for she was the first adult to appreciate my gift. I decided to become a writer that very moment."

Fredricka, a playwright, remembers, "I was different from my neighborhood pals, but they admired me, treating my creativity as natural. I wrote skits from a bottomless source of ideas, with juicy roles to fit everyone's personality. The kids weren't jealous; they enjoyed performing my dramas. My parents praised me, typing and copying the plays for the little actors and actresses.

"I'm lucky to have been accepted as a special and gifted child. I've known many writers who, as youngsters, were made to feel weirdly separate because of their creativity. This is sad, because unthinking, cruel comments can cause deep wounds and leave emotional scars in people who should revel in their differentness.

"Whenever I meet a child who is bubbling with ideas, I take time to appreciate his or her original imagination. All artists should encourage young people. You may be the only person who offers a reassuring word."

Jason, a columnist, remembers his youthful creativity as causing trouble. "I was obsessed with making up dirty rhymes and taught them to my buddies, who thought I was hilarious. Friends' parents would overhear my obscene singsong ditties and banish me from their homes. I embarrassed my parents and brought punishment down on myself.

"My impish preoccupation with gutter language eventually faded after repeated sentences to the isolation of my room.

"Today, when I find myself too serious or gloomy when working on an assignment, I change direction and write limericks—sometimes as offensive as when I was a kid. The difference is that I don't chant them through the neighborhood. (I'm much too dignified these days!)

"I was a child with talent, sidetracked into mischief. More sensitive parents might have directed my rhyming abilities into writing approved songs, but mine were too horrified to look beyond the obvious. Along this line, I've noticed that children with alert, inquisitive minds will often fabricate and exaggerate their adventures. Parents might bear in mind the possibility that these tall tales are a creative signal instead of immediately becoming alarmed about lying."

Childhood Signals

Invisible Friends. Did you have an imaginary companion as a child?

Inventing an invisible friend is a sign of creativity. Many parents think making up pals is a symptom of mental disturbance. However, visualizing a complete, separate personality is an ambitious act of the imagination. The child who does so is revealing the use of inner resources for comfort and companionship.

Adult writers describing their imaginary childhood friends present them as complex personalities who told long, involved tales to their owners, gave advice, and remained alive longer than most children's made-up friends. Perhaps the longevity is due to the fact that future writers usually don't begin using their talents until adolescence, whereas musically or artistically gifted children can begin practicing their craft even before grade school. The would-be writer spends more time feeling an urge to create while lacking the essential tools than other creative children.

"I had a friend called Whisper," shares Lauri, a playwright. "Whisper was a kindly fairy who spoke to me from a knothole in my climbing tree, telling me stories about a little girl who performed magic tricks and made herself invisible. When my older brothers teased me too much, I ran to my tree and Whisper's caressing voice. That comforting sound was very real to me, and I had no idea that I was making it all up. I knew that Whisper would appear one day. She would be a dazzling princess, so commanding that no one would ever tease her friend Lauri again. I have used imaginary companions in several of my plays for young audiences. After a performance there are always some bright-eyed children wanting to tell me about their special pal."

Maurice, a cookbook writer, remembers a fantasized, mischievous alter ego he blamed for his misdeeds. "My folks would rant and rave about one of my antics and I'd innocently deny any wrongdoing, insisting that Talk Too Much was at it again. I half-believed that my friend was really there and urging me on to greater acts of havoc. When I was seven, I started taking responsibility for my actions because my teachers wouldn't put up with my excuse. I held a funeral service for Talk Too Much, much to the relief of my parents."

Recalling a childhood imaginary friend can keep you in touch with your ability to suspend disbelief, and rejuvenate your sense of the endless possibilities for innovation.

Having Books as Friends. Did you obsessively reread favorite books as a child?

Writers are usually voracious readers—for information, relaxation, and the inner joy of reading. Writers with a love of reading were usually read to as children. Their parents and teachers encouraged the solitary act of reading as one of life's satisfactions. The magic of the written word continues to attract throughout life.

Many writers have described their emotional attachment to special books during their youth.

"Every month or so, my mother bought me a new Dr. Seuss book," recalls Ted. "I was struck by his incredible drawings and giggle-producing words. His books were my companions, far more interesting than television. I dreamed of telling tales as elaborate and exceptional as those of my hero. I struggled to invent unusual characters for my stories but never could compare with Dr. Seuss.

"I'm a waiter by night and write during the day. My lifelong dream is of creating a story with the appeal of a Dr. Seuss book. His books entertain but also teach lessons about man's strange behavior."

Bill, a psychologist and part-time writer, says, "I trace my career choice to a favorite childhood book, *Winnie the Pooh*. I know now that I loved the hero, Christopher Robin, because he was a special little boy, humanizing objects to overcome his loneliness. I identified with Christopher's sweetness. I couldn't show my 'soft' feelings because I lived on a block where boys were tough and mean. Any sign of 'weakness' was an invitation to a thrashing. For me, *Winnie the Pooh* was a lesson in empathy. My decision to become a therapist was based on a desire to help men reclaim their Christopher Robin gentleness and help them to be less afraid of their repressed feelings.

"I maintain a link to my inner child by piling a bunch of pillows on the bed, getting a glass of milk and a plate of cookies and gleefully wandering through the pages with Christopher Robin and Pooh.

"When my patients suffer from pessimism or depression, I insist we read aloud a book from their childhood. It renews the hope and wonderment we all require for healthy living."

Do you remember your favorite stories or books from childhood? Can you remember what quality drew you to reread a treasured book? Think of how the story may have delighted or comforted you or perhaps revealed a truth, however simple. Has it been too long since you reread your cherished books?

"Two books captured my heart as a young girl," related Brandy. "They were *A Wrinkle in Time* and *Snow Treasure*, both children's adventures in which the heroes overcame seemingly impossible adversities.

"Told what a precocious, gifted, and intelligent child I was, my parents pressured me to study medicine, science, or law. Even in high school, those professions seemed flat and boring, lacking in fun or excitement.

"Writing is my real challenge. Finding just the right word or painting a character with depth and believability really stirs me. I quit college after the first semester. A professor advised me to gain life experiences if I wanted to write about real people. He thought the university environment was too protected for would-be writers. Those were exactly the words I yearned to hear. I'm clerking in a boutique and absorbing a world of information about people's quirks. I write screenplays and novels at night, and it's the time I feel most fulfilled.

"My parents consider me a failure. They continually argue

that I'm wasting my talents, writing instead of finishing school. They can't understand how I can be happy being a writer. I often read reminiscences by painters, writers, and actors; they tell about parents' warnings against following the call of artistic talent. Creative commitment, ambition, and determination to compete were met with dire predictions of rejection and poverty. I may be unpublished, but never a failure. I live a rewarding life, devoted to writing. My childhood heroes succeeded against unbelievable odds and so will I."

The printed word seems to have held a fascination for future writers during their childhood, a pleasure retained in adulthood. The creative child, unaware that special gifts are his heritage, seems to look more intently at those around him and experiences life more intensely than those born without unique gifts. The artist-to-be is usually attracted to stories, whether written or spoken, satisfying the need to travel in one's imagination.

The Need for Stimulation

Are you easily bored by idle chatter?

Most creative people are interested in ideas, concepts, and diverse opinions. They rarely enjoy superficial conversations that add nothing to their knowledge or fail to stimulate exciting discussion.

"Time is precious," remarks Katherine, a speechwriter. "I can't waste time in conversations that meander and have no substance. I have friends who occasionally call and who, no matter how much they talk, have essentially nothing to say. I try to be polite, but I would rather interview strangers, gleaning opinions to use later when writing speeches. It's not that I never engage in small talk—I enjoy chatting with potential interviewees to relax them before posing questions about their private opinions. Cocktail parties—a welter of shallow exchanges—really exhaust me, so I avoid them. I don't think I'm a snob. I just have so much to write that I can't afford the time for conversation that isn't communication."

Julie, a confessions writer, loves to gossip because she collects ideas from personal intrigues. "A technical writer would probably consider gossip stupid. However, I happen to have the kind of face and personality that invite strangers to reveal amazing details—I'm *creating* when I'm listening to others. (I always ask their permission to weave their experiences into a story, and most people gladly give their okay.) I enjoy hearing people's stories, but conversations about fashions or possessions bore me to tears. Every writer has a slightly different definition for a tedious conversation."

David, a writer of fantasies for teenagers, says, "For me, 'intellectual discourse' is boring. I can't stand pseudosophisticates who try to impress one another with long words. That kind of talk makes me sleepy. I love being with teenagers. They're brimming with emotions and like to share their dramatic turmoils with a sympathetic adult. I've served as a hotline resource person for runaway kids. When I tell adolescent callers that I write stories for young adults, the most common response is, 'Will you put me in your next book?' Believe me, I hear plenty of one-of-a-kind stories to use in my novels."

Whatever your concept of an interesting exchange is, respect your boredom barometer. Never squander time by allowing yourself to be dulled by boring conversation. If you can't turn the discussion around, remove yourself from the situation. It is not selfish to protect your mind.

Shyness

Are you comfortable in most social situations?

Many writers we've known are distinctly uncomfortable in everyday social situations. Some say they prefer to observe people rather than participate. Many admit to feeling shy and introspective, envious of "regular folks" who enjoy exchanging pleasantries.

Because writers have often felt apart from normal society and have experienced the unpleasant sensation of being different, they regularly assume that the ability to socialize comes easily to everyone but them. But self-confidence in social situations is a learned skill and can be an enjoyable experience. Actively taking control of a social situation and addressing questions to strangers is a worthwhile alternative to standing around feeling stiff and awkward.

John, a writer for real estate magazines, recalls, "I was at this incredibly dull party. The combination of people just didn't work, because it seemed like everyone was a stranger except to the host and hostess. I was thinking up an elaborate excuse to leave when I spotted an old fellow who sat straight-backed and looked grim. The party was in the country, and he reminded me of my grandfather, who had farmed for sixty years. I thought the old guy must have a story or two and sat beside him. I broke the ice by asking how long he'd been a farmer. Soon he was telling me the history of local irrigation and his twenty-five years as the man in charge of irrigation for the county. Most people, including myself, know nothing about water rights, but it is a fascinating subject when explained by an expert who loves his job. I wrote an article about his valuable work and sold it with no difficulty. The party turned from dull to interesting because I set aside my boredom and reached out to a stranger."

If you feel like an outcast in the midst of happily chatting people, turn yourself into a casual interviewer, asking others about their childhood, their job or hobbies. By the time the stranger asks you to talk about yourself, you'll feel more at ease with the give and take of conversation. No one can force you to enjoy social situations, but if you approach them as an opportunity to learn more about people, they will eventually enrich your ability to characterize and your interviewing technique.

The Porcupine Complex

Are you highly sensitive to criticism?

Writers spend inordinate amounts of time depreciating their talent, questioning their abilities, and worrying about acceptance. One side effect of this perpetual self-criticism is that writers tend to bristle when others—critics or readers—comment unfavorably about their work, since it confirms their worst fears. They may have solicited the comments, unconsciously hoping for praise. (At the other extreme, some writers become paranoid when praised, thinking the complimenter is attempting to fool them.)

Many creative people grew up without encouragement and were castigated as daydreamers. Such treatment can lead to an oversensitive, thin-skinned response to all comments about one's creative processes.

"I don't let my wife or best friend read my completed manuscripts," comments Bruce, a novelist. "My wife knows how touchy I can be about criticism and when she read my manuscripts, she tried to soft-pedal her opinions. I would angrily accuse her of being vague. My friend Eric thinks everything I write is superb, so he can't be an objective reader. Several years ago I relieved them of the silly burden of reading my copy. My two published novels have been edited by the same person. Her remarks and suggestions are clearly meant to improve the manuscript. She doesn't have to witness my winces, groans, and desk pounding when one of her sharp notations makes me feel like a jerk.

"Sometimes I think I shouldn't read comments about my works because I waste too much time ruminating on them and feeling discouraged. It's a problem with no solution.

"Writing cronies of mine with more experience have explained that a writer must approach criticism realistically. One said, 'If a critic scolds you for disorganization or shallow characterization, take your emotional reactions firmly in hand and *pay attention.*' Although most writers view it as painful, criticism is not always a negative experience. Taking a creative writing class is an excellent way to learn how to accept criticism as helpful and constructive."

"In college I took creative writing on a whim," shares Marilyn, a short-story writer. "We were assigned to write a poem about how we looked at life. My paper came back with the notation, 'This poem is a definite credo.' I didn't know if credo was good or bad and had to look up the word in the dictionary. I was happy to find that it meant a set of beliefs and was a compliment from the teacher.

"The instructor said we had to become accustomed to criticism and he had a method to make it anonymous. He had students read each other's material. No one knew the identity of the author, so we all commented on it freely and the writer felt he didn't have to squirm with embarrassment. The class liked the system and we learned to value the objective comments about our writing."

Many beginning writers have brought their work to us, asking for critiques and advice on where to submit it. Over the years we've come to the conclusion that most new writers don't want to hear anything negative, but secretly hope that we'll find their writing so excellent that we'll gladly take care of the boring business of sending out their material. This unspoken desire is not bad, but it is very unrealistic and leads to disappointments. It is also childish because it assumes that because we're older, established writers, we have the time and inclination to do the legwork for beginners. Most writers are too busy for secretarial work for other writers. We direct them to read *Writer's Market* and learn for themselves.

Another unprofessional reaction to criticism is when writers become touchy and defensive when they hear an objective evaluation of their work. We speak kindly, but refuse to be dishonest. We encourage them to rewrite and return with revisions. Those who do are genuinely grateful for our time and attention. Those who continue to dream of instant praise rarely call again.

If a teacher, fellow writer, or established author is willing to set aside time to discuss your writing, be grateful, be attentive, and learn from the experience. The individual attention you receive is a gift, since most writers do not charge for their opinion. If a critic tells you that you use too many words or your prose lacks authentic emotion, reread your manuscript and improve it.

Gene, a gag writer, reports, "There are degrees of criticism. Some remarks are really a disguise for hostility. When I started writing jokes some nonwriter acquaintances put me down with innuendos that comedy writing belonged in the basement of the arts. I was insecure and believed their drivel. Writing funny gags is one of the most difficult forms of entertainment. It takes a great deal of skill to make readers laugh. Today, when a dolt tries to demean me by denigrating humorous writing, I begin a lengthy discourse on how I'm going to use them in a gag about the prisoner/guard relationship between bosses and employees. Soon the put-down artist in question is thinking about his nine-to-five existence. My girlfriend finally explained that 'regular folks' are often secretly envious of creative people, and take potshots at our work to avoid admitting jealousy. I always took my creativity for granted and never dreamed people would be jealous.

"I have a friend, Marcia, who's working very successfully in nonfiction. She has managed over the last five years to build a reputation for dependability and originality. In another six months she plans to quit her banking job to do magazine writing full time. When she ran up against such things as the secretary who said, 'Articles are great, but everyone throws magazines away. Why don't you write a book instead?' her heart used to sink and her self-esteem drooped until she devised a soft revenge (that is, used her verbal skill to retaliate instead of dropping a cash box on her coworker's head). She would say, 'You know, you're probably right. Why don't we write a book together? I'll bet you'd find it a breeze.' Her tormentor slunk away after muttering excuses about not having enough time, et cetera. She doesn't feel vulnerable to asinine remarks anymore."

The consensus of writers we have known or interviewed is that we all suffer some negative reaction to criticism. A published work culminates hours of research, planning, writing, honing, polishing, and revising. This creative investment is infused with our own personal experiences, observations, perceptions, and unique views filtered through our imaginations. We offer the finished product as an example of our best personal performance, exposing our souls. It is normal to feel defensive, resentful, and misunderstood when one's creation is attacked.

Older writers say that they still have to cope with unpleasant feelings from negative comments, but have learned to set these emotions aside and keep working.

"If you pleased everyone, you'd be a static writer," pronounced an eighty-year-old poet. "I *want* certain people to hate my poetry about the denial of death. If they loved it, there would be no need to shake their complacency. Forget about criticism and use your time to write."

You Are Special

Forty years of our research, studies with humanistic scientists, and clinical practice have made it clear that a very small portion of the populace is born with the special gift of creative possibilities. *This is not an elitist statement, but a genetic fact of life.*

Creative people quickly deny their specialness, not wanting to be set apart from their peers. But it is imperative for a writer to accept his specialness. Those born with the gift of perfect pitch and the consequent affinity for playing musical instruments and composing delight in their special talent. This genetic gift is no different from the gift that propels creative thought in writing. Creativity cannot be taught, only fostered and encouraged.

Our definition of a special person is one who is born with

and develops many or all of the following characteristics:
- finely tuned sensory perceptions
- keen intuition
- sensitivity to subtle changes in others
- never-ending curiosity
- thought patterns that involve consistently pondering and sifting ideas
- technicolor dreams
- a drive to define life's meaning
- dissatisfaction with the status quo
- appreciation of the preciousness of life
- intense drive to forge emotional connections
- a vivid fantasy life
- a need for solitude

These traits are unrelated to intelligence, education, environment, physical appearance, race, or age. There are brilliant people with high IQs who will never create anything and people of average intelligence who are powerhouses of ideas.

The special person, like everyone else, is subject to emotional traumas, childhood neglect, fame, physical disfigurement, poverty, acceptance, wealth, rejection—all of life's positive and negative events. Negative experiences can strangle creative exuberance; they can sometimes cloud and interfere with the expression of special gifts. But psychologically speaking, creativity is solidly planted inside your soul, as distinctive and irreversible as fingerprints or eye coloration. You may discover, however, there are some obstacles to overcome in order to free talents repressed by negative events.

"I was an energetic child," relates Judith, "and I invented a make-believe business to occupy myself. My play business was a complicated insurance company, involving all kinds of forms. My father brought home an old typewriter and set up a table in the basement for my enterprise.

"I wrote long-winded letters to prospective clients, explaining their life insurance requirements, and pretended to mail the missives. Next, I made up clients who ordered policies and then I set up a billing and collection procedure, using Monopoly money. I invented devious reasons to never pay off claims, becoming 'Mr. Hencepay,' a play on my intentions to pay hencely.

"I also wrote, acted and directed plays which I produced for the other children in the neighborhood. I was a dynamo of creative energy.

"When I was eleven, my father lost his job and we moved to a smaller house. There was no basement or room for my desk, typewriter, and bulky files. A new place and new friends eased the loss of my playtime insurance career—or so I thought. My father died the following year. My mother went to work, and I had a part-time job. I gradually lost my creative joy: obviously that kind of enjoyment was for carefree kids.

"At twenty-five, I was a bored housewife, spending afternoons hypnotized by the soaps. I had acquired the trappings of contentment—two healthy children, a successful husband, a large house. But my spiritual malaise developed into a gloomy depression with no apparent external reason.

"A friend suggested psychotherapy. In the fifties, making a psychiatric appointment was the same as admitting insanity. But I had no choice.

"After a few sessions the therapist said, 'You're creative but live on the surface; a special person locked away from her center. Our job must be your creative recovery. Your depression masks feelings buried in your unconscious.'

"Laborious recall revealed the combined loss of my creative play arena and the repressed anger surrounding the move had evoked a rage toward my parents even though I knew they had no choice. My father's death caused guilt feelings, which I had denied. I learned young people often magically assume responsibility in parental deaths, particularly when they are angry. The underground guilt system grew, burying my exuberance. I unconsciously relinquished my creativity in emotional payment for murderous impulses.

"With the analyst's help I relived the trauma of moving, anger, fantasies of my father's death, and resolved the guilt which had deadened my central self. The psychic energy I was using to recant my gifts was freed to flow into my creativity. Creative impulses stirred and my depression disappeared as we moved through the layers of emotional debris.

"My creative enthusiasm was reborn in therapy. I was totally unaware that childhood traumas could affect gifts. With my new respect for the power of the unconscious, I monitor my inner world regularly. Other writers, blocked by repressed memories, might gain insights and move ahead without professional help, and I admire them. My problem was too complex and shrouded to resolve by myself."

Accepting your unique talents doesn't require a formal proclamation. Rather it can be a quiet, sustaining inner glow that can be shared with other gifted friends who are unthreatened by your differentness.

"Special" status counts you as a member of perhaps less than 5 percent of the population. You did not earn your genetic present. You received it at conception through the complex mechanisms of heredity. Being a gifted person carries a creative responsibility—a personal obligation to explore and fulfill your artistic possibilities. It is your good fortune to be a special person, but your devotion to work is what will make the most of it.

"Occasionally I envy normal people," says Bruce, the novelist struggling with criticism. "They take life in stride, unburdened by endless, distracting brain activity. They seem unhassled, unconcerned with people's motivations, which I mull over continually. They never have to excuse themselves or just disappear during a party. (I lack the social graces to explain my actions as I rush away to capture a certain phrase on paper before it falls through my memory sieve.) Others seem to accept fate; I shake my fists at the winds of chance. I'm impatient, constantly irritated with the inferiority and dullness of my daily productions.

"My wife listens patiently to my whinings about perception overloads. She teases me and dreams out loud of a serene life married to a easygoing, regular guy, content to watch television without yelling at the announcer or blurting comical dialogue for the actors. She talks about the possibility of a surgical procedure to remove my creativity, which would lend a modicum of peace and quiet to our household. My self-pity evaporates at that point, and I get back to work."

Special people are born with the seeds of creativity. The atmosphere for germination and growth of your creative bouquet may be less than ideal. Our educational system and society's job market tend to ignore creative talents and aspirations, giving meager encouragement and validation.

Writers must be self-motivated. Only you can develop the discipline necessary for success. To have the confidence to maintain a writer's identity, to become a full-fledged member of the writing family, you must accept your genetically given gifts and listen to your inner music.

The following chapters are meant to help you increase your creative self-esteem, and hence your creative output.

Your insights and resulting increased creative energies will form a support system of comfort when you must deal with the built-in disappointments of your craft. You are not really alone, but connected with all other living and dead writers by the persistent urge to transform ideas into believable, interesting, and emotionally moving language.

CHAPTER TWO

Your Competitive Spirit

SERIOUS WRITERS develop plans for acceptance, publication, and adequate payment for their material. In order to achieve these goals a writer must have a realistic attitude toward the publishing business, a business that has to struggle to survive in the crowded field of communications. Writers must submit quality material that will appeal to the reading public and make money for themselves and the publishing company. As a writer, you are in fierce competition with other freelancers who have the same desire for publication and payment that you do. In order to make a living as a freelancer, you must enjoy competing for sales or you will soon give up.

A good competitor consistently presents his best material with the confidence that it will win the prize of publication and a check. Writers in harmony with their competitive drive understand that others will often be chosen over them, but they continue to dedicate themselves to the goal of success.

Being a hard-driving competitor does not detract from your artistic sensitivity. The two qualities should work together. A competitor examines the obstacles, plots a course to minimize the chances of failure, and then works diligently to train himself to be a winner. The writer's sensitivity is then directed toward creating original works.

A writer who competes intelligently values his talents enough to submit material instead of hoping some editor will discover him. He considers it vital to acquaint himself with his arena of competition. This means studying writers' magazines, reading current issues of target publications, and poring over the current *Writer's Market* for up-to-date, accurate needs of publishers.

The realistic writer, fully aware that his query and manuscript presentation are competing with those of other competent writers, always submits manuscripts that have been typed with a fresh ribbon and are free of typos, smudges, and penciled-in words. The manuscript is a physical representation of how you value your work and ultimately yourself. Sound competition means offering a finished product that will impress editors with the seriousness of your intentions.

Success will result from a combination of originality, disciplined work habits, dependability, and a meshing of creativity and competition.

Competitiveness, which springs from man's potent aggressive drive, is a healthy attitude that helps propel us toward success. Unfortunately in our society aggression and competition are often associated with violence and anxiety, causing many sensitive artists to cringe and change the subject. But knowledge of and acceptance of your aggressive and competitive spirit are vital to success.

Inner harmony between aggressiveness and creativity is possible when you understand the positive elements that feed competition.

Overcoming Basic Fears

"People ask me to read their poetry," relates Jamie, a published poet. "They often make flimsy excuses that it's not very good to buffer any criticisms.

"Modesty about creativity is silly, but I make allowances for beginners. I get excited and give compliments when I read a good poem, one that pricks my emotions or concisely targets on an issue. I'm glad to share my knowledge, dissecting mistakes or wordiness.

"Next, I inquire into the would-be poet's plans. Typically, he looks bewildered and mutters about writing 'just for personal pleasure.' My philosophy is 'Write for a potential audience.' It doesn't make sense to write without attempting to get published.

"As we talk further I usually discover an abject fear of competing hidden behind the modesty. Shy writers will admit they think it's unartistic to hustle intensely personal pieces. Or I will find they harbor morbid and exaggerated fantasies about rejection. I give my standard lecture about the absurdity of such attitudes, including the folly of investing too much self-importance in their words—or their frailties. I refuse to accept anyone as a serious writer until he studies market lists in the writers' magazines, reviews current poetry journals, types his works (many have not progressed enough to realize the necessity of a return self-addressed stamped envelope!), and actually submits. I lose patience with the endless procrastinators, who remain in their cocoon of fear rather than pay reality dues in the writing business. I've gotten plenty of rejections; sample chapters of a recent novel have been turned down by seven publishers so far. I may be disappointed, but I'm never discouraged enough to stop competing.

"Some writers may avoid competing because the finished product—printed writing—looks so aesthetic. The mental labor, the stresses and traumas—rewriting, submissions, rejections, acceptance, and editing—do not show. But we are entertainers, and no professional—singer, comedian, or announcer—exposes the preparations of the act to the audience: the auditions, the rehearsals, the makeup applications, and microphone setups."

Jamie is not afraid to compete. He is comfortable with his aggressive nature and with pitting his talents against those of fellow poets and novelists.

"I was one of the many beginning writers Jamie helped with his practical advice," recalls Matt, a greeting card illustrator and writer. "At first I was offended by his 'crass' approach—viewing one's wares with a businesslike attitude.

"Jamie looked at my samples and told me to study the competition, to gauge rivals by reading greeting cards available on drugstore racks and in stationery shops. I discovered my 'bright and fresh' ideas were not all that original. It shook my fantasy of the first batch of cards prompting an excited editor's phone call offering the highest pay and insisting to review my portfolio—a scene I'd replayed in my mind like a movie for years. Friends in other areas of writing have admitted to having the same unrealistic dreams.

"Jamie thought the fantasy of instant success was pretty funny and said such a wish would effectively keep a writer from entering the fray of normal competition—'If I can't be discovered immediately, I'm not going to play!'

"He further advised, 'You have to expect regular rejections in this crowded creative field. Keep enough sample cards circulating so rejections are offset by an occasional sale. People don't like competition because they are programmed in school to *win* first place (sale), or be a complete *loser* (rejection). But there are many shaded areas that refusals to buy can fall into: overstocked, change in direction, not quite sharp enough— none of which editors have time to explain.

"I've been selling greeting cards for five years, with two barren years before the first sale. Competing is easier because I'm not there in person when an editor rejects my work. It's kind of a lightweight form of testing talents, sending your work while remaining safe and snug at home. Writers who make sales when mine are turned down can't taunt my failure; they're scattered across the country and don't even know me. Competing with fellow writers is a rivalry where the contestants and judges are faceless, at least."

"Whenever I sell a card, I try to outperform that verse or drawing, making it my adversary. Jamie taught me to value competitive spirit as much as artistic talent."

Understanding Aggression

Do you avoid competition so as to make yourself less vulnerable to rejection? Are you uneasy with or unaware of normal aggressive drives?

A redefinition of aggression that will serve your creative endeavors should help you overcome fears of competition.

We are born with an aggressive (survival) instinct, neither good nor bad, but a biological fact.

Hunger stimulates infants' insistent (aggressive) demands for oral satisfaction. A baby cries for nourishment without concern for parental convenience. Babies are totally self-centered in an emotional state of primary selfishness, dependent on innate aggression to attract attention.

As an infant develops into a toddler, a child, and an adolescent, the primary me-oriented aggressive drive for immediate satisfaction—meant to insure survival—must be channeled and controlled to enable the growing person to function reasonably with others. Undisciplined children are extremely aggressive, because parents haven't taught them how to wait or share.

Historically humans needed large quantities of aggression to survive in an unfriendly environment. Today we don't require the same amount of aggression to fight off animals or defend against enemies. However, our biological makeup has no knowledge of social change: this necessitates external rules to tame our powerful aggressive instincts.

As parents "socialize" their child, the child gives up primary selfishness, and gradually replaces it with consideration for others, the ability to wait for satisfactions, sharing, and a conscience system of right and wrong—sublimating raw aggression into civilized behavior.

Aggression is further channeled into achievement, mental and physical competition, and the ability to defend oneself by talking and negotiating instead of automatically using physical force.

Cultural Programming

Each society defines how and to what extent its members may practice aggression. We are products of our biological family and its extension—our society—which sets standards of conduct. Children reared in countries constantly threatened by invasion and terrorism are culturally programmed for defensive and offensive aggression (e.g., Israel and the Arab nations). The upbringing of youngsters in "safe" societies does not emphasize aggressiveness against bordering countries (e.g., the United States and Canada/Mexico).

Historically our society also delineated aggression as a gender inheritance, labeling aggression as masculine and passivity as an innate female trait. But psychologically, every human is born with a mixture of aggression and passivity.

In our culture both sexes are given free rein to express feelings until approximately age three. Boys are then taught to develop defenses against feelings labeled soft or feminine and they eventually learn to repress them. A definition of masculinity, passed down from generation to generation, reinforced the belief that it's shameful for a male to have "soft" feelings. Revealing such feelings was considered weak and sissified.

Crying, a natural reaction to intense emotion, is even now frowned on as unmasculine.

Boys' aggressiveness becomes exaggerated, impulsive, and explosive as other normal feelings are blocked from release. They adopt aversions to passivity, secretly envying girls, who are allowed the full spectrum of their wide range of soft emotions. Boys' aggression becomes a valuable asset—as a defense against the jealousy generated by repressing their other feelings—since it's their principal acceptable feeling.

Girls' aggression appears milder because it is only one of many emotions released through physical and verbal activities. Females inhibited from expressing the majority of their normal feelings would most likely exhibit overly aggressive tendencies.

Bill, the psychologist, secretly wrote love poems full of romantic longings during his childhood. Although he could fight and roughhouse on a par with his streetwise friends, he hated their lack of gentleness and their need to out-strut, out-boast, tease, and jeer at one another.

Bill rode his bike to faraway neighborhoods, escaping peer judgments, and joined girls in hopscotch and skip-rope games.

"The girls' games involved competition, but with grace and agility, not brute force. I behaved like a gentleman so they'd let me play with them. I loved the vacation from always being a jock.

"I grew up believing aggression was hurting feelings, yelling instead of talking, fighting, and being destructive. Boys who didn't like strong-arm competition or crunching body-contact sports were called fairies.

"During my teens, I gave up aggression as repulsive, and I retreated into reading. I didn't understand that normal aggression and its counterparts, kindness and empathy, could exist together. My determination to avoid aggressive pursuits kept me from competing in creative areas. In therapy and training I learned that aggression is normal and doesn't have to be violent when it can be expressed with all the other emotions. I could then compete in the writing world, realizing that one doesn't grimace menacingly and jam a manuscript in an editor's face. Aggression is a positive propelling force that motivates me not to beat out anyone, but to prove myself able."

Cheated Boys and Girls

Boys usually learn self-esteem through athletic prowess, feigning bravery in the face of pain, winning at any cost, and hiding normal responses. Competing, a badge of masculinity, is replete with overtones of violence and injury.

Society defines femininity in double terms. A woman's self-esteem rests on the kind of person she is, rather than what she produces. Girls are motivated to compete for high grades, but subtly learn that high intelligence threatens male egos. The competitive spirit must be tempered to maintain feminine appeal. Many women reach maturity denying pleasure in competing, fearing it might stigmatize them as unfeminine. The socializing female message has been, "Compete, but not too vigorously."

No wonder we have difficulties using aggression effectively after growing up thinking our degree of aggressiveness is a function of our gender.

Julie, the confessions writer, recounts her cultural programming: "I am a Southerner, raised with complicated, rigid male-female role expectations: women are male ornaments, pampered and patronized; men are admired for logic, control, and independence from women.

"Yet in reality women compete fiercely for successful husbands, pretending gentleness and naive innocence while scheming with horse-trader shrewdness. Charm disguises aggression like a heavy layer of makeup.

"As a child, I irritated my mother and her frilly friends, trying to understand their different conversations and behavior when men weren't around. An outside-the-norm tomboy, I introduced myself into boys' games. My relatives and teachers warned me that unladylike, pushy behavior would surely end in spinsterhood.

"Throughout childhood I ignored the admonitions against open competition but was unconsciously haunted by them as an adult. At twenty, I moved to New York to get away from constricting Southern mores. I began writing confessions—my reading passion during a lonely adolescence. While I researched markets, a charming Southern inner voice repeatedly spoke: 'My dear, it is coarse and degrading to expose ambition. Ladies never, ever sully their hands in business.'

"The unconscious cultural mechanism I had consciously rejected was still an internal force that silently eroded my desire to test my author's mettle. Dramatic, moving plots dried up. My thinking became sluggish, my energies were drained by city survival and a secretarial job. I rationalized the evaporation of my creative intentions as a casualty of the adjustment to big-city life.

"This vegetative state was finally disrupted when a coworker invited me to celebrate the sale of her first sculpture. The other guests, like me, were employed by dehumanizing organizations. But this mixture of would-be actors, writers, and artists didn't talk about their jobs, but about plans for creative recognition. They vibrated with enthusiasm as they shared tips about auditions, workshops, agents, new markets, and classes. I contributed nothing, mumbling excuses about no time to write. A vivacious older woman overheard and remarked, 'You have to *make* time, or never fulfill your destiny!' She introduced herself as a gothic novelist, and related her adventures as a beginner.

"At eighteen, she came to New York from Utah, with four manuscripts and a driving ambition to be published. 'I thought living in the hub of the publishing world would be a big plus,' she explained. 'It wasn't. I telephoned editors, asking for appointments to be read. Barely disguising their annoyance, they directed me to write letters describing my novels. They weren't interested in reading completed manuscripts. I didn't believe them and I looked for an agent, but no one wanted to represent me. I was mystified because I assumed if you wanted an agent one would accept you as a client without question. Experience has proven that ethical agents won't take you on unless they think you're a salable writer. Eventually, I sent query letters, which got me a few readings and form rejections. An assistant editor really helped by sending a personal note, which explained that a clichéd plot, purple prose, and lack of action prompted the rejection. She suggested taking writing classes and studying current titles. I went to school and bettered my writing techniques. I had neglected reading, failed to keep up-to-date with my competitors, and was offering tired plots instead of fresh ideas. This is a common fault among young writers who think their works are golden, and if only someone had the wisdom to agree.'

"Our rapport deepened during the evening and I confided

my quandary: an internal restriction against competition that seemed to sap my creative juices. She said to think of myself as a writer, not a Southern female rebelling against the establishment.

"The next day I tacked a hand-lettered sign over my dusty typewriter: WRITER! PRODUCE! COMPETE! SELL! Lassitude disappeared with my new self-definition, sweeping aside those blocks to my original ideas. I can only repay my mentor by passing her advice on when I speak to beginners' writing clubs.

"Today, I love the excitement of competing. My sign remains, a reminder of the cultural influences that almost short-circuited my career."

Regaining a Sense of Wholeness

Cultural concepts of innate psychological characteristics can cause repression of assertiveness in some females and overly virulent expressions in males. Writers must be comfortable with all their feelings to produce authentic material. Creative people are better equipped than most to overcome unworkable, inhibiting cultural designations and to attain inner harmony between passivity and aggressiveness.

Review your external programming by examining the pressures that attempted to squeeze you into sex-stereotyped behavior.

List the personality traits and feelings you learned were appropriate to each gender. Recall, verbally or in writing, the cultural influences that caused you to alter your inclination to aggression or passivity.

As a catalyst, here are some gender-delegated emotional aspects: anger, assertiveness, automony, caring, compassion, consideration, defensiveness, dependence, despair, discipline, empathy, fear, gentleness, hostility, hysteria, initiative, intimacy, intuition, judgment, leadership, logic, loyalty, patience, perfectionism, perceptivity, practicality, responsibility, sensitivity, spontaneity, tactfulness, and tenderness.

A woman denying normal aggression will be ineffective when writing scenes involving violent emotional or physical eruptions. A one-dimensional male will lack genuineness when he tries to describe empathetic, intuitive scenes.

Those who enjoy internal harmony between aggression and

passivity (competition and sensitivity) are comfortable when demanding appropriate fees and yet flexible when asked to consider revisions. A creative person who lacks assertiveness will often offer no resistance to an editor who offers a low fee or advance. Writers who fear they may appear offensive if they bargain with a self-confident attitude will end up with smaller checks than writers who speak with an authoritative tone.

As with all opposing emotions, there is a happy medium between too much aggression and too much passivity. When you have attained a balance between these psychological forces you will be a fuller person because you will be using all your energies for creativity and competition instead of repressing innate feelings.

"I was too aggressive with editors when I began in the business of selling articles," says Bradford, a writer so successful that he has had to use different pen names when appearing several times in the same issue of a magazine. "I come from a family of intensely competitive business people in the wild world of dress manufacturing. They did most of their business on the phone with lots of threats and demands for immediate service. They manipulated buyers, pushed the workers around, and seemed to enjoy the hysterical atmosphere at the office. My uncle always said after a big deal, 'Always keep the pressure on everyone—that's how you get to be a success.'

"I decided to sidestep writing query letters to editors; I thought it outdated. I called editors directly. I had a forceful voice (like the rest of my family) and pretended to be a personal friend of the editor, conning secretaries into putting me through. My brash approach worked with some editors because I was so convincing about my original ideas and promised them excellent copy. After I mailed an article I would wait for just a week and start calling the editor for a response, acting just like my relatives in the dress business, wheeling and dealing. I soon learned that editors didn't like my invasive, intense approach—they told me I sounded like a huckster. I had to tone down my aggressive nature, even though I'd been taught at home that pushiness was a positive trait. Publishing is more sedate and orderly than the garment trade. I channeled my aggressive drive into researching more and more original ideas for articles and stopped using the phone to badger editors. They treated me with more respect when I wrote stimulating queries and waited to hear about acceptance or rejection by mail. My family can't understand how I can make so much money without yelling into the phone!"

Personal Inhibitions

It is during childhood that we first receive our training in aggression and competition. Our family's child-rearing practices dramatically influence our self-esteem and our opinion of what are acceptable emotional responses.

We are aware of our conscious thinking, our likes and dislikes, our positive and negative traits, our interests, habits, friend and love choices, and easily recalled memories.

Our unconscious mental activity is usually completely unknown to us, unless we have been psychoanalyzed. The unconscious part of the mind is like an emotional tape recording, imprinted with all childhood events. Most people have infantile amnesia. Some cannot remember adolescence, blaming memory loss on aging. The unconscious retains the forgotten, profoundly affecting conscious decisions, feelings, and choices. The positive facet of the unconscious stimulates creative thought and works silently on problem solving.

In adulthood, unconscious activity exerts power over conscious behavior as it replays the emotional tape recording of the past. People unconsciously become involved in relationships mirroring first emotional connections. This psychological phenomenon is called *repetition compulsion*.

Marriage is the most obvious example of the compelling need to repeat the emotional past. One's mate invariably psychologically resembles one's mother, the primary caretaker during developmental years. A woman raised by an alcoholic, abusive mother vows abstinence and avoids drinkers. After marriage, she discovers her husband's personality to be addictive and infantile, matching traits of her mother. She is consciously miserable, but the unconscious finds satisfaction in copying long-ago attachments.

The imprinting on your invisible tape recording is considered "normal" for the unconscious system because whatever is experienced and recorded is the only criterion of life's meaning. It makes no moral judgments; it only seeks to arrange adult experiences emulating childhood feelings. People raised in a happy, loving home where their self-esteem was nourished through praise and acceptance experience pleasant repetition patterns. However, the majority of people, particularly sensitive and gifted ones, are reared with neurotic conflicts—parential ambivalence, harsh restrictions, and rejections.

If you discover unconscious patterns, you can consciously ward off negative repetitions, in particular those that interfere with creativity or competition.

Freeing the Competitive Spirit

Competition begins in infancy. The baby joins an established two-person relationship and competes for attention. Toddlers compete for mothers' exclusive attention with siblings, fathers, visiting friends, or even a book or television program. Youngsters' aggression is devoted to defending their position as mother's favorite. Consistently losing or winning her demonstrated love influences children's self-esteem and is unconsciously recorded as "normal."

During the *family romance* period between the ages of three and five, children become sensually enamored of the opposite-sex parent, actively competing with the spouse who has the love of the prized parent. The way parents handle children's competitive spirit during this period sets the foundation for future behavior.

"I couldn't see myself as competitive," states Dena, "even though college instructors urged me to submit short stories to writing contests. I felt edgy and put off submitting until the deadline was past. I knew I was being foolish, and again and again filled out contest applications, but never managed to complete them.

"A sorority sister majoring in psychology irritated all of us, always relating our every action to childhood traumas. One afternoon while playing Scrabble, she accused me of deliberately losing. I denied it but she persisted until I admitted holding back large-scoring words, afraid to hurt her feelings if I won. 'Where did you learn such ridiculous thinking?' she demanded, always probing. Her basic good intentions helped me squeak open a door to my unconscious and started me thinking about my upbringing.

"The problem was my twin sister. We were always together, outwardly acting the same, differing only in how we liked to play. I liked to draw and color while Dierdra was physically active. Mother forced me outside to play with Dierdra, instead of 'wasting time doodling.' She kept whispering that my sister would feel bad because she couldn't draw pictures. In school I was smarter but learned to temper my scholastic performance to match Dierdra's level. I just gave in to make Mother happy. I expressed my anger over the unfairness by passive torture; I became deaf when Dierdra asked questions, I'd 'forget' to meet her after school, I'd pretend to be tired when she wanted to run and play outside. Gradually, my normal competitive spirit was squashed, replaced by a tendency to let others win. Mother's overprotectiveness of my sister's feelings made competition forbidden—outshining Dierdra promised to cause terrible suffering.

"The amateur psychologist said, 'You think your friends will collapse if you compete aggressively, just as your mother warned.'

"The memories, insights, and my friend's blunt remarks made me angry about Mother's demands and how they still affected me. I could reason that by her own lights she did her best, but I was still furious.

"After I cooled down, I called Dierdra at her school—we had insisted on different colleges, secretly glad to get away from each other. I told her about the memories and why I was afraid of competition. To my surprise, she said that Mother had warned against her being a good athlete, lest I feel inferior. Dierdra said, 'I felt chained by your lack of coordination. I have the same problem—holding back instead of going all out.' We decided to give each other permission to enjoy our individual talents in competition.

"Learning to laugh at my noncompetitive unconscious system took time, but I finally freed myself."

Jed, a retired physician, relates, "I was extremely competitive during college and medical school, and professionally successful for thirty years (doctors compete for patients on the basis of their reputation for competent treatment). I retired at fifty-five and, after I'd had my fill of golf and fishing, I got an urge to write a novel about my family's history. I had published many technical articles and was confident creative writing would come easily.

"I spent a year gathering copious notes about my colorful immigrant family. My habits of organization paid off and the first draft was completed in four months. A fellow writer read it; he liked the story, but said the novel needed tightening and smoothing. This challenge seemed exciting. However, rewriting became obsessive, each sentence demanding a poetic polish that eluded me. At the end of each day I was depleted and dissatisfied, more tired than in medical practice. I kept muttering, 'It's not good enough, not good enough,' preparing myself to admit failure.

"My wife, patiently living with my suffering, insisted I set writing aside and take a vacation. Other writers will understand how undeserving I felt. The failure of not writing well seeps into a person's sense of accomplishment and creates an unproductive vicious circle. But my wife took control and managed the trip. After a few relaxing days she gave me *The Person, His Development throughout the Life Cycle* by Theodore Lidz, saying, 'You need this book.' I read and reread the book's explanation of unconscious forces, reflecting on my obviously neurotic reaction to rewriting.

"My emotional history revealed a creative bent in childhood that was devalued by parents and relatives. As struggling immigrants, they revered education, professionalism, and financial security. Artistic expression was considered frivolous. I automatically became a scholar to gain their respect and pride. I unconsciously came to value ambition, financial gain, and material security above all. My introjected parents were a mental barometer that disapproved of creativity—still operating after fifty-five years. Unconsciously I was programmed to believe creative competition was unrewarding and undignified. As I contemplated those childhood ethics, vague feelings of guilt for letting down my hardworking, sacrificing parents emerged. I was supposed to die attending patients, not leisurely scribbling a story!

"Insights of this magnitude take time to absorb and further patience to divest unconscious effects. I tackled the crippling generational attitudes, devising my own maneuver to overcome the difficulty of switching my sense of competition to the artistic sphere. I addressed a loving, lengthy, simply-worded letter to my deceased parents, explaining the usefulness of creativity. I argued persuasively about changing customs—and even values—from one generation to another and listed my past accomplishments, proving I had earned the right to be creative. This letter device separated the unconscious constraints from my conscious desire to perform. I labeled the envelope 'Resting Unconscious Directives,' and filed it.

"The plan's simplicity helped it to succeed. I come from simple peasant stock, so my unconscious voice speaks a straightforward language, such as, 'This is bad,' 'Helping people is good,' 'Don't waste time.' My unconscious would not understand or accept intellectual reasoning.

"I tackled the novel again, repeating to myself, 'Permission granted to create.' My 'insurmountable' writing block faded, and I finished the job joyfully. My manuscript hasn't been accepted yet, but that seems unimportant compared to the triumph of overcoming unconscious forces."

Uncovering Unconscious Dictates

You can expose the unconscious denial system that restricts aggressive pursuit of creative endeavors.

Free association is the quickest route to unconscious recall. This technique circumvents the normal sifting of ideas before they are verbalized. Writing, typing, talking into a tape recorder or to yourself can be employed for free association.

Choose a quiet, comfortable place and sit or lie in a relaxed position. Close your eyes and visualize a white screen. Mentally print on the screen the words *competition, aggression,* and *assertiveness* and then focus on them. Let your mind float, and say whatever comes forth, uncensored, no matter how trivial, unconnected, or inconsequential it seems. This cathartic blathering releases repressed thoughts and discloses unconscious memories. You may recall scraps of conversations or disapproving glances, which remind you of other episodes related to aggressiveness. If the thoughts seem to stop, visualize yourself trying to attract your mother's attention while she talks animatedly to a faceless man. This will take you back in time to your first experiences with competing for attention. Concentrate on remembering anxieties, strategies for attention, and feelings of frustration or victory in this mental movie.

"I was overconfident," explained Arthur, a screenwriter. "I sent my first film script to a Hollywood agent, expecting a sale within a week, and literally packed my bags. He returned the script after two months, with a noncommittal rejection note. I was dumbfounded. Several other agents passed over my script.

I couldn't face the fact that maybe my screenplay wasn't the best movie ever written. I began to feel paranoid, ranting about the stupidity of agents who couldn't see the genius of my work.

"I tried the free-association method after a friend said that I was probably setting myself up for failure. All my memories were positive, showing no hindrances to intelligent competition. My single-parent mother encouraged and praised my childhood efforts. She recopied my 'cute' three-year-old observations as poems and pasted them in a scrapbook. She foretold a brilliant future for me all through adolescence. My unconscious told me I was superior, talented, and loved. Why weren't my mother's predictions coming true?

"My father's new wife published children's stories. I thought she might open some doors since I had apparently sent my material to dunderheads. (What a bigheaded jerk!)

"She read the script and began a critique—no central sympathetic character, stilted dialogue, and nonfilmic scene changes. I was deflated and angry. My overwhelming desire to be approved of was petulantly revealed on my self-centered twenty-year-old face.

"She said, 'You expect other people's evaluation to be the same as your mother's opinion of your talents. It won't happen, because you have to *earn* accolades. Your mom treated you like a prince, extolling your gifts beyond the facts. I don't mean to judge her, but she taught you to expect too much too soon.'

"My stepmother was right, but I was too humiliated to agree. She did force me to think, and I recognized that my superconfidence and expectations of effortless success were built on Mother's dreams. I dug out the scrapbook, appalled by the time she had spent rewording baby talk into brilliant-sounding sayings.

"I had to learn to view myself realistically, to fight the lulling unconscious message of my princeliness. It was very difficult, because we all like to think of ourselves as wonderful. Given a choice, I wish I had problems with feeling inferior so I could work to better myself instead of dealing with my mother's assurances of superiority. From the way she talked, I thought the literary world was waiting with open arms to offer me fame and fortune.

"From time to time I still write a line and stop to reflexively pat myself on the head for excellence. I consciously stop, call myself 'egotist,' direct my adoring unconscious to take a walk, and begin editing my sloppy sentences. I remind myself that I'm a young, untried, struggling, studying film writer in competition with experienced, successful, older veterans.

"And I never let my mother read my scripts!"

The process of uncovering your unconscious attitudes toward competition can be frustrating. You may spend several sessions digging up restrictions on your sense of competition. The effort is worthwhile, because these restrictions can be a real impediment to your success.

Once you become aware of your internal enemies against aggression, your imagination will be stimulated to find ways to deal with these unconscious forces, such as Arthur's directives, or Jed's letter device. Although we cannot change the unconscious's determination to replay the emotional past, we can interrupt its influence and reroute mental activity from the negative to the positive.

Draw or visualize an image of your negative unconscious that personifies the stultifying influence within, and gives you something tangible to battle against. Writers have imagined the figure to be a person, a gnome, an animal, a machine, or even disguised as pretty flowers.

When you have an image, speak harshly to it, proclaiming your independence from its control. Enter into the mental picture, prepared to pummel it, swear at it, and stamp out its power. This fantasy allows full emotional expression, an excellent outlet for normal anger. Some writers severely hampered by fears of competition perform this exercise daily, before working.

"I feel refreshed," states Jason, the columnist, "after a bout with my unconscious, which I imagine as a puppet. It has an aristocratic nose and glaring eyes. I bat it around, yelling that I can accomplish anything, even though 'Percy' disdains aggressive competition. Writing is passive. An extroverted mental romp burns off psychic energy. The puppet figure and name popped into my mind when I tried to envision the snooty inner voice that doubts my gifts."

Janet, the college student, reports, "I made up a picture of a frail, handwringing lady, afraid of her own shadow. She was a combination of my meek grandmother, apprehensive mother, and my insecurities. I can't imagine pushing around this fragile composite image, so I poke fun at her quaking personality. I always feel more confident after this exercise."

Sally, a songwriter, discovered a frightening vision of her unconscious—a looming Viking warrior, spear aimed to strike. "I scared myself until I discovered I could shrink the terrorizing fantasy figure into a miniature. The hateful fantasy figure resembled an older sister who had been jealous of my ability to write cute songs when I was a child. She tortured me with threats and gruesome faces when I would sing them. Before I start to write lyrics, I mentally place the Viking in a locked steel box. The vague anxieties that accompanied creative competition before I used the personification method have now subsided."

Unconscious thought patterns contain negative promises, warnings, and doubts. The inner voice intrudes, thwarting aggressive plans for competition. You can converse with the inner voice, firing questions and observations at it like a prosecuting attorney.

A conversation like this can uncover absurd unconscious restrictions, leaving you in conscious control.

Jonathan, the mystery writer whose parents and playmates made him feel different as a child when he revealed his rich imagination, discovered his unconscious image to be a blue fog.

"It felt suffocating, much like the feelings I had as a misunderstood child. I couldn't see why I was put down for my creative ideas, and no one ever gave me a reason, which may account for the image of the vague fog. My mother's favorite color was blue and the house was decorated in different shades of blue, which may account for the color. It would be simpler if my unconscious image were more concrete, but the foggy blue cloud is what comes to mind when I confront my unconscious wish to stop writing and competing. It's my internalized enemy. A conversation with my fog goes like this, when I feel like giving up as a writer:

Jonathan:	Why shouldn't I compete?
Blue Fog:	People will know you're crazy when you show them your trashy writing.
Jonathan:	Trashy?

Fog:	Your mysteries are no good, just nonsensical fantasies. Lies, too.
Jonathan:	You're the voice of my parents and they were wrong!
Fog:	You'll never sell anything again!
Jonathan:	You want me to give up and be a respectable person?
Fog:	Yes. Forget writing. Do something constructive.
Jonathan:	Stick it in your ear . . . your opinion doesn't mean anything to me. I'm a good writer and you're a bad parent.
Fog:	But I . . .
Jonathan:	Get lost.

After his imaginary conversation Jonathan experiences a rush of creative freedom, explaining, "When I speak forcefully, the foggy image breaks up and drifts away, the ghostly voice losing its power. I was reluctant to experiment with this cleansing technique because at first it sounded silly. However, it works—removes unconscious doubts and clears my mind for productivity. As a pragmatist, I believe in using anything that helps keep me creative."

Helen had sold several inspirational religious articles. She felt nervous and afraid to seek article assignments from more lucrative general markets.

"My free association led to memories that told me why I could only compete on a small scale and never try for larger challenges. I specifically remembered my father's chauvinistic anger when I skated in ice hockey better than an older brother. Dad demanded I give up 'boys' ' athletics and stick with volleyball. I couldn't wait to escape his irrational domination. I didn't know his disapproval would embed itself in my psyche, forbidding competition in my professional life.

"On my imagination screen my father was reduced to a tiny man, skinny legs dangling over the edge of a big chair, cowering as I bullied him, just as he had done to me when I was a little girl. After the insight and imaginary conversation, my fears of competing dissolved."

Rationalization

It is sometimes a surprise when translating the messages on the emotional tape recording to discover a subtle block to becoming a wise and consistent competitor. The most devious form of unconscious restriction is *rationalization*. Rationalizing is an ostensibly sound explanation for one's behavior that is actually a cover-up for unconscious motivation.

An example of rationalizing is the writer who denies any ambitions for recognition but is secretly jealous of published authors, convincing himself that established writers had easy access to editors and acceptance. Rational excuses of this kind are a protective device to defend against admitting the desire for recognition. The rationalizer fears he will exhibit too much aggression if he declares a need to be recognized. It is an unproductive form of modesty.

Amanda, a journalist, reports, "Our family was extremely wealthy, and my parents worked for the government for a dollar a year. Their voluntary jobs as advisers were never made public, at their insistence. The children were constantly reminded that a good life was one devoted to the betterment of the world. We had a relative who was in the entertainment business, and she was dismissed as a show-off. I went to private schools whose philosophy was the same as my parents'. It was uncouth to seek personal acclaim for your work when you were already blessed with wealth. I wanted to be somebody, not a ghostly figure in the background, and was made to feel selfish and ungrateful for my aspirations.

"The way I overcame the family rationalization about avoiding recognition was to give up the money held in trust for me, enough to live on for my entire life. I think my family felt guilty about having so much money, yet they didn't give it away— they eased the guilt by devoting their lives to sacrificing time and personal possibilities. They were insulted when I turned my back on their way of life and started from scratch as a reporter. It took years to become a successful journalist without the approval of my family or the comforts that money can buy, but I was determined to break the chain of denying ambition. I love being recognized as a writer. I can enjoy spending my money because it's earned, instead of given to me just because a great-grandfather made a bundle."

Another form of subtle but self-defeating rationalization is found in writers who believe that inspiration is the key to success. This fantasy puts a damper on disciplined daily writing and also sidetracks the competitive drive. The excitement a writer gets from an infusion of ideas, as if from a magical source, is undeniably delightful, but this arousal of creative thought happens very rarely. Waiting for the exquisite sensation of inspiration means a writer will produce very little while comforting himself with the rational excuse that good prose only flows from magical moments. The same thinking when applied to the tasks of competition—market research, writing queries, rewriting and resubmitting after rejection—will hamper determination to succeed as they will also depend on inspired action. Those who suffer from this romantic myth will have to confront their laziness which is being protected from examination by an unworkable rationalization.

Personal Challenges

Any problem with competition that is the result of early influences can be solved by another adult human: you. Children, because they are dependent and vulnerable, cannot argue with parental teachings. But as a creative, independent adult, you can fearlessly review the tape and examine its fallacies. Your responsibility as an artist is to ferret out the forces that restrict your professional progress.

When you have a clear picture of the unconscious motivations that block off normal aggression used for competition, denounce them as foreign to your conscious plans. You can then employ determined, vital energies to keep competitive—by honing your writing skills, presenting clean, clear copy, and keeping in touch with the needs of the reading public.

Chapter Three

Use Your Rejections as a Catalyst

ALL OF US, beginners or established authors, receive rejections. The sheer number of competing artists means that you will have to deal with rejection. Refusals arrive—euphemistic, humorous, on brusque printed cards, scribbles across queries, and, sometimes, personally signed letters.

Two writers talking: "Boy, I got the nicest no-sale today, from a senior editor, no less. I must be coming up in the world."

"Well, at least my latest form rejection had a handwritten 'sorry' across the bottom. Somebody actually cared about my feelings."

However kindly dismissals are couched, they make writers feel rebuffed, deflated, and unappreciated. We all handle non-acceptance with varying degrees of despair, depending on our self-confidence, our experience, and our mood of the moment. Few are secure enough to brush aside rejection with aplomb, although it is a goal to reach toward. Negative responses to creative offerings just plain hurt: we suffer sickening stomach thuds, the sting of being excluded, and the anger associated with unexpected failure.

Some writers, particularly those who feel isolated from others, become paranoid. They think there must be a secret society of editors who have a conspiracy against them, and ignore the reality of the large numbers of writers competing for a limited amount of space in magazines and the strict budgets of book publishers.

Professional writers cultivate a sharp business sense for selecting possible publishers. They handle rejections with the nonchalance of a gambler who figures a fair percentage of loss in his craft.

Reactions to rejections are a lot like our responses to other kinds of criticism. A rejection is the harshest type of criticism; the editor may make no specific unfavorable comment but turn your work down totally—the ultimate negative response.

People working in other fields also receive negative reactions to their work or refusals to buy their products and yet they are able to pursue their careers with optimism. They don't take one unsuccessful sale as a personal tragedy, like so many writers do. They're able to avoid feeling devastated because their product is not as invested with creative effort and does not represent their person the way a writer's material does.

Since we must all expect rejections, it is imperative to develop sensible defenses against feeling annihilated by them. Writers must be able to overcome the mini-death (depression) that often accompanies rejection in order to continue writing with confidence and to maintain a belief in their work as artists. We can approach rejections as a catalyst for improvement, as a spur to try even harder to sharpen our style or present more convincing characters. Rejection can be a reminder that we must always strive to learn more about the art of writing and should view ourselves in the process of continuing education.

A rejection from one editor need never mean a total defeat of your efforts; another editor may find the same material acceptable. Writers who have been in the business for many years have commented that they've learned not to feel defeated if a project is rejected thirty or forty times but continue to send the manuscript around until some editor finds it valuable. Giving in to depression after a piece has been sent back several times will get you and your manuscript nowhere.

You can learn to bounce back, regain emotional equilibrium, and strengthen your dedication to your craft through practical measures and an awareness of unconscious motivations that may cause rejections.

False Notions About Rejection

Open-Ended Acceptance

Many unpublished writers assume that successful authors enjoy automatic acceptance. While previous publication does demonstrate experience, each new submission to a publishing house undergoes close scrutiny, regardless of past performance and regardless of whose name is on the wrapper. All manuscripts are read for clarity, style, originality, and audience appeal. You have a fair chance for acceptance if you present quality material, to the right place, no matter who you are.

Inside Connections

Another misconception fostered by writers' feelings of being excluded is that "connections" bring advantages that struggling unknowns who don't have relatives or friends inside the publishing business can't hope to enjoy. Although connections made from past sales and friends who are familiar with your talents offer a slight edge (such as being considered first if two authors suggest the same topic), all authors are susceptible to rejection.

Sometimes connections can be a minus. Several years ago an acquaintance discussed with us the problems of stepparenting. We gave her an article we had written detailing expected difficulties with blended families. Calling to thank us, she said she wished a book were available to help solve everyday stepparenting hassles. We pointed out that our book proposal on the subject had been rejected several times during the last three years. She promptly sent the outline to her brother-in-law, a publisher of textbooks who was expanding his list to include trade nonfiction.

We waited six months before he replied offering a contract. Later he confided that the proposal had sat on his desk unread for five months. He hated dealing with relatives' submissions. "Friends and relations and friends of friends of relatives send me terrible material. I'm forced to defend negative decisions, always causing ill will. I can simply refuse strangers' work and let it go at that. You almost missed a sale because my sister-in-law mailed your idea."

Agents

An agent's representation is also often construed as insurance against literary rebuffs. Agents are usually savvy, matching clients and receptive editors, but they cannot sell unappealing manuscripts. They don't teach basic writing skills, do extensive editing, or specialize in offering personal comfort. Their business function is to search out potential publishers, negotiate advances and contracts, and mediate between author and book companies (and in rare cases magazines). A sympathetic agent may protect an author's sensitive feelings by leaning heavily on announcements of favorable news. However, reliable agents never guarantee immediate success because of their services.

Ethical agents won't take you on as a client unless they're confident they can represent you successfully. They must make a realistic assessment of the salability of your material before accepting you. Some agents who are extremely busy will charge a reading fee to examine your manuscripts and also will include a critique detailing the faults and merits of your work. A reading fee is not a scam; agents are in the business of making a living just like everybody else.

If you decide to seek an agent to represent you and find one who is enthusiastic about your career, make sure an attorney reads your contract, and request a clause delegating the American Arbitration Association to resolve any legal difficulties that may occur in the future. They make a fair and binding decision which both parties must agree to abide by.

As with editors, one agent may find your manuscript unappealing but another may judge it superior and gladly accept you as a client. One rejection is not the signal to give up your career but only an expression of a personal preference. Some agents list their priority of interests—plays, film scripts, novels, nonfiction—so study their specifications carefully before spending the money necessary to send a sample of your material.

Rejections as Judgments

An additional defeating distortion is that rejections prove a writer's lack of talent.

Even the most talented writers have difficulty getting publishers interested in books or articles that have a potentially limited audience. And financially successful publication is not always equated with good writing. (E.g., a porno-violence writer can earn big bucks from mass-appeal novels.) As we have noted, publishing companies are in the money-making business and would quickly face bankruptcy if they were not shrewd about what the reading audience will buy. As a free-lancer, you are also in business, with a responsibility to develop an interesting idea that will convince an editor of its marketability.

Erroneous beliefs surrounding acceptance and rejection must be shelved. Rationalizations gnaw into gumption and tenacity. They may momentarily soothe hurt feelings, but in the long haul toward success, excuses are a waste of time.

Let's listen again to Gene, the gag writer.

"Fifteen years ago, I wrote a poem about beauty contests. It was turned down at least fifty times. I thought it relevant and funny and continued to send it around. A contemporary women's magazine accepted it last week and the editor let me know that it was one of the sharpest poems she had read. You can never predict.

"I assumed the subject matter was ahead of the times and didn't blame editors for their lack of foresight. I have a suggestion for would-be and beginning freelancers. Writers, regardless of their main interest, should write poetry. To my mind it's the highest form of writing, helping you learn to reduce concepts to bare bones, and forcing clarity. Besides, market-wise, it's the most rejectable. Writers should create as many poems as possible, pick out the best for submission, and keep them circulating. Study the markets (largely literary magazines) carefully—don't send sexually explicit verse to a clergymen's magazine—and sooner or later some will be accepted. Lots will be returned, often with no comment and rarely with a criticism, because editors receive thousands of submissions. This approach teaches rejection acclimation. A poem usually requires less of a time-and-energy investment than a play, novel, article, or essay and is most likely not your main writing form if you want to make money. Thus the rejections are easier to handle. Experience gained with poetry rejections builds up shock immunity. After several hundred rejections and few acceptances, you'll have a thicker skin when a big project is turned down. You also learn another valuable lesson: the fact that your material is not returned immediately does not mean it will surely be accepted. It only means the editor has a great deal of material to read and hasn't gotten to your envelope yet. Don't tantalize yourself with this myth, ever."

Practical Reasons for Rejections

There are two major causes of rejections: writers' faults and editorial variables. Pretend you're an outside observer and examine your writing habits. Sidestepping essential procedures is a form of psychological undoing, unconsciously setting oneself up for frustration and mental anguish.

Writers' Faults

We will use magazine editors to dramatize all publishers' complaints.

Editors depend on freelancers—90 percent of some publications is written by independent contributors. The work involved in producing a monthly magazine is staggering, and overworked editors live with tremendous business pressure. Writers would receive a mind-blowing education if they could follow an editor during an average working day.

We visited the office of a women's magazine and even though we had an appointment with the senior editor, she was constantly interrupted by important telephone calls that demanded immediate decisions. She gave us a tour of the office; the business conversations we overheard were tinged with worry about deadlines, advertising accounts, writers who'd neglected to turn in articles on time, and art layouts. This highly charged, frenzied atmosphere revealed to us why editors have little time to be concerned with a writer's sensitive feelings and instead send out form rejections to quickly deal with undesirable submissions.

Shotgun Submissions

Editors and their assistants are rightfully annoyed and bewildered with queries and submissions that are simply irrelevant to their magazine's requirements.

Magazines that accept freelance material are listed in the current year's *Writer's Market*. The listings give each magazine's precise specifications for nonfiction, fiction, columns, fillers, cartoons, and photos. Writers following these instructions open the assignment door or make direct sales. Writers who ignore editorial particulars and insist on sending material that "will interest everyone" risk having the door slammed in their faces.

Competition for advertisers and readers is fierce and editors must entertain, satisfy, and keep a fickle audience. Read and *follow* the listing directions completely—it's your primer for acceptable material and prevents you from being labeled "amateur."

Those who ignore this often-repeated advice suffer from *narcissism*, a psychological disorder that flows over into business practices. Narcissistic individuals have an excessively admiring view of themselves, their possessions and productions. This state of self-love is a primary condition of infancy, which, in normal growth, develops into a realistic view of one's personality and a mature consideration for others' feelings. Children who are spoiled and never learn to earn love continue to remain in a narcissistic state: as adults they assume everyone is as interested in them as the parents who gave them too much attention and not enough realistic frustration.

Most people are put off by narcissists' lack of interest in anything but themselves—there's no give and take in their conversations, as they only enjoy talking about their interests, bragging about real or imagined accomplishments. The narcissistic writer doesn't bother with such details as editors' requirements but floods them with manuscripts they consider to be the work of genius. When a narcissistic writer is rejected, he can't imagine it is his wonderful words that fall short, so he develops a rationalization to explain the rejection: the editors are too stupid to recognize superior talent when they see it. Because of this self-deceiving attitude of narcissistic writers, they rarely succeed.

Ignoring the Demographics

Experienced freelancers become familiar with a magazine before writing a line of a query. If local distributors don't carry a particular magazine, check the library. Request several sample copies from editorial offices when you can't locate a magazine. Never submit to any publication without cover-to-cover study.

Advertisements reveal more about editorial policy and readership interests than any other item in a magazine. Magazines could not exist without advertisers, and editors cannot alienate their supporters. A planned article on non-nutritional processed baby foods will not sell to magazines that feature full-page ads for prepared infant food. A health-food magazine promoting natural foods would be more receptive.

Ads indicate readers' average age, income, education level, and hobbies, providing writers with a general lifestlye profile. For example, the ads in many women's magazines are for cosmetics, perfumes, clothes, vitamins, hygiene products, food, and diet aids. This reveals to writers that the readers are women, interested in improving their appearance, getting or kooping a good figure, attracting men, and enjoying parties. The writer who sends in a romantic love story with a single career woman as the heroine will likely receive acceptance over the nonresearching writer who submits a story, however delightful, of an older woman returning to college.

Typical men's-magazine advertisements for cars, alcohol, stereo equipment, grooming products, cameras, cigarettes and cigars, and sophisticated clothing target the reader as a man with money to spend on luxury items, who enjoys looking attractive, dates frequently, and has interests related to music, machines, and travel. The writer seeking publication in such a magazine should slant his manuscript toward adventure, love conquests, up-to-date information on music, computers, and automotive innovations. The editor would most likely dismiss a story on how to apply for a job, since most of his readers are educated and already employed.

Editorial Philosophies

Pay particular attention to the editorial or letter from the publisher that appears in the front of the magazine. This statement offers a glimpse into the journal's overview and concerns and gives you information about the editor's interests.

As an example, the editorial comments in a medical magazine will reflect the current concerns of physicians about politics, patient management and financial planning which gives the writers clues about the editor's preoccupations.

A magazine directed toward teenagers will discuss in the editorial the possibilities of the future, self-discipline and how to understand oneself, which illuminates for the author the philosophy of guiding young people in their values and options.

Switch gears to another publication if your ideas contradict the editor's philosophy. It is considered unprofessional to submit material intended to alter an editor's ideals.

Magazines are read for relaxation, entertainment, and information. The writer's duty is enrichment rather than pointing out an audience's misconceptions. There is a podium for controversy in Alternate Publications, also listed in *Writer's Market*.

Study the articles to grasp the magazine's overall style and tone. A retirement magazine's tone will be upbeat, enthusiastic, and stimulating, avoiding overly serious, depressing topics. The target audience is well-adjusted retirees who are interested in travel and tips on maintaining health into old age.

A magazine whose audience is religious and family-oriented will have a mixture of inspirational articles and stories, plus pieces on how to understand and handle family living. The intelligent writer thus submits pro-religious, uplifting, and practical-advice pieces to this type of magazine.

Special-interest magazines like those directed to recreational-vehicle owners, gourmets, writers, pilots, dentists, affluent travelers, or skiers appeal to one specific interest of their readers and don't want general articles about how to enjoy life.

The language used in the articles and stories points to the range of acceptable vocabulary. For example, magazines appealing to highly educated, intellectual readers require a more complex style.

Careful reading of several recent issues provides a good overall impression of editorial preferences and readers' interests.

Your Calling Card

Busy editors often prefer article queries rather than complete manuscripts. The query letter should clearly state your point of view and the unique information that will contribute to the reader's knowledge or entertainment. Experienced writers present ideas creatively but concisely, whetting the editor's interest to read the completed piece. Proper research will give you a good idea of an editor's proclivities for anecdotes, humor, interviews, and facts.

You must be creative with your query letters. You are competing with telephone calls and business interruptions for the editor's attention. A boring letter almost surely generates a rejection slip. Become a student for a few weeks if you find you have problems writing a stimulating query letter. Read a variety of articles, books, and short stories. Construct outlines, then three or more paragraphs explaining exactly what the author wrote about and why you read the piece through, what was original in the plot or style, and why an editor should purchase the manuscript. Compare your query with the finished product, checking for accuracy and appeal. Like writing poetry, this exercise hones your ability to condense ideas.

A professor who had written many technical papers shared with us some advice he'd received from his mentor. He presented his first paper to his old professor just before he sent it off to a medical journal. He expected praise and a pat on the head, but instead the professor handed back the paper and asked the writer to explain in one sentence the central idea of the manuscript. After he delivered a brilliant and concise statement describing the theme, the older man explained that nowhere in the manuscript had the writer told the reader what he intended to explain in detail. The author devoted time to learning how to simplify his ideas into one sentence and then use that sentence as the first line in his query letter. He also noted that a well-written query gives him an excellent starting point when he begins to write the article.

Editors appreciate a list of previous publications with query letters. Tearsheets of published works will give the editor an impression of your style. A novice presenting an original slant or idea will not be ignored, however.

Building a Reputation

Seasoned writers acknowledging assignments reiterate the article's delivery date—a thoughtful gesture welcomed by editors. Many assignments, even to well-known writers, are made "on speculation"—no payment guarantee until editorial approval of the finished piece.

To establish a solid reputation for dependability, make every effort to meet your deadline. Explain any unavoidable delays, reinforcing your understanding of the editor's situation. Many editors are treated like unfeeling machines by writers, but, of course, they are people too, trying to perform a difficult job. If you show consideration for their responsibilities by explaining delays, they will respect your mature, professional attitude.

"I've sold articles to a family-oriented, religious magazine for ten years," reports Helen. "The editor is friendly, quick to reply, and receptive. But he has a strange quirk, which drives me nuts. He consistently returns articles for elaboration, no matter how long and informative. I'm always prepared for at least one rewrite, even though I try to please his thirst for additional statistics and anecdotes the first time around.

"At a seminar I talked to Jerry, a dentist and part-time freelancer. He refuses to work for my picky editor, because he hates to make revisions. He admitted writing scathing letters to editors who suggested improvements. I can't afford a prima donna stance. My sales supplement the family's income. The editor's demands invariably add refinements proving his expertise. Writers should be honored when editors patiently correct flaws instead of flatly refusing manuscripts or 'expediently' printing them with all their dirty laundry on display.

"Some of my colleagues ask for a kill fee when assignments are rejected. Most editors don't pay this nominal fee for the writer's investment because they can't afford the expense. My editor of long standing pretends total ignorance of kill fees!

"On balance, I have a polite, respectful relationship with him. He probably thinks I'll never send a fully fleshed-out article and I know he'll always peer critically at my offerings. I guess we have a mutually profitable arrangement."

Unsolicited Material

Short stories, poems, cartoons, and fillers don't require queries, but careful study of the magazine's format is just as imperative for success as your article research.

The assistant editors who review unsolicited submissions are swamped, so they appreciate receiving clear, clean manuscripts, revealing professional self-esteem, serious intentions, and respect for readers.

Kiss unsolicited work goodbye when you mail it without the obligatory self-addressed, stamped return envelope. Publishers cannot afford to return manuscripts they didn't ask for and many a manuscript sent without proper postage ends up in the wastebasket.

We received the following inquiry about a manuscript dealing with male-female relationships. There was no return, stamped envelope—a courtesy when requesting information.

Dear Dr. Rosenbaums,
   Please help me finished this artilce. Would it be corect for a women to have mens for friends even tho she is married to

someone ellse? I need this infornation most quickly as you can write back.

Your buddie in writing,

In an attempt to educate the writer, we suggested that he'd make a better impression with correct spelling, businesslike language, and a return envelope. He replied, amazed by our criticisms and pronouncing us "unfeeling snobs." This would-be writer was his own worst enemy: he sets himself up for rejection because he didn't invest the time to learn how to write a professional letter.

Blocking Success

Inappropriate goals are another psychological setup for rejection.

Many beginners squelch their publishing potential by submitting only to top markets. Then they give up their dreams of success after their first few form rejections, never thinking about the fact that very few neophytes gain immediate access to the big time.

Any writer finds it difficult to crack the top-paying general-interest magazines. The most lucrative markets have the most people vying for them, and they have a stable of freelancers with solid, long-standing reputations. These writers have earned the status they enjoy, having labored up the ladder for many years, and even now they must *continue* to compete for acceptance.

A college journalism student convinced our local newspaper editor he could write informative movie reviews. His main objective is building a portfolio. "When I apply for a writing job, I'll have concrete proof of my abilities. I consider writing reviews as my apprenticeship."

Jason, the columnist, remembers, "As a novice, I wrote five 'witty' columns, spent a small fortune on copying, envelopes, and postage, and sent them to the country's ten largest newspapers. All were summarily returned. My brilliant efforts treated like rubbish!

"After a period of disillusionment, I set my sights on a more reachable target. My subject matter was actually geared to small-town Americans rather than sophisticated city dwellers. Large newspapers, with entrenched syndicated columnists, leave little room for competiton. I studied syndicates and sent a new batch of columns to a service selling to Midwest weeklies. They liked my fresh approach and offered to carry me on commission. I soon had markets matching my material. The money arrived in droplets, dashing my dreams of lugging bags of cash to the bank. But in five years I have erected a solid reputation with several weeklies, received a lot of fan mail, have a sturdy sense of accomplishment, plus a dependable income. Now I'm branching out to the medium markets—daily papers in higher-population areas.

"Too many writers blackball their chances by shooting for the stars when they should shrewdly examine attainable possibilities. There's a place for everyone—you just have to find it."

Judith's first short story appeared in a literary journal. "It was thrilling to see my creation in print. This validation gave me courage to approach paying markets. I made the usual mistakes, sending manuscripts to *The New Yorker*, *Atlantic Monthly*, and *Reader's Digest*. A veteran soap opera writer advised me to start sending stories to small-circulation magazines. She helped get my head out of the clouds. My first sale netted thirty-five dollars, but it could have been five hundred, the joy of acceptance was so sweet! I'd still be frustrated, striving for only top markets, had I not listened to my experienced friend. One day I'll try for the 'best,' but only after my talents are perfected."

Avoid setting yourself up for rejection, aiming for the heights before you're seasoned. You will have to consciously overcome our society's judgment that only the biggest and the best have value. Any sale affirms your writing skills and will add to your credentials. Editors will understand you have paid your dues in the lower and middle markets and won't reject your current work just because you haven't yet made a big sale. Devotion to practical writing skills, intelligent market study, and proper manuscript mechanics will eventually lead to publication. A sale is a sale!

Novelists and nonfiction writers need to be knowledgeable, too, about book companies' interests and submission rules, also detailed in *Writer's Market*. If a company says that it doesn't want complete manuscripts or poetry and cookbooks, *listen*— and stick to the rules. We are fortunate to have such an up-to-date market manual to aid us in finding the right publication for our properties. If you ignore the publishers' specifications, you will waste postage, frustrate editors, and collect more rejection slips.

By necessity, publishers are conservative, carefully weighing sales potential and competition. If you think you have a new slant for a book on fathering, check published titles and, where possible, upcoming books on the subject before sending queries or outlines. Can you compete? Six recent books on the subject might turn your plans to other subjects.

Flexibility

"Readership trends fluctuate," observes David. "A few years ago I sold several teenage stories loaded with heavy psychological messages and Freudian concepts. Today's young people are turned off by esoteric theories and psychiatric jargon, and are more interested in practical advice for their future. So I've developed a different vocabulary and new means to get across the same old message—know yourself before rushing to alter the world."

Originality

"Many excellent writers are rejected because of boring plots," explains Robin, an editor for twenty years. "Many first novels involve transitions from adolescence to adulthood, marriage breakups, or personal attacks on the opposite sex. 'Growing up and getting away' novels saturate the bookstores. I'm looking for uniqueness, but I can't give a formula for the special quality I seek. I consider sparkling plots the author's job, whether the novel's genre be mystery, romance, gothic, or contemporary.

"I can tell whether the author is a reader after reviewing three manuscript pages. Reading makes for excellent writing. Nonreaders' style is stilted, self-conscious; it lacks believable dialogue, and comes across as old-fashioned. My colleagues and I are especially open to experimental writing. We all agree that authors should take more time assessing current trends and inventing original plots and characters."

A Checklist

To avoid setting yourself up for rejection, review your approach:

- Do you carefully read editorial requirements before submitting queries, or, if appropriate, completed works?

- Do you research magazines' styles, readers' interests, ads, and vocabulary before knocking on the door for admittance?
- Do you check recent publications to weigh the originality of your idea, and its competition?
- Have you learned to write clear, interesting synopses?
- Do you represent yourself with businesslike letters?
- Have you established a reputation for dependability?
- Do you choose markets open to beginners or keep trying for the top?

Unconscious Motivations

Consciously, you may follow the rules strictly, but unconsciously break the very one that dooms you to rejection.

Do you think you work against your best interests? Employ the unconscious personification routine to make sure you don't set yourself up for rejection.

"After two sales to a family-living magazine, my next three ideas were turned down cold," shares Peter, an articles writer, cartoonist, and photographer. "I picked up a current issue and immediately saw the format had changed, focusing on single parenthood, working mothers, and children's independence. My rejection letters had been signed by the outgoing editor, who was obviously putting in time before the new staff took over. I couldn't use this as an excuse, because a rereading of last month's writers' magazine informed me of the hiring and firing at this magazine. My suggestions were out of sync with the 'modern' approach. I quickly queried the new editor with ideas more in line with the redirection. She replied, accepting one on speculation and releasing my previously-paid-for material since it no longer fit their needs.

"I had wasted precious time and possibilities, because I hadn't kept informed. There seemed no rational reason for my laziness. After all, I'm in business and should always be aware of editorial changes. Mistakes like this are costly. I have to continue selling a minimum of three pieces a month to keep my full-time freelance business going.

"Searching for the source of my creative undoing, I turned inward to my unconscious negative force, an ugly, ferret-faced, cloaked figure I call 'Rat.' I can get in touch with my unconscious voice easiest when walking outdoors, away from household distractions.

"My conversation:

" 'Hey, Rat, I know you're in there. Why do you fool me into assuming everything will stay the same? You like me to feel lazy, right?'

" 'Nothing really changes when you're a loser. Work is so tiresome. All that attention to detail has to wear you out. Forget this creative stuff,' said the rasping voice of the Rat.

" 'You're evading. Tell me why you like me to be lazy.' (My unconscious never actually lies when I pose direct questions. It doesn't seem to think the truth will affect matters).

" 'Dope. You always were kind of slow. You can barely spell your name. Better sell insurance or maybe go on welfare.'

" 'You pretty much hate my gifts, don't you, Rat?'

" 'That's because you're a no-talent guy. Why bother when you're going to fail anyway.'

"I stopped this stream-of-consciousness conversation, having uncovered enough information to satisfy myself: The Rat thinks I'm stupid, worthless, and untalented. I fantasize pushing and trapping Rat in a giant mousetrap where he writhes until our next bout.

"My unconscious's voice has my father's tone. He controlled children with biting sarcasm, laced with low expectations of our futures. He never praised my writings or drawings, often warning me to find a simple job that would not tax my low IQ. He thought all artists were shirkers, lazy and irresponsible morons. My unconscious thinks writing is an escape from 'real' work. It silently spaces out my alertness, reinstating the doltish, crestfallen self-image my father instilled. An uneducated, rigid person, my dad truly believed he was toughening up his offspring for adult life. The funny thing is that I have a sister working as an actress, and a brother who writes science fiction."

A Practical Rule for Finished Work

Sometimes writers are rejected because they don't carefully re-read and rewrite a project.

After you've revised your final draft to your satisfaction, file the finished manuscript away. Reexamine it again a few days later in the role of a demanding English teacher, delighting in spotting errors, wordiness, redundancies, and preachiness. Red-pencil your work until it shines.

"A client returned a speech on how to be an assertive disciplinarian without physical force three times because it was boring, unclear, and repetitive," recalls Katherine. "I fumed about her perfectionistic attitude. After all, other customers were pleased with my speeches, written so the speaker appeared to be talking casually.

"My confidence began sagging after the last rejection, which labeled my writing too vague for her audience of educators. Resentment began to interfere with my concentration. To clear my mind, I began a free-association tape recording, searching for the unknowns that were causing the rejections. I formed a fantasy audience of listening teachers. As I spoke, a shrill, angry voice emerged, revealing long-forgotten hostilities toward bossy instructors. Hiding under the surface was a mass of discontent and anxiety connected with my school days when I was a bored and disruptive student. I hated most of my teachers and thought school was a prison. My flabby writing was a secret attempt to withhold interesting information from the 'bullies.' I was my own victim, frustrating myself by writing and rewriting nonsalable materials. I faced a decision: cling to childish hatreds and lose sales or approach the assignment maturely. Did I want to make money or involve an innocent client in my neurotic problems?

"To get rid of the old angers about teachers and school, I wrote a speech for mean, disinterested teachers, recounting their sins against certain students (me). The technique was successful, freeing my energies to put together an acceptable speech. The client said it seemed almost as if it were written by a different person, and she was right. I should have been aware that any string of rejections meant I was being controlled by hidden motivations, but when the unconscious takes over, it's really hard to understand why you're failing. I've never been surprised by the crazy stuff recorded on my invisible tape, just shocked that it can manipulate me so powerfully."

Lauri, the playwright, concurs: "I'm hindered by an internalized mother, who's alarmed by my preoccupation with perfection. As a child I collapsed in tears, tearing disappointing drawings or stories into shreds. Mother was upset by emotional outbursts and scurried around trying to smooth over situations with, 'You ask too much of yourself, dear. Don't try so hard. Let's have a nice plate of cookies and forget about this.' When I have a play rejected because I've produced less than my all-out best, I know I have succumbed to my unconscious voice.

"Now, when beginning a play, before blocking out characters, scenes, costumes, and scenery, I dictate a stern reprimand to invisible Momsy, and fantasize her tied and gagged so she can't interrupt with her placations against my ideal standards.

"My central self, which fights against unconscious promises to relax, urges quality—which means revisions, and a continued effort toward high-caliber writing. My children laugh at the moans, thuds, and screams they can hear coming from my inner sanctum. I overheard them explaining to friends, 'Mom's just doing a play. Writers have to yell to get their work done.' "

Rejections decrease in proportion to the amount of time invested in researching the market and in uncovering psychological roadblocks that interfere with success. When you are confident you have overcome these external and internal roadblocks, rejections can be viewed in a businesslike way.

Editorial Variables

Even solicited manuscripts get rejected. Editors cannot predict their responses before reading a work in its entirety. They may express great enthusiasm for a proposal but dislike your final offering.

Usually, a magazine editor will reject the entire piece, whereas with a nonfiction book or novel, the editor will suggest changes and work with the author to produce a polished product. "I received a humorously written query for an article on sticky social situations," states Joseph, a magazine editor. "I gave a go-ahead 'on spec' even though the writer was unknown. When the piece showed up, the material was too caustic for my readers—the idea was excellent, but the language and treatment were inappropriate. My return letter stated, 'The enclosed does not meet our editorial requirements.' That's life. I know many writers think editors are heartless, but in truth, we are just extremely busy. I can't teach writers about my readers' tastes—that is their responsibility."

Some editors reject submitted material because of changes in the focus of a magazine, stories with similar plots, or too much material on hand.

Maurice authored two mildly successful cookbooks—elegant pastries and gourmet diet menus. "My editor rejected a cocktail party book proposal as 'too risky in today's tight market.' I called him for clarification and learned their marketing department was declining all cookbooks using expensive ingredients. He reported, 'People are concerned about rising food costs—they're looking for bargains, not extravagant ways to spend money.'

"I'm flexible and write for a living, so I changed directions from gourmet to the basics and submitted a proposal on preparing eggs a hundred appetizing ways. Their contract offer included a smaller advance than usual. I accepted, because I liked working for them and knew they were short of money. Besides, I'd rather have a book assignment than no contract at all."

Sometimes proposals, manuscripts, and queries get lost in the mail, misplaced in files, or stuck in a stack of unread properties. After a reasonable wait of six weeks, writers can inquire about their material. Editors depend on secretaries, mail deliveries, and memories, just like the rest of us.

Buffers Against Rejection

Samples Only

To cut down on your rejection ratio, never write an article until you have found an interested editor. Write sample chapters of novels, finishing the story only after a publisher has expressed curiosity to read a completed manuscript. Screenplays can be sold by first presenting treatments—lengthy explanations of plot, action, characters, and dialogue. Short-story writers, cartoonists, lyricists, and poets can afford the luxury of finalizing their productions before submission. Unless you are driven to finish a project for your personal enjoyment, writing a complete novel, article, or script without editorial interest is a waste of valuable time.

Quantities

Serious writers circulate quantities of material. Chances of acceptance increase with the sheer number of your submissions. When your output is a mere one or two queries or manuscripts, excessive worry or paralyzing preoccupation are all too likely to result. Freelancers have no control over an editor's personal idiosyncrasies, when submissions will be considered, or, ultimately, publishing decisions. But we *can* be in command of an elaborate network of submissions.

"Book companies took forever replying to my lengthy nonfiction outlines," states Joann, "I changed policies last year and now I write one-page synopses, sending copies to at least fifteen appropriate publishers. In *Writer's Market*, publishers note whether they will accept simultaneous submissions or not. My synopsis is obviously a copy, so I don't mention that I've sent the same query to other places. To date, no one has been offended by my practice. My cover letter offers interested editors an extensive outline. The responses usually arrive within two weeks with an average of three or four proposal requests. I then have a name to write to and am confident the material will receive prompt attention. My new approach saves time and postage. I no longer hover around the mailbox, waiting for that one editor's answer. I have induced novelist-pals to follow my lead and they report similar results. We take refusals with a more blasé spirit because with thirty letters in the mail, there's lots of action.

Rituals

"When a rejection arrives, I stop all writing and activity and follow a self-esteem-boosting ritual," shares Marilyn, the short-story writer. "With three children, a job, and a part-time writing career, I have little time for self-pity. The editor's comments (if any) are noted and the story filed for rewriting. No critique means the editor didn't appreciate my style. Every piece submitted has intrinsic value or I wouldn't bother to send it. Immediately I search for a new market, mailing the story that day. Piles of returned manuscripts don't litter my desk and I don't save rejection slips. This routine keeps me optimistic. If I find myself slumping from a rejection slip, I take out some work that's been published, reread it, remember the amount of the check, and feel validated once more."

Normal Reactions

Many writers ask if their responses to rejection are normal.

"I get so down in the dumps, I can't think straight, let alone write."

"My husband accuses me of wallowing in self-pity. He

thinks I use rejections as an excuse to avoid my typewriter. He doesn't understand how my confidence is shattered when sample chapters are turned down."

"I get overly excited when an editor requests to read an article. I fool myself, believing a sale is imminent if a piece is held over three weeks. (What a dreamer!) Then, when he turns it down, I'm as shocked as if a stranger had slapped my face. I crash with a resounding thump, and walk around in a glum cloud for days. Someday I'll learn to be more realistic."

These reactions are commonplace and normal for creative artists who must expect rejections. Surprise and depression should be brief and nondebilitating.

Recovery

Distancing

Distancing is the ability to separate yourself from creative sensitivity (used to produce material) and treat submissions as a business operation.

Set aside all expectations and daydreams that build false hope when mailing submissions. Reroute your energies to the creative work at hand. Freelancers who attain a realistic attitude worry less while waiting for replies.

"I separate the act of writing completely from the practical selling aspects," says Ted, a children's storybook author. "I've forced myself to put creativity and business in two compartments wearing different hats. My creative hat directs energies toward free-flowing imagination and fantasy worlds of adventure. I wear my business hat to update file cards, list manuscripts' whereabouts, and plan further submission targets if rejected. I keep my manner efficient, treating submissions and returns as salable properties, not pieces of my soul. Distancing protects my emotions. (When I make a sale, I gleefully throw the business cap in the air, and celebrate like a kid.)"

Sectioning

A rejection simply means one editor responded unfavorably. It does not imply the next reader will react the same. And the rejected manuscript is only *one* piece of writing; a small portion of your possible creative productions.

"I used to experience feelings of total inferiority," recalled

Bill, "whenever an article was returned. Over the years I've gained a better perspective, realizing the impossibility of pleasing every editor. When a publisher returns unwanted work, he isn't aware of the writer's emotional investments, research time, and anticipation. The business side of creative life demands sectioning off expectations—removing your ego from your completed works. That way, you can maintain self-appreciation when assignments are sent back.

"Some authors love their creations *too* much, and they can't believe anyone could fail to appreciate the beauty of their style. This is narcissistic, thinking everything you do is perfect just because it's yours.

"Currently, I'm working on a novel, and I'd love it to be a bestseller—who wouldn't? But the book, even if it were published and even if it were a bestseller, would not be read by that many people on the planet. I'm a realist and so I accept the limits of one writer's impact. No matter how valuable your message may be, you can't change the world with one book. I've reached the point where it's not a personal put-down, but just a rejection of one of my many ideas. No publisher's refusal is the end of the world."

Outlets for Anger

Angry responses to rejections are normal, although usually unfulfilling. Raging at editors is inappropriate—it won't help you make future sales and it never changes an editorial decision. Editors are usually dedicated professionals with sound reasons for rejecting a property. They don't like to be attacked for their decisions and will respond angrily, making a note to avoid dealing with an author who cannot control his temper. Misdirecting anger toward friends, family, or pets is unfair and eventually causes guilt.

"I wrote an entire book for a university press without an advance," recounts Sheila. "The editor was supportive and helpful during manuscript preparation. The highly technical material required several months of library work to assure accuracy. After I delivered the 250-page manuscript, the editor informed me it would be sent out for reader evaluation. This was news to me! Three out of five commentators responded negatively and the project was dropped. I was livid. My hard work was dismissed without a penny's remuneration. The nervy editor then suggested that I submit another proposal.

"I live alone without any understanding friends close by. Filled with righteous indignation, I furiously typed a succinct, rude letter to the editor and her misinformed experts. I was convinced I'd mail it, though of course I didn't. But the act of writing it helped release my boiling fury. Rage often needs some physical expression. I spent the next hour chopping wood. Guess what face I fantasized on each log!

"My fantasies help discharge my aggression; I'm perfectly comfortable with murderous thoughts. After all, thoughts are not deeds, but rather a visual image of the things we would like to do at that moment but never intend to carry out. I resolved never again to write a full-length manuscript without an advance or promise of a kill fee."

Jed's friends talk out their anger at being rejected. "We have mutual gripe sessions about unenlightened editors who disdain our masterpieces, and since we're all storytellers we invent gruesome misfortunes to befall them. Our conversations help us vent our spleen and clear our minds to return, refreshed, to our writing. We understand the need to air frustrations so we accept and even applaud each other's sadistic but harmless rantings."

A good, long scream does wonders for the spirits, releasing explosive feelings. Of course, you must consider the surroundings. An enclosed car is an excellent environment for a scream. Apartment dwellers can scream satisfactorily into a pillow.

Moving On

Rejections will always befall writers. Expect them. Present your work free from practical and psychological roadblocks to success. When the inevitable occurs, persevere with resubmission rituals and the knowledge that each piece is only a small portion of your expected lifetime production.

Chapter Four

Your Psychohistory: An Aid to Creativity

NO ONE HAS ever been (or will ever be) exactly like you. Nor can any other person ever experience your feelings, sensations, or thoughts. People's reactions to life events are as individual as their fingerprints. For example, siblings reminiscing about family rituals or parental treatment are usually surprised to discover great divergences in their perceptions and conclusions.

Everyone's memory contains a transcript of his profoundly personal experiences. The average person uses his past experiences as an aid in daily problem solving, for avoiding unpleasant or uncomfortable situations, and for sharing social information.

For the writer, memory performs all these vital functions and more. Writers depend dramatically on memory to recall and record idiosyncrasies in people's characters, to describe moments from long ago with clarity, and to capture moods from the past. A writer's personal psychological history is a hidden treasure, because the creative imagination can take any experience and develop it into a unique story. Inside every memory rests the spark of a story, play, poem, lyric, screenplay, novel, or article, waiting for the bellows of your imagination to fan it.

Unfortunately most of us have large areas of our past that have been forgotten. Of course, there are insignificant events which we all forget because they are common to human nature and would be so much clutter in the mind. But we also lose track of many very meaningful events, experiences that could be invaluable to us as writers. Unless we invest the concentration and patience required to uncover centers of disremembrance, some important segments of experience will be forfeited to oblivion.

We do not always forget discriminatingly, only blocking out traumatic or frightening memories. Sometimes, in order to protect ourselves from overwhelming feelings, or to continue a negative illusion, we also forget beautiful and sweet incidents. We silently construct sentinels to stand at the gates of memory. Creative people, however, function most effectively when they're in touch with all of their significant feelings and past experiences.

Your inner tape recording is a hidden gold mine that can be discovered, explored, and transformed into creative works by constructing a personal psychological history.

Overcoming Repression

We cannot recall every emotion or situation stored in the brain because of their incredible number. Selective recall is a mental process we use to remember a specific event, someone's name, or an important date. Events that are charged with emotions which can be easily recalled intellectually but without a feeling connected to the memory are under the pressure of repression. *Repression* is a psychological barrier unconsciously erected to protect a person from overwhelming sensations of anger, pain, grief, loss, jealousy, or shame. As with other protective devices, this defense requires psychological energy to maintain.

The mechanism of repression begins in childhood, when the fragile ego doesn't have the strength to accept or deal with devastating events. For example, children who are abandoned by a parent can't cope with the thought that the parent didn't love them enough to stay with them. They defend themselves against this pain by repressing the realization that the parent is gone for good and talk about the absence as if it were temporary, or that the parent is planning a surprise for them and only traveling to make plans for the child's happiness. The real feelings of bewilderment, anger, fear, and rejection are solidly entrenched behind the fantasy that the parent plans to return. It's only when children reach a certain level of maturity in puberty that their psychological resources are strong enough for them to give up the illusion and face reality. Teenagers have the intellectual ability to understand that the parent left a marriage, not just the child, and can make personal, moral decisions about the abandonment. They will have developed strengths to handle the anger and pain, and thus can allow those feelings to escape from their psychological prison. The energy that was used to repress the feelings can be channeled into relationships, achievements, or creativity.

Whenever we repress memories and their associated emotions, they assume exaggerated proportions. This occurs because much of what we're afraid to recall is moments from childhood when we were helpless and victimized by our limited verbal, physical, and emotional resources. A devastating event is terrifying to a child, but as adults we have the mature inner strengths available to cope with and confront revealed truths. Children often respond to loss, anger, or rejection as if the pains were a miniature death. Some adults think that if they allow themselves to relive repressed feelings they'll feel as if they were dying again. However, you have obviously survived your past and will not be damaged if you penetrate the walls of recall.

Retrieving and writing down the contents of your psychological history will present you with an endless source of rich material for ideas, characters, and plots. The release of memories and descriptions of your past should not be used to pinpoint personality flaws or neurosis, but rather as a springboard for totally unique creative material.

Jenny, a novelist who writes about contemporary women, was frustrated with the lack of authenticity of one character's reactions. The story had reached a point where the heroine's husband died. Jenny was unable to convey the combination of despair, anger, fear, and guilt that she thought her character would be buffeted by when her mate was killed.

Jenny talked the problem over with her lover, which led to a conversation about death.

"What do you know about loss?" asked David.

Jenny let her mind wander, remembering the death of her aged father. She couldn't equate her mourning over his long-expected death with the feelings of a young wife losing a healthy, vibrant man.

"There's a buried memory from my childhood," recounted Jenny. "I haven't thought of this in over thirty years, but during World War II English friends of my father's sent their daughter to live with us. They wanted her to be spared the daily terror of the buzz bombs. She became like a sister to me. We loved each other and shared all our fears and secrets. After about six months she became terribly sick with some unpronounceable blood disease and died at the age of nine. My parents tried to hide her illness and hospitalization from me. They wouldn't let me go to the funeral. I was brokenhearted and couldn't understand why my wonderful new sister had been taken away from me. I was furious with my parents, secretly blaming them for not saving her life—a normal belief, I guess, when a kid is seven. My parents told me that I began to wander away far from the neighborhood, getting lost. When I was found I was always crying, asking strangers about my kidnapped sister."

While Jenny talked about her "forgotten" childhood episode of sudden loss, she reexperienced the original sorrow and pain. She also began to understand the roots of her peculiar relationship with friends. "I always act as if they're going to disappear without telling me. Now I see that this fear comes from the actual disappearance of my dear friend from England."

David thought the story very touching and prodded Jenny to begin a novel about young children's feelings, fears, and daily life contrasted against the background of a world war.

The sample chapters Jenny sent to a publisher were quickly accepted. The editor commented that the descriptions of the tone of the times, the little girls' fantasies about invasion from Germany and Japan, and the bonding that took place between the children were completely credible. "This writing is obviously not from your imagination, but autobiographical," wrote the editor.

Before Jenny began the novel she listed every memory of herself as a seven-year-old during the 1940s. She was delighted and amazed that even though she had not seen the small town of her youth for twenty-five years, the images of neighborhoods, playmates, school, parents, war events, rationing, smells, and noises were easily accessible to a concentrated effort.

"I had consciously avoided thinking about my unhappy years," reported Jenny. "My parents were preoccupied with money worries, fears about relatives in Europe, and were quite harsh and unloving. I have come to understand that my perceptions of them, the fears I lived with, and the oasis of sisterly love make a beautiful statement about children's needs. When I finish this novel I plan to delve even further into my background. I've learned that reliving the unpleasant times is not that painful."

Jenny's uncovered memories stimulated the idea for a novel, afforded insight into her present-day behavior with friends, and proved to her that a painful past does not have to be repressed. What about the original novel that brought Jenny to this problem? The reason she was unable to adequately write about the husband's death and the wife's mourning was that Jenny had barriers erected against all feelings of grief. When she opened herself to the past, the barriers were knocked down and she could continue the novel with renewed dynamism and empathy for her character.

Your Psychohistory

Before you begin your psychological history, decide which mode of expression will be the most comfortable for you. You can jot the answers on a tablet or type them up if you think better at the typewriter. Some people are more at ease talking into a tape recorder and listening at a later date. Using the most comfortable combination will add to the flow and richness of your recall. This questionnaire is long; some of your answers will probably be lengthy while others may be brief. Since this is not a test but a tool for increased creativity, the amount of time you spend on each question or whether you answer all the questions is insignificant. Each reader should select a quiet place conducive to thought, comfortably pace himself, and let the information flow at its own speed.

You will discover a more spontaneous recall if you respond to the questions with feelings rather than intellect. By this we mean if you are asked "Did you feel loved most of the time during your childhood?" and your first reaction (feeling) is "No," but your next thought is "But I was told that I was loved, so I must be wrong" (intellectual reasoning), go with the emotional response. It's how we felt as a child that's important, not what we were told we should have felt.

There is no place for guilt or worry about hurting someone's feelings when you recall and record negative emotions. This is your personal reaction to life events and belongs entirely to you. Ignore any invisible critic who peers over your shoulder to inhibit your candid response.

The following questions are those a psychoanalyst would ask a client over a period of time as he attempts to piece together the experiences that formed the person's view of the self and to jiggle the memory of buried thoughts and feelings.

What is your earliest memory from childhood? It doesn't matter if the memory is from three or twelve, just the first thought or scene that comes to mind.

Describe the setting: people, scenery, pets and furniture you visualize.

What action occurs inside the memory?

Close your eyes and mentally view the memory as a movie. Can you recapture your emotions connected with the scene? If this incident prompts other scenes in your mind's eye, keep writing until your imaginary screen goes blank.

What was the order of your birth—first, second, fifth?

How did you feel about your birth position?

Can you recall another sibling's birth and your reactions?

Do you have strong negative feelings about any of your brothers or sisters?

Can you trace the origin of this dislike?

Which sibling do you feel closest to and what are the reasons for the positive bond?

How did your parents handle bickering between their children?

If an only child, describe your feelings about this situation.

Did you feel safe and secure as a child?

What periods or events caused you to feel unsafe or vulnerable?

What elements in your family life produced security?

If you did not feel safe, what event or person caused your fearfulness?

Were you afraid of anything specific, such as dogs, boggiemen, strangers, darkness, or thunder?

Was there anyone whom you could talk to when you were afraid?

Describe the ruminations, fantasies, or actual encounters

with alarming experiences, including physical sensations.

What situations cause you to feel afraid today, whether real or imagined?

Did you feel loved by both parents?

If so, record the special feelings that assured you that you had a loving niche in your parents' hearts.

If you felt unloved by one or both parents, did you discover an explanation for this lack?

Did you believe you were unlovable?

Visualize scenes where you felt unloved and record the attendant emotions.

Visualize scenes where you felt hatred for your parents.

Indicate the mixture of love and hate you felt for your parents.

Were the ambivalent feelings confusing?

Did you witness affection between your parents?

What kind of affectionate behavior was considered normal in your household?

Describe how you observed it differed from that of other households.

How does your background of affectionate behavior affect your present living and relating?

If your parents did not display affection, how did they relate together?

Did they argue bitterly but stay together "for the sake of the children"?

How did you feel about their daily life?

Did you wish you lived with another family? What were they like?

Were you an abused child, either physically or psychologically?

How were you abused?

What did you think about the adults who abused you?

Did you feel you deserved the abuse or did you experience anger, plot revenge, or actively run away?

Did anyone know about the abuse?

What fantasies did you have about being rescued from your abusers?

As an adult, do you still feel wounded by this abusive experience?

How does it affect your relationships with adults and children?

Were you an adopted or foster child?
Was the adoption a secret to you?
How did you feel when you were told you were adopted?
Did you feel unloved because a biological parent gave you away?
What were your fantasies about your real parents?
If you were a foster child, what were the circumstances that separated you from your parents?
Were your foster parents kind and understanding toward you?
Did you ever see your biological parents again?
Were you separated from siblings when you became a fosterling?
Did you ever see your brothers or sisters again?
Do you feel grateful or angry toward your foster parents?

One parent died.
Do you remember the circumstances of the death and the funeral?
What fantasies did you build around the lost parent?
Did you imagine the parent was not dead and would return one day?
Describe the scenes you constructed of this hoped-for reunion.
Record secret conversations you imagined between yourself and a deceased parent.
Did you come to terms with the idealized version of your lost parent, or do you still maintain the illusion?
What conversation would you like to have with a deceased parent?
Did you feel angry at your surviving parent? How did you express your anger?

Were your parents divorced?
What feelings did you have about the breakup?
How did you feel when your parents fought?
Did you feel responsible for and guilty about their marital split?
Describe the adjustments you went through when one parent left the home.

Did your parents force you to take sides?
Were you forced into a mini-adult role?
What were visits like with the parent who left home?
How did you deal with your feelings of anger or abandonment?
Did you dream your parents would reunite?

If your parents remarried, did you think of your stepparent as an intruder?
How did you relate to this new parent?
Describe how life changed when your parent remarried.
Did you plot to break up the new marriage?
Did you have stepbrothers or sisters? How did you all get along?
Did you ever learn to love your stepparent?

Did other adults play a significant part in your childhood?
Describe them and how they treated you.
What did they add or take away from your life?
Did any of them act as a substitute parent?
Did you have maids or babysitters?
What positive or negative memories do you have about these caretakers?

Did you feel especially favored by any adult?
What kind of treatment did you receive as a result of being thought special?
Was anyone jealous of your special treatment?

Did you ever feel you did not belong to your parents?
Did you suspect a secret adoption?
Who were your fantasy "real" parents?

How did your parents respond to your childhood questions?
Were they patient and attentive?
Did one of them refer you to the other, or otherwise try to brush you off?
Did they laugh at you?

Did you make up jingles and stories?
Did you share your creations with anyone?
Did other people appreciate your creativity?

How did your parents respond to your childhood creations?
What kind of things did you create as a child?

Relive a scene in which you present a parent with a creation.

Who was your most important playmate?
  What games did you play?
  How did you play, fight, and make up?
  Did your parents like your friend?
  Did his or her parents like you?
  Did you spend the night together?
  Did anything surprise you about your friend's parents?

Did you have an invisible friend?
  When did your imaginary companion arrive?
  What were the qualities of your exclusive pal?
  Did you ever confide to anyone about your companion?
    What was their reaction?
  When did you stop relating to your imaginary friend?
  Did you think you were strange to invent an invisible friend?
  If so, where did you get that impression?

Did you have imaginary enemies as a child?
  Did you believe there were monsters in the closet? What
    were they going to do to you?
  Did you tell anyone about your fears?
  Describe all imaginary worlds, people, or animals that you
    believed were real.

Describe the neighborhood of your early childhood.
  Did you feel comfortable in the neighborhood?
  Who or what frightened you in the neighborhood?
  Did you have special hiding places?
  Did you play in the yard, a playground, the street or the alley?
  Do you remember any adults?
  What was the general atmosphere?
  Do you remember the first time you strayed from your house?

Recall the situations that caused your parents to become angry.
  What phrases did your parents use toward you when they
    were angry?
  How did these labels, nicknames, or warnings make you
    feel?
  Have you ever used the same phrases against your own children or anyone else?

Did you enjoy the discovery of "bad" words?
  How did you use swear words?
  Did you have a friend who shared a glee in making up stories
    with forbidden language?
  Did you receive punishment for using inappropriate lan-
    guage?
  Did you like to shock others with "bad" words?

How did your parents respond to your illnesses?
  Where you a sickly child?
  How did you react when confined to bed?
  What special treats did you receive when bedridden?
  Did you ever pretend to be sick? Why?

*What were your experiences with doctors and dentists as a
child?*
  Were you afraid of them?
  How did your parents react to your expressions of fear?
  How did the doctor or dentist react?

Were you ever hospitalized?
  Did you know the reason for your hospitalization?
  What experiences did you have in the hospital?
  Did you think your parents were going to leave you there?

Did you have a physical handicap?
  How did your parents treat you differently because of the
    handicap?
  Explain how this has added to or taken away from your life
    experiences.
  Did you think you had a physical handicap because you felt
    different from the other kids?

What nighttime rituals did you perform as a child?
  Did they involve parents and siblings?
  Were you plagued by nightmares?
  Does one particular dream stand out in your memory?
  Did you ever have a repeated dream? Describe the dream. Do
    you ever dream the dream today?
  Were you able to call to your parents when you were afraid
    during the night?

Did a parent or other adult read to you??
  What were your favorite books?

Who was the reader?
Did you imagine the characters from the stories in your
mind's eye?

How did your family value food?
Did you have a favorite food?
What foods did you dislike?
Did you look forward to holiday menus?
Was food used for treats or punishments?
Were mealtimes pleasant or upsetting?
Did your parents make you feel guilty if you didn't like the
food they prepared?
Do you still feel like you must clean your plate?

Who teased you?
How did you respond to teasing?
What were you teased about?
Whom did you tease and how did it feel?
Do you enjoy teasing and being teased today?

Did you play sex exploratory games with your playmates?
What kind of sex games did you play?
Did you ever get caught? If so, describe the adult's or other
children's reactions.
How did this affect your sexual curiosity?
If you were not discovered, did you feel guilty or joyful?

How did your family celebrate birthdays and holidays?
Did you believe in the Tooth Fairy, the Easter Bunny, and
Santa Claus?
Describe your reactions when discovering the truth about
these childhood myths.

Did you fall in love in early childhood?
Who was the person?
How did it feel?
Did your parents or siblings make fun of your romantic feel-
ings?
Did you wish you could get married even though you were
still children?

What role did religion play in your family?
Was religion frightening or comforting?
Did you imagine a Godlike figure watching your actions?

Did you have a guardian angel protecting you?
What questions did you ask about religious rituals, dogmas,
   or promises?
Did you reach any personal conclusions? At what ages?

What made you laugh?
Did anyone in your family have a sense of humor?
Did you do funny imitations when you were growing up?
Did you think cartoons at the movies or on television were
   funny?
What was your favorite kind of humor or character?
What kind of humor did you dislike?
Do you think you have a sense of humor?

Did you ever torture animals?
Did you do it alone or with a playmate?
Did you ever get caught? How were you punished?
Did you feel angry at someone else when you picked on ani-
   mals?

What were your favorite radio or television shows?
Did you make up your own stories about the characters?
What fantasies did you concoct about yourself and your he-
   roes?
Did you wish your family was like the characters on your fa-
   vorite shows?
Did you believe the people and stories were real?
Did you memorize and repeat jingles from the radio and tele-
   vision?

Did the movies affect your perception of life?
What were your favorite movies and movie stars? Why?
How did you respond to horror films?
Did you have fantasies of meeting your idol?
Did any movie stimulate your creativity?

Was there ever a fire in your house?
Do you know what or who caused the fire?
What damage was done?
How did the members of your family react to the crisis?
Are you afraid of fire?

Can you recall the first day of school?
Did you go to school alone?

What did you look forward to about going to school?
What jolts did you receive on the first day of school?

Describe classmates and teachers during elementary school.
What events stand out most clearly?
Were you ever a teacher's pet?
Was your creativity encouraged?
How did your school handle punishment?
Were you ever unjustly accused?
What hobbies or skills did you acquire during these early years?
What did you think about being a good sport?

Did your family move during your childhood?
Did your parents discuss the move with you?
Did you want to move?
How did you adjust to your new environment?
Did you miss your old friends? Did you ever see them again?

Were you ever ashamed or embarrassed by your parents?
How were they embarrassing?
Did you tell them you were ashamed?
How did you wish them to change?
Are you still ashamed of your parents?

Did your family include you in conversations during your elementary school days?
What did you talk about?
Did they encourage you to read?
Were your parents pleased with your work around the house and in school?
Did you feel you had to earn good grades in order to be accepted by your parents?
Could you disagree with your parents' opinions?

Were you allowed to express feelings in your home?
How did you express your feelings of dependency, happiness, anger, sadness, or frustration?
Did you ever have temper tantrums?
Were you allowed to pout?
If you were constricted, how did normal feelings find an outlet?

Did you have pets?

What kind of animals?
Did you take care of your pets?
How did you feel when they died?
Did you replace them?
Did you consider your pets as people?

Did you belong to a group of kids?
What activities were you involved in?
Were there both boys and girls in the group?
What kinds of mischief occurred?
If a loner, how did you occupy your time?
Did you enjoy being alone?
Did your parents worry because you spent so much time alone? Did they try to change you?

Did you ever steal anything in elementary school?
Did you need it?
Did you get caught?
What did you do with stolen items?
Did you feel guilty?

Were you in love with another child, teacher, or a hero?
What attracted you to this person?
Did he or she know about your love?
What daydreams did you have about the two of you?

What were your dreams of growing up?
Did you think you were going to be a writer?
Did you talk about your dreams with anyone?
Did you have dreams of being rich and famous?

In one sentence, describe yourself between the ages of six and eleven.
What reactions did you have when puberty began?
Were you informed and prepared for body changes?
Did your new sexual feelings feel comfortable or disquieting?
Were you a late or an early bloomer?
Did you suffer from acne, excessive sweating, awkwardness, or temper explosions?
How did your family help or hinder your adolescent growth spurt and personality change?
Did you feel guilty about sexual fantasies or masturbation?
What rituals did you devise to deal with the guilt?

Did you have aggressive fantasies? Who were the victims of
your aggression?
Were you afraid of your aggressive thoughts?
Did you question the social circumstances of your life? What
was the response of your elders?
Did you write during the teen years? What was the content?
Were you validated as a creative person or put down?

Did you have a best friend?
How were you alike?
How were you different?
What secrets did you share?
Are you still friends?
Did you make plans together for the future?

Did you fall in love as a youth?
Was it mutual or unrequited?
Were you comfortable with the opposite sex?
Did you know how to talk with someone who attracted you?
What qualities attracted you to your first youthful love?

How did peer pressure affect your teen years?
Did you go along with others' actions, decisions, and man-
nerisms just to feel accepted?
Were you a leader?
Were you ever rejected by a clique?
Were you ever the target of malicious gossip? How did you
handle the frustrations of being gossiped about?

Did you work during high school?
How did you spend your money?
How did you get along with your employers?
What did you learn about the realities of life?

Did an adult ever try to seduce you?
Who was the adult?
Was the seduction expected?
Did you encourage or discourage the seduction?
How did you feel about the adult before and after the at-
tempted seduction?
Did you feel guilty?
Did you tell anyone about the seduction?

*Did you have to struggle to gain independence from your par-
ents?*

Did they trust you?
Did they accuse you of sexual activities?
Did they learn to treat you as a separate person?
Did you fight with them about their opinions?
Did they let you talk about your differences?

Were you personally affected by any of the wars or military actions of your country?
Did you ever enter the service?
What experience did you have?
Were you injured?
Did you see people die?
How did you handle loneliness, fear of death, and authority figures?
Did you lose a loved one because of war?

How did you leave home?
Was it a period of good will between yourself and parents, or a time of anger?
Did you attend college or begin working?
Did you travel around? Did you learn a lot about people?
Record the adjustments from the security of the "known" to the "unknown."
How did you handle personal freedom?

Describe your first sexual encounter.
How did it match up with your fantasies about sex?
Was it a satisfying experience?
Were you in love with your partner?
Did you feel good about yourself afterward?
Do you enjoy a healthy sex life?

Did you identify with either parent?
What qualities did you pick up from your parents?
Are you shocked when you act or talk like one of your parents? Why?
If you did not identify with them, who did you want to be like?

As a young adult, did you experiment with different jobs, travel, and meeting new people?
What were your positive experiences?
What were your negative adventures?
What did you learn about handling money?

How did your experimentation add to your growth, knowledge, and common sense?

If you are single, how do you feel about being unattached?
Do you take pride in your independence?
Do you ever feel lonely?
Do you enjoy solitude?
Describe your friends, both single and married.
Did you make a personal decision to be single?
Do people criticize your enjoying the single life?
Do you feel defensive?
Do you enjoy traveling alone?
What are the benefits?
Do you talk to yourself?
Do you ever feel jealous when you witness the bond between
lovers?

*If you are married, what expectations did you have for this
union?*
Describe your courtship.
What did you talk about?
Did you hide imperfections?
Did you expect to change your mate's habits?
What was the biggest shock after the honeymoon?
What marital problems confronted you and your mate?
Do you love each other?
Did your mate admire your creative bent?
Is your mate a creative person?
Do you compete against each other?
Do you talk about your feelings?
Are you friends?
Are you satisfied with your affection-romance-sex relation-
ship?
Do you try to control each other?
Can you have a fair fight?
Do you get along with your in-laws?
Do your parents respect and accept your mate?

How did becoming a parent change your life?
Did you plan your family?
Did you enjoy the pregnancy and birth experience?
Do you treat your children as you were treated as a young-
ster?

Do you have a favorite child?

Do you have an aversion to one offspring? Does that child remind you of someone from your past?

What dreams do you have for your children's futures?

If divorced, describe the circumstances and eventual adjustments of this trauma.

Did you want the divorce?

Did you feel ambivalent about the dissolution?

What were the biggest adjustments after the divorce?

Did you maintain a friendship with your ex-mate?

Are you a single parent because of the divorce?

Are you a visiting or visited parent?

How do you treat your visiting children?

Do you feel guilty toward your children?

Do you talk about feelings with your children concerning the divorce?

If you have a photo album, review the pictures and record the memories associated with the scenes.

The Results

The answers to these questions will give you a document of your unique makeup—a personal psychogram. When you get to Chapter 6, which deals with psychological problems inhibiting creativity, you'll be able to understand your particular problems by tracing them back to the events that formed your adult personality. Insight and understanding can bring changes in feelings, responses, and reactions. Although you cannot consider yourself psychoanalyzed simply by having answered the psychogram's questions, you will have a valid blueprint of the causes for certain types of behavior that disrupt creative expression.

The psychogram is also a tool to spark your thinking about the complexities of your character overall. We often take thinking for granted as we use the mental process to plan, create, ruminate, and consider options. As a creative person you have an artistic responsibility to set aside time during every day to think, without the distraction of music, television, driving, or walking. Think about your life, how you pursue your creative goals, how you repeat past mistakes, how the events of your childhood influence your decisions today, how you can improve yourself, your relationships, and the way you express yourself.

Active thinking about your life, which the psychogram facilitates, gives you a sense of control over your destiny. As a child you were the recipient of decisions, events, emotions, and circumstances, with little control over your environment. As an independent adult you can understand how these events formed you, but can take charge of current affairs.

Many writers we have spoken with or treated have felt a surge of creativity after they explored their memory transcripts and spent time thinking exclusively about themselves. This surge occurs because the energy used to repress memories flows into the ego, and because the memories also contain elements for different ideas about stories, plots, and characters.

You may feel there are some important questions omitted from this questionnaire; if so, feel free to add them to our list, as every memory adds to the wealth of information about your history. Your document should be reread occasionally as a reminder of your emotional history and to further spark ideas.

Jeffrey remembered that his classmates taunted him because he was always studying, reading, or lost in his daydreams. They called him "the queer one."

"I had read about 'queers' and was convinced I must be a homosexual, not realizing that the kids substituted 'queer' for 'strange' or 'weird.' During the recording of my psychological history I had the insight that this fear of being gay had blocked my understanding of homosexuality. As a heterosexual person, why should I avoid learning about another sexual preference? The recall and recognition of my naive acceptance of my peers' label released my forgotten queasiness about my sexual identity.

"I studied homosexuality, reading novels and nonfiction works on gay life. I began to empathize with the stresses and social pressures that plague homosexuals. I spent a year interviewing gays and eventually wrote sympathetic articles for and about gay people. I met an incredible number of creative, happy-go-lucky, and miserable and frightened people. Because I was empathetic and nonthreatening, they felt comfortable enough to confide their feelings and dreams to a 'straight.' This complex and interesting writing area would never have been opened to me if I hadn't been willing to confront my early feelings and fears."

Margaret had confined her writing to poetry. She'd been successful for many years and never thought about expanding her horizons.

"Out of curiosity, I decided to answer your questions. I had no reaction to the part concerning imaginary companions and skipped that section. My husband told me I was thrashing around in my sleep that night. He asked me what was the matter and I spoke in my sleep, saying, 'There's a big monster coming at me!' 'Can I help you?' Tom asked in response to my frightened child's voice. 'Oh, no. It's okay. Helpy is right here.' 'Who is Helpy?' 'My friend. Helpy always gets me out of trouble.'

"When Tom told me about our middle-of-the-night conversation, I was really surprised. It seems impossible, but I had forgotten about my made-up friend, Helpy, for at least thirty-five years. I was flooded with memories of Helpy, who had been my imaginary playmate from the age of four to about eight.

"I began a children's story about invisible friends and how wonderful they can be when kids are lonely. I discovered that I had a knack for children's writing and I feel certain I would never have added this facet to my career if not for that dream which nudged Helpy back into consciousness."

When you review your personal history, look for experiences that can be turned into material different from your usual avenue of expression. Can you use your new information to further understand a particular problem in relationships? Could this be researched and turned into a story, article, or book that would help others cope with living problems?

"I was confronted with strange reactions concerning my possessions while answering the section about present-day responses to past events," says George, a screenplay writer. "I become angry when anything of mine is rearranged or moved. I feel invaded. Tracing back to my long-ago childhood, I reflected on a two-year stint in the hospital because of heart disease when I was eleven. I remembered spending hours watching the dust particles filter and dance through the window. This was before the days of television. To amuse myself and keep from going crazy, I wove stories about the particles, giving them personalities and motivation. Whenever a nurse or doctor entered my room, they disrupted the air and its minuscule pieces of dust. I would become angry and sullen, which they assumed was related to my illness.

"I never told anyone about my obsession and forgot it until I honestly probed my exaggerated reactions to people moving my possessions. My fantasies with the dust motes were the only things I had any control over when I was ill. I realized my love of writing screenplays was a creative expression of being in control. As a film writer, I invent characters and dictate their actions, just like I did in my hospital bed. These thoughts sparked my curiosity about recuperating patients and their need to control something in order to overcome feelings of helplessness. I visited hospitals, spending most of my time with children. My own need to control seemed to lessen as I delved deeper into the fears of bedridden patients. My family certainly expressed relief when I no longer had fits about misplaced belongings. I learned to laugh at myself and my overreactions.

"The creative outcome was an article for parents explaining the anxieties of sick children, a short story about using one's imagination to make up tales when observing cloud formations, and even a humorous piece about a man who lost his temper when he lost things, blaming his family for hiding his treasures. Learning to laugh at my peculiar reactions has lightened my overly serious demeanor."

Whenever you borrow material from your chronicle of the past, your writing will gain authenticity, because the content will be infused with your personal perceptions and feelings. One's creative imagination can always be called upon to exaggerate and build your original experiences.

Any emotional state that you have uncovered can be woven into your work with a twofold consequence—you'll be purged of unresolved feelings and you'll create an original piece of writing.

Chapter Five

Guilt and the Creative Process

WRITERS GUARD TIME JEALOUSLY, hoarding hours for their creative pursuits. Part-time freelancers, working to meet financial responsibilities, budget writing hours like gold, fearful of wasting this precious commodity. Homemakers raising children plot and plan writing time away from constant family demands. Fortunate full-time authors talk endlessly about arranging blocks of creative hours.

"If only I had more time!" is part of every writer's litany. All writers dream of the freedom to explore their creative potential, yearning for time to fully develop all the ideas which compete against everyday responsibilities.

An unsettling dilemma confounds many writers who take pains to arrange special time for writing and then suddenly find themselves unproductive. It doesn't make sense to a creatively dedicated person to find himself unable to carry through intentions to devote specific hours to writing. Psychologically, the writer is suffering from unconscious forces which inhibit creativity and ultimately wastes valuable time, another form of a writing block.

Unconscious Guilt

Unconscious guilt, one of the most powerful negative forces, wastes more creative time than any externally imposed circumstance. This form of guilt swamps creativity, sending its reproachful waves across the psyche to drown the spirit. Artists must have clear minds unhampered by negative emotions to concentrate on imagination's inner voice, but guilt drains these psychological energies and stifles creative flow.

We learn to feel guilty during childhood when parents reprimand our misbehavior. As adults we should feel appropriate shame when we deliberately perform a harmful act toward another person. When we admit we are wrong and thus guilty, we have the choice of living with the guilt or of making amends to disperse the unpleasant feeling of shame.

Unconscious guilt is a sense of going against the "rights" imprinted on our emotional tape recordings, even though those messages may be at odds with reason. For example, a writer who was made to feel like a bad child for daydreaming may feel guilty when "wasting time" by drifting into imaginary scenes necessary to plot a story. Consciously the author knows that daydreaming is a healthy, helpful aid to creativity, but unconsciously the writer is programmed to feel guilty about being "unproductive." One of our authors was a constant "dreamer" in childhood and was yelled at and told "do something constructive!" As a result, she felt worthwhile only when busy proving to her parents that she was producing something that people could see.

Remorse and guilt, unconnected with the present or concrete situations, are a relentless hostility turned against the self, a wasteful, destructive emotion, akin to anxiety and depression. Unconscious guilt can be overcome by examining the seeds and restructuring psychological programming which nourishes shame.

Unconscious guilt is best understood with a knowledge of the structures of personality that evolve and develop during childhood. In Chapter Two we discussed the emotional tape recording and the unconscious compulsion to repeat past emotional experiences. The growth of the conscience, or sense of right and wrong, is also imprinted on the emotional tape recording and has an impact on thinking and responding to external events and pressures throughout life.

The Structures of the Personality

We begin life as instinctual beings, self-centered and unable to withstand frustrations controlled by the primary part of the psyche called the id.

The id represents bodily needs and desires fueled by innate sexual and aggressive instincts for survival. Because the biological base is instinctual, the pressures from the id are experienced as body tension, unrelated to thought or concern for others. For a person to fit into the social order, the id's demands for immediate gratification must become tempered and channeled during childhood.

The secondary mental process of the personality is called the ego. Our sense of self, or ego, begins at birth and continues complex maturation throughout life. The ego is responsible for conscious thought, language, memory, reason, and decision-making and gains depth and scope as a child emerges into adulthood. The function of the ego is to find solutions that will satisfy instinctual strivings in a way which will also be acceptable to environmental conditions. One's ego strengths depend upon the quality of nurturing in infancy, love or hate relationships during the toddler and juvenile years, those whom the child molds and identifies himself with, the skills learned throughout life, and the ability to cope with reality. Love, work, and creative accomplishments further stabilize our sense of self as adults. The ego, through experience and socialization, protects us, regards external events and reacts, either through action or flight. A balanced ego characteristic is common sense. Impulsive, uncaring recklessness reveals an id-controlled person whose shaky ego is incapable of restraining the wish for instant pleasure.

A mature ego's province is testing reality—choosing methods to obtain satisfaction without causing peril or harm to self or others. The ego juggles and weighs options, postponing insistent demands from the id, which says, "I want everything. Right now!". The ego decides when patience is required to satisfy wishes and to feel acceptable in the eyes of others.

The third system of the psyche is the superego which assists the ego in decision-making. The conscience, or sense of right and wrong, is comprised of introjected dictates from childhood caretakers. During infancy and the juvenile years, parents exert control over their offsprings' behavior, teaching them a system of ethics. Eventually, these become internalized as a superego, which judges the person's actions and directs acceptable behavior. When a person disregards the rules of the superego, he feels unconscious guilt. The superego is, of all the personality systems, the most accessible to recall, because it is the last psychological formation, externally introduced to the ego and id.

The three systems, id, ego, and superego, do not function in separate compartments, but are in constant, dynamic interaction.

Ego Control

A writer retires for the evening, planning to get up early to finish an assignment—a mature ego decision praised by the work-oriented superego. The id's preference would be to never work, but just play.

The alarm rings in the early hours, and the pleasure-prone id lulls the drowsy author into burrowing under the covers. The voice of the conscience whispers, "Up! Up! You made plans to work. Get moving!" The awakening ego sorts the pros and cons—the id's desire for sloth or the superego's work injunctions. The ego chooses to stick to the plan to work, and the author hastens preparations to begin writing, alert and pleased to have overcome id's seductive siren.

Id Control

Another writer with similiar intentions lost his resolve and drank to excess the previous evening. Alcohol depresses the superego's admonitions against overindulgence. After several generous drinks, the writer is governed by his id. The pleasure-seeking id encouraages continued drinking, and the ego, without the conscience's support, gives in to the unrealistic fantasy that he will be able to work in the morning regardless of how much he drinks tonight.

The next day's hangover prevents the writer from performing. The superego, no longer repressed by drugs, harshly berates the ego, bringing on feelings of guilt over the previous night's excessive drinking. The remorseful author feels disgusted with himself which compounds into a sense of worthlessness. The self-reproach and physical lethargy caused by his hangover combine to ruin the writer's joy and creative output. In order to appease the superego and to regain some self-esteem, the guilty author vows to never overdrink again.

A Balance

A healthy arrangement between the three psychic components,

the id, ego, and superego, occurs when the healthy ego allows the id appropriate, moderate satisfactions, after sifting and tempering demands, with a just superego consenting to decisions, infusing well-being into the psychic triad.

Gene, the gag writer, has great confidence in his ability to create laugh-producing material. His assuredness has thrived with continued success, made possible by ongoing research of current events for popular subjects of humor, his consistent work habits, and dependable submissions.

"My internal judge finds me satisfactory, so I don't have to struggle with feelings of inferiority. I allow my id to run wild when outlining humorous catastrophes, by relaxing all the social rules and thinking like a mischievous kid. Hilarious, crude, and sadistic situations come tumbling from that primitive sphere which delights in others' misfortunes. But my ego's creative imagination tones down the gag's more primal aspects, so that my audience can comfortably identify with my subject.

"My story-telling family's sense of humor leaned toward the absurd and man's foibles. Fortunately, I identified with them, and the voice of my superego supports and praises my career. I feel a strong inner balance. I have great sympathy for fellow artists hounded by unfriendly inner turmoil."

Superego Construction

We do not choose those—our parents or their substitutes—who construct our superego standards. Parental influences on the conscience include their own values and personalities as well as the racial, national, and family traditions they themselves inherited. The superego also incorporates ethical systems learned from other relatives, schoolteachers, religious leaders, peers, and heroes.

The Artistic Battle

The artist's role is revolutionary. Visionaries, we predict the future, presenting readers with a glimpse of what is to come by interpreting social trends, human nature, and historical patterns, punching holes in our readers' complacency, revealing unpleasant truths, exposing possibilities and destroying our pretenses. Writers are thorns in the side of society's status quo. We move beyond the minuscule world of childhood acceptance of parental pronouncements. Writers' rebellion against permanence automatically pits them against rigid, personal superego rules. The artistic dilemma occurs when writers experience unconscious guilt when overthrowing outmoded introjected standards and soaring beyond programmed restrictions.

This dilemma confronted Bruce, the novelist. "Incongruency reigns inside my complex ethical system. My mother immigrated to America from Italy with a head full of Old World superstitions where evil spirits and ghosts lurk everywhere. She passed these on to her children with dire threats about damnation and hell's fire whenever we misbehaved or showed disrespect. At the same time she adored me and never told my dad about my mistakes or troubles in school. My father was Irish, strict to a fault, quick to punish and slow to forgive. My maternal grandmother lived with us and is an additional voice of my superego. She believed that praise was the Devil's agent and that children should be corrected constantly. No one could ever please her. I hear her combined Italian and English phrases putting me down as a wastrel writer, ignoring the fact that I also hold down a responsible job and provide for my family.

"Catholicism was our family's way of life, and evil thoughts were judged to be as sinful as evil deeds. My Catholic education reinforced a thousand guilts. My one relief from feeling like a sinner was the weekly confession with the parish priest. Since he gave forgiveness and a penance, I thought he was wonderfully powerful. But the sense of feeling good only lasted for a day, when I'd start building a list of sins again.

"A constant flow of motherly love saved me from being stifled by this weird mixture of my father's stringent rules and rejections, my grandmother's condemnations, and the Church's unreachable personality goals. My mother's generous affection kept my ego healthy and strong enough to sustain the barrage of negative, restrictive criticisms. Even her superstitions were tempered with genuine care and concern for my safety.

"I envy my wife, who grew up in a quiet household with more kindly parents. She never feels vague, unsettling guilt from her unconscious or feels unbalanced by internal demands for unrealistic perfection. She has helped me sort out the unreasonable demands from my conscience whenever I get bogged down and lose my creative energy."

Our parents' insistence on compliance to family rules heralds the formation of our superego. Infants begin testing the limits of their expanding environment as soon as they can crawl, requiring adults to set rules and reinforce the lessons ovor and over again. Parents, teaching acceptable behavior, set perimeters of movement, allow limited, protected exploration, and restrain curious toddlers from dangerous objects. They insist on socially acceptable behavior, require bowel and bladder control, teach manners and repetitiously impress on the child the consequences of unacceptable behavior—verbal rejection, isolation, or physical discipline.

Children's emotional tape recordings are imprinted with all the "no's" and "yesses" heard and felt during the rule-learning years. An evolving personality forms an ego-ideal—a self-conception of approved conduct—to maintain a bonded connection with the parents who give love and thus control tho child's conco of worth.

Too Strict

Harsh, perfectionistic parents who angrily curtail curiosity or treat the child as evil or sinful foster a critical, demeaning superego that is constrictive and overly punitive. The ego quakes before the thunder of negative appraisals, and the person presents himself as meek and compliant, fearful of taking chances.

"I was an abused child," relates Tina, a writer specializing in pet care and training. "I grew up in a foster home with pitiless discipline and no affection. I was regularly told how lucky I was to be taken in. Infractions brought loss of meals, sometimes for a day or two. The two other foster kids and I lived in a state of frightened obedience. We were not allowed to ask questions or to refute the unloving adults. We never dreamed of telling the visiting social worker about our abuse. I found out later that abused children fear telling authorities about their plight because they expect retaliation, believing that all adults are cruel and hateful.

"In a fourth grade art class, the teacher handed out paper and told us to make up a design from our imaginations. I didn't even know what a design was until she said it had to be like something you would see on a dress or a striking drawing in an advertisement. I was stuck, afraid to expose my creativity. The teacher was exasperated with me as I sat, staring blankly at the empty page. Finally she gave up in disgust. This incident remains with me still. I thought then that my indignant foster parents were trying to kill my spirit and would hate me even more if I made something special.

"I began hating them instead of believing I was a bad seed. I knew I couldn't be as awful as they said.

"Another voice, a nurturing voice, grew in my superego when we three victims of this strange family whispered encouragements back and forth during the night, comforting each other. We made up stories, casting ourselves as beloved daughters of a king and queen. We parented each other, easing some of the oppressive judgments that our foster parents were piling up on our superego tapes. The inner strength and support gained from our secret community gave us the courage to escape when we were in our teens.

"Those hateful voices still persist in my conscience ('you are evil, unworthy and unwanted'), but I have long since learned to silence them as nonsense, listening instead to the soothing voices of my psychological sisters. The superego voice is most angry when I receive a check for an article. It insists that I should find my foster parents and pay them back for their sacrifices. I have a silent chuckle as I deposit the money in the bank."

Too Lenient

Wishy-washy, overprotective parents, afraid to harm their child's sensitivities, permit disobedience and allow selfish behavior without censure. The child's superego is faulty, excusing misbehavior and allowing the id full freedom, without normal checks and balances which exist in a child who is taught to earn love through appropriate behavior. The person who has no internalized "no's" lacks a guilt system and is uncaring about others.

Arthur, the young screenplay writer with an overly idolizing mother, comments, "I assumed everything I said, thought, or did was perfect because I was so wonderful. I was selfish, refusing to share my toys with playmates. Soon, I had no friends, but Mother said the other kids were too rowdy and not good enough for me. When I was caught stealing from lockers at school, my mother bullied the principal into waiving punishment. I could do no wrong, so I never suffered guilt twinges or regrets when I walked over someone's feelings.

"Her kind of love was really a great disservice, because she never demanded the behavior necessary to function maturely. I struggle every day, building and shoring up an ethical system which takes others' rights into account. I must completely reject my unworkable superego's grandiose opinion of me. I will never allow my children to grow up in such a sick atmosphere of total acceptance."

Inconsistent

Vacillating, inconsistent parents who allow bad behavior one day and severely punish the next similar incident produce a confused, unreliable sense of right and wrong.

"My superego is a sieve," relates Peter, an articles writer. "My father provided a strange model. He boasted about stealing from his boss and cheating on his taxes. I began stealing from the drugstore in my teens, since it was an approved activity handed down by my father. When I was caught and arrested, he came bellowing into the jail and began punching me. On the way home he shouted, 'Dummy! If you steal, don't get caught.' He also frequently berated my lack of brains and general stupidity. Whenever I sit down to write, I can hear his voice doubting my talents. When I receive a check, the superego which contains his input tells me I'm stealing money, since I don't deserve to be paid. I fight against the former judgment and laugh at the latter. The holes in my conscience come from Dad. As an adult I patched up the gaps to feel like a worthwhile person.

"My mother was super moralistic, but cowered in her husband's presence, never defending her position. She stressed work, equated it with self-worth, and I developed a very strict work-oriented superego. This helps with the discipline necessary for creative work, but it makes me feel guilty when I relax."

Guilt Roots

Several of the questions in Chapter Four were directed to uncovering guilt roots, such as sibling rivalry which may have caused punishment from parents, family deaths or a divorce in which a child may have felt a responsibility, anger toward parents, or words or phrases adults used to encourage acceptable behavior but which caused a child to feel ashamed. There may be a feeling of guilt associated with having been the victim of abuse, sexual shame over activities or fantasies, guilt imposed by strict religious beliefs, hostilities toward those smaller or more helpless, guilt induced by unrealistic parental expectations, thievery, seduction experiences and struggles for independence.

We hope you completed your psychogram to discover more about your unique experiences and that you were able to recover some real or imagined childhood culpabilities.

"I discovered a buried guilt when reviewing memories connected with torturing animals," reported Dena, a college student.

"Outwardly, I was a sweet little girl, busily pleasing my mother, giving in to pressures against competing with my noncreative twin sister. I was very angry, but expressions of feelings, either verbal or physical, were not allowed in our house.

"I had a sneaky, malicious ritual, performed when no one was around. I would stroke my mother's favorite cat into purring contentment. When she was lulled and relaxed I shrieked at the top of my lungs while hurling her into a nearby bush or tree. The cat's nimble reflexes saved her from injury. I took cruel delight in scaring her half to death but she finally ran away, causing my mother grief and bringing glee to my nine-year-old heart.

"I never faced my guilt over torturing an innocent animal until working on the psychogram. Quite honestly, I had forgotten the much-repeated torment, but the repressed incidents affected my writing. I characterized little kids as one-dimensional—innocent and naive—disregarding the reality of the normal mix of good and bad traits. I avoided my own childhood cruelty by writing only scenes involving nice children.

"I felt ashamed, but also realized that I was an unhappy child who took out her rage on a cat because other avenues of expression were *verboten*. I forgave myself, reliving old feelings and the self-reproach.

"Friends have asked how I was able to move on so quickly from remembering the event, feeling guilty, and forgiving my action. I think the key to forgiving myself was understanding *why* I had behaved so cruelly. Children usually act on their feelings by physical means if they cannot talk about their hurt. I know I wouldn't harm an animal or a person as an adult, so it was a simple matter to look back on myself as a small child and connect the torture to its roots of restricted behavior demanded by a parent who was afraid of anger.

"For myself, the experience freed up creative energies and I revised the personalities and actions of the children in my plays and short stories. I sold a one-act humorous play to a magazine for elementary school children about kids plotting to steal money from parents, but in the play they find out they want more attention paid to their feelings instead of more money."

If you cannot go back to a person in the past who made you feel guilty or apologize to those whom you may have harmed, just accept the wrongdoing as a reaction to childhood pain. Guilt is wasted emotion if you can't do anything about a mistake. Most people are too hard on themselves. You should be able to forgive your mistakes without a lot of breast-beating. If you heard your own story told by another, you would probably be quick to forgive.

Relieving Guilt

Guilt results whenever a person goes against conscious or unconscious superego guidelines. A conscious standard may be a remembered phrase against stealing (Thou Shalt Not Steal), repeated at home, school, and in church. An unconscious dictate may be stern, visual disapproval when a child sought attention.

The juvenile who steals is forced by nagging qualms from his internalized judge to confess the crime. Parents relieve the child's guilt by declaring a penance—loss of privileges, returning stolen goods to owners, banishment to a room, or physical punishment. The child's emotional balance is restored after disciplinary tactics are consummated.

Adults who feel unconscious guilt do not have parents to punish them to relieve the tension caused by disharmony within the psyche. They unconsciously find methods to punish *themselves*—interfering with creative pursuits.

Penalization to appease the angry superego can be disguised as vague preoccupation, debilitating illness, fatigue, unhealthy relationships, and creative blocking.

"I grew up in an antisexual family in the thirties," remembers Judith. "My parents never appeared in front of the children unless completely dressed. They never kissed each other in our presence. We girls were quickly admonished if we didn't sit with our legs crossed. As small children, our arms had to be outside the covers when we went to sleep. A peculiar contraption held the sheets and blankets tightly over our bodies so 'little hands' could not rove. Neither my sister nor I dared question the reason, afraid to expose our secret masturbatory inclinations.

"My parents never gave us any sex education, but we received many solemn warnings against touching ourselves 'down there,' and the horrible, unnamed diseases which attacked girls who had 'relations' before marriage. My sister wasn't very bright and believed all their unhealthy sexual lectures. I was of the opinion that I had been kidnapped into a house of crazies, and nothing they said impressed me. I couldn't wait to get out in the world and find my real parents, who, I fantasized, were warm, sensual, attractive people, unlike my pinch-faced, dried-up kidnapper-parents.

"Years later, in analysis, my therapist explained that my genetic creative inheritance was so intense that it gave me special perceptions to weigh and refute my parent's antisexual teachings.

"A difficulty erupted when I tried to write romantic, sensual scenes between lusty partners. I would feel spacy and unable to depict the lovers' reactions authentically. I got in touch with one of my unconscious voices that was horrified that I was embarrassing my upstanding parents by blatantly describing joyful sexuality. My frigid parents lurked inside my ethical system, their voices barely audible, but their agitation still able to infringe on my creativity.

"I visualized their imprisonment in a continuously playing 'X' rated porno film. As they squirmed, my real movie star parents urged me on to write unhindered by preposterous sexual notions. Even though my parents were deceased, their asexual message remained imprinted on my superego."

Reshaping Superegos

Adults can reshape their internalized justice systems, evaluating the morality imposed by parents and other authority figures. You can retain the intelligent, workable judgments and reject the ludicrous. Children are unequipped to discriminate and sort out the barrage of parental "no's," believing all to be true. Maturity brings the objective appraisal needed to change the superego into an effective, flexible and helpful mental activity.

Evaluating Your Superego

Disconnecting the Obvious Triggers

In order to clarify your superego's standards, prepare a list of the rights and wrongs in relationships, work, and business which you automatically accept as normal.

Jonathan, the mystery writer whose family rejected his childhood fantasy world, writes his conscious, easily identified moral standards.

Right	Wrong
Honesty	Exaggeration
Hire good accountants	Stealing
Honoring elders	Criticizing parents
Avoiding prurient thoughts	Masturbation
Realism	Daydreaming
Continual work	Vacations
Containing feelings	Emotional outbursts

"I can appraise these rights and wrongs fairly objectively," laughs Jonathan. "My parents confused honesty with imagination and thought I was a bad boy who lied constantly. I would be a pretty boring writer if I couldn't exaggerate and elaborate.

"I agree about not stealing, but I was keenly aware of my parents' hypocrisy. They retained genius accountants who manipulated every tax loophole available. They even deducted my summer camp tuition as a 'charitable contribution.'

"I honor deserving elders. Why should I be kind to irritable, nasty old people just because they have lived a long time? An observing eye that notices self-aggrandizement or pompous stuffiness is a fundamental tool for a writer. I infuriate my superego whenever I describe an old fool with piercing accuracy. I think my parents read my stories just to see if I have exposed their true natures.

"My independent thinking discounted all that trash about sex being unhealthy. One's sexual nature seems to easily overcome Victorian parental squeamishness.

"I am realistic about business and relationship expectations. I do retain emotional scars regarding wasteful daydreaming. I start up, guiltily, and try to look constructively occupied whenever caught in the act. Consciously, I remind myself daydreaming is acceptable and profitable. Daydreaming is an inherent writer's device used to consider various possibilities of character development and plots.

"My superior-acting parents believed that vacations were slothful, and so we never traveled or visited far-flung relatives. They derided spendthrifts who gadded around the country, wasting time and money. Perhaps this is the reason that, as a child, I invented a fantasy world populated by carefree individuals. It took several years after leaving home to feel I deserved vacations. I always felt I should be back at my desk, resolutely grinding away at the wheel. Thanks to insisting, creative friends, I learned vacations are necessary for writers to renew their imaginations. I now consider holidays a priority for continued high-quality work even though I still hear my superego's voice *tsk, tsking*.

"As a youngster, I was humiliated by sarcastic remarks when I cried or lost my composure. My punishment was verbal isolation—my parents' ignoring me as if I were invisible. This tactic makes a child feel dead. I learned to control my emotions and avoid the pain of their disapproval.

"I still have difficulties with spontaneity, because my parents were so effective in their punishment. I feel safest emoting on paper. This is the last vestige of my superego which hampers my present-day living. My encouraging, patient wife has helped me overcome this resistance to getting out my feelings. When I do allow myself to express feelings, she praises me instead of rejecting me. Her loving approval gradually bumps aside and replaces old parental prohibitions."

Your personal right-and-wrong list may be very different from Jonathan's, since our families are all so dissimilar. Examine each notation and follow the message back to its conception. Consider how each injunction has helped or hindered your writing approach or subject scope, motivation to work, dedication to the craft of writing, attitude about receiving money for your skills, identification as a gifted person, relationships with editors and your view of yourself as a worthwhile individual.

Buried Triggers

The next procedure in superego evaluation is to record situations that quash your creative spirits, interfering with productivity—a form of self-punishment. The circumstances arousing superego displeasure will reveal buried or unconscious guilt triggers.

Bill, the psychologist, says, "My guilt mechanisms are devious, and it takes me a few hours to realize that I have entered a cycle of guilt and punishment. I feel especially proud of myself when writing flows smoothly. At this point, I need to take some preventative measures by personifying my unconscious superego for a little chat. It looks like a menacing scarecrow, surveying my life with disgust.

"My parents think delving into the mind and dredging up the past is a useless and unmasculine occupation. From my early childhood my father had talked of my future as a surgeon, saying, 'A surgeon works with his hands, rescuing people from disease and death. He gets back money and gratitude.'

"When I chose clinical psychology as my profession, he was disappointed that I hadn't lived up to his dream. He has always been a laborer and has a childish awe of doctors. Being tactless, he said, 'I don't trust men who talk about feelings! That's sissy stuff!' I cannot argue or defend my career to this rigid man. Our relationship is superficial and we keep peace by chatting about sports and television shows.

"But his negative opinion about my work is firmly implanted in my superego. When I don't do my homework and fantasize victory over his judgment, my unconscious superego slithers silently into my sense of orderliness—if only it came with clanging bells! I forget my original ideas, lose manuscript pages and sometimes even manage to break the typewriter's carbon ribbon. I end up discombobulated. In effect I appease my opposing superego by punishing myself with incompetency. I might as well quit and go for a walk.

"I despise the guilty child inside me, taking an emotional whipping from irrational parents. But I'm entirely to blame when I allow my unconscious to censure me, because I can consciously control its influence through fantasy. So can anyone else who is willing to take the time to prevent unconscious guilt and punishment."

Many writers received no validation from parents when they pursued artistic goals. Noncreative adults often forcefully demand their children find secure, financially guaranteed careers, treating a devotion to the arts as irresponsible and unpredictable.

Brandy, the aspiring screenwriter, constantly fought against her parents' wishes. "They think I am unmoved by their disapproval and I foster that image to keep them at bay. My ethnic background involves an ingrained technique of parents controlling offspring by manipulating spirit-crushing guilt. My parents are experts at it. They never attack my 'profitless' life straightforwardly, but chatter on about relatives and friends whose 'good' children are professional achievers. Letters from home always contain news about who's in medical or law school and all the nice young ladies making their families proud by getting married and producing beautiful grandchildren. Their unspoken lament is, 'So, why were we not blessed with such a daughter? She has the brains of a genius but quits school to live a bum's life in L.A.' After I read their letters I would feel ungrateful and selfish, which was their intent. My confidence would plummet and I felt worthless and disinterested in writing. The internal critic would say, 'See the big deal writer! How much money does she have in the bank? A child who stabs a mother's heart.' This increased my guilt and paralyzed my writing efforts.

"A boyfriend whose parents delight in his writing talents was horrified by my family's guilt-inducing tactics. He thought their obvious maneuvers and coarse attempts to control their adult daughter were actually funny. He read the letters aloud, moaning and groaning and clutching his chest and taught me to laugh at their emotional frame-ups and the unconscious results when I took their manipulations to heart.

"We had long conversations about self determination. He said parents should bring up kids to lead their own lives. 'You've made your choice. Stop accepting their opinion. Ask yourself if you're happiest as a writer, and if you are, why you should take their advice and give up your vision. They threaten you with the loss of their love if you persist in being a black sheep. Truth is, their continued harassment will eventually drive you away from them. Would you take this kind of putdown from friends?' He helped me overcome the guilt and the influence of my superego through rational examination and a big injection of laughter. We called my superego 'You-Should-Do,' because it's so full of what I should do instead of what I want to do."

Brandy's conception of an acceptable self or ego ideal was taught by her parents. Her independent self-view as a writer was contrary to her superego's judgment which made it easy for her parents to make her feel guilty. With her friend's help, she exchanged parental expectations and "shoulds" for a healthier self-definition of worth.

Redefining the Ego-Ideal

Visualize your ego-ideal by imagining a picture of yourself living, loving, and working in a style which would satisfy your parents or other authority figures. How do you differ from this portrait? Most of us do not conform to the exemplary image of parental anticipations. The disparity can cause a free-floating guilt that erodes our self-esteem and creative motivation. Make an effort to accept yourself rather than wasting time and energy comparing yourself to unrealistic, internalized expectations.

"My mother was an ardent feminist," shares Gilda, a novelist, "and our home was a lecture hall for women's rights, hostile male power, the necessity for women to have high-paying professions, and women's ultimate superiority. I was groomed to be her gift to the women's world, challenging the establishment and championing her cause. My ego-ideal is an outspoken, sharply dressed, confident professional, sans male attachments. The comparison to the real me is shocking, at least to my mother.

"I am shy, I dress like a slob, I didn't attend college, and I am madly in love with my husband. I am a housewife with two children, content to write between chores. My mother feels betrayed and doesn't hesitate to wonder aloud how she failed, how a feminist could produce a daughter so disgustingly, traditionally dependent on love and happy with her situation.

"My unconscious superego voice harps at my lack of interest in changing the world for women's rights, but I smile and pat its frenzied head. My life is so fulfilled that the superego's clamoring has little effect."

Remaking the Superego

Make a final appraisal of your superego's life-style expectations, moral dictates, and judgments about your personality by reviewing your lists of learned rights and wrongs and situations which trigger unconscious guilt. Pick out the reasonable, workable, self-sustaining standards and discard the inhibiting or negative criticisms. Then before a writing session, personify the unworkable superego as an enemy to be locked up and silenced.

Uncovering guilt roots and triggers prevents unconscious powers from depleting your creative energies. A creatively responsible ethical system, constructed from an adult position, will have goals and standards fitting your capabilities. You will feel appropriate guilt if you decide to devote at least ten hours a week to writing and do not fulfill the bargain. Set reasonable goals in order to congratulate yourself on meeting requirements. Free will and creative autonomy are gained in proportion to the replacement of untenable superego "shoulds" with your own principles.

Chapter Six

Psychological Blocks Against Creativity

ALTHOUGH WE CANNOT give a definition of a normal personality, we know that a person should strive toward a full life, one in which there is an enjoyable balance between love, work, creativity, and play. The balance is different for everyone and can easily be upset when psychological problems interfere with our ability to explore, develop, gain pleasure and work—the elements which make up a quality life. Emotional distractions not only cause unhappiness, they can be periodic nuisances or frightening adversaries when they stunt our ability to create.

Writers are prone to psychic distress because the quality of introspection that is common to creative people makes it impossible for them to ignore the inner world. Perceptiveness and sensitivity, delightful and necessary attributes of writers, also make them acutely aware of their own inner states. Added to this mental preoccupation are the writer's rich imagination and fantasy life which can lead to exaggerated reactions and responses in relationships and daily situations. The very qualities that we treasure and depend upon for our art and craft can be unavoidable silent enemies when turned against the self.

Writers are continually aware of details, nuances, and subtle changes in the feelings of others and themselves—using this awareness to enrich their craft. We cannot compartmentalize these sensitivities, but must deal with them in everyday life, understanding when we suffer with neurotic tendencies, and overcoming the negative aspects of our personalities.

Many writers who accept their special gifts and are comfortable with the label, "creative person," assume that their emotional distresses are an unavoidable part of their artistic personalities and allow their emotional turbulence to blow them about like a feather in the wind. Writers *are* more susceptible to psychological problems than noncreative people, but the artistically inclined person need not suffer silently with emotional problems as though they were the price of creativity. There are active means to deal with blocks against creative enjoyment. Your psychological history is the first step for uncovering the reasons for inner turmoils. With a dedicated attempt to understand and control unconscious forces, you can overcome emotional hang-ups and invest the freed up energies in your writing.

You do not have to pay a price of unhappiness to maintain a creative identification. You should be willing to pay the price of gaining insight into your problems, clear away the emotional garbage and continue to grow as an artist to reach your full potential as a person.

No one emerges unscathed from the complex journey to adulthood. You most likely discovered emotional scars and the roots of current day problems when recording your personal psychogram. Some of those experiences, even the unpleasant ones, may actually have directed you into the writing life. And other memories may still be perplexing, and difficult to link to the present day problems that are eroding your creative efforts.

By adding to your self-knowledge you will increase productivity rather than reduce it. It is a myth that insight destroys the mystery of the creative process, because awareness and understanding transform defeating emotional problems into writing vigor by releasing energy. Consider the exploration of your inner world as an exciting challenge that will ultimately add to your creativity rather than harming your talents.

Internal Disruptions

When you choose the craft of writing, you also accept isolation as a companion. Authors know they are alone and must depend solely on self-motivation to face the complex and difficult task of sorting out and externalizing thoughts into informative or entertaining language. This voluntary isolation, imperative to the act of writing, is still a difficult adjustment because it often causes frustration, irritability, and loneliness.

Paradoxes and Irritations of Isolation

Bruce, the novelist, confesses, "Freelancing is full of paradoxes for me. I require absolute peace and quiet. I hate any disruption which breaks my concentration. Yet, I can be my own worst enemy, disturbing my own serenity.

"An example of this constant contradiction happened last night. After dinner I was working on my book and vaguely heard the telephone ringing in the living room. Try as I might to ignore the barely discernible conversation, curiosity ate at the edges of my thoughts just enough to divert my concentration. I couldn't shake off the distraction. My curiosity finally propelled me into the living room, to casually ask about who had called. My family laughed, having predicted my appearance, accustomed as they are to my nosiness. I returned to my desk, angry for allowing trivia curiosity to break the creative flow.

"Another one of my emotional discrepancies is the desire for both solitude and socializing. I often think I would love to be a hermit and never talk to another soul. And yet I enjoy and need to be with other people. This conflict leaves me feeling nervous and never quite satisfied with how I use my time.

"A believable contemporary storyteller must have involvement with people, must be informed about national and world events, fashions, fads, and popular gossip. Facts and ideas can be abstracted from reading, listening to the radio, and watching television but the tone of vital, busy people and the texture of atmospheres can only be absorbed through inter-relating—observing and actively participating in human affairs.

"I have to balance my all-important alone time with socializing for my own pleasure as well as my craft.

"I rail against time—my job robs nine hours a day from my writing. I also need time for my family; my wife and two teenagers need love and attention. We also need something resembling a social life, although my wife regularly makes 'doctor's mate' excuses for me, attending functions alone because of 'medical emergencies.' The paradoxical pulls between everyday responsibilities and creativity often makes me nervous and irritable.

"Living with teenagers means dealing with the normal adolescent commotions of friends and dates, telephones constantly ringing and the ever-present loud rock music. My daughters' inconsideration (I know it's directed toward me) leads to shouting matches in which I find myself acting more childish than the kids. When I let myself get angry, then I feel too upset to concentrate on writing. My wife's solution is a separate studio writing apartment. I can't afford one, so I continue to suffer bouts of irritation. Besides, I have an embarrassing suspicion that, even if I were rich enough to afford a studio, I'd keep on working at home because I'm afraid of missing something!

"I often read authors' dedications to their wives and children, filled with effusive words of gratitude for patience and understanding. A more honest inscription would be: 'Thanks for not divorcing me and living with my selfish temper tantrums so I could finish this damn thing!' "

Many writers think they must be weird when they are pulled by the opposing desires for isolation and the need for companionship. Since these qualities are important for a sense of balance, a freelancer must learn to appreciate both demands and then set priorities. Most authors accept their limitations, realizing that they can write only a certain number of hours during the day or night. After an extended time at the typewriter or writing pad, the brain begins to tire, signalling the writer to stop. If possible, mark a specific time in which to write, and discipline yourself to a routine of concentrating on some facet of writing, whether it be research, thinking, attending to correspondence, writing, or revisions. When your writing time becomes a routine, the other activities that attract you can be enjoyed without guilt. Very few freelancers live in a vacuum, so you must be flexible about the hours earmarked for writing. Crises occur with our friends and family which must be dealt with, just as you expect loved ones to give up their normal activities to care for you in difficult times. The amount of curiosity writers possess can bedevil them into believing that they are missing some excitement while they toil at writing. We cannot be in two places at once, so must accept the reality that there will be a certain amount of adventures, people, and stimulating events that *will* be missed while we are creating. This condition is the same for anyone whose craft demands isolation from the world around.

The positive side of setting up priorities for a social life and writing is that freelancers have the freedom to choose the time and place in which they will work, whereas those who are employed from nine to five have no control over a large segment of their daily lives. You as a freelancer are in active control of the options of how you will spend the precious gift of time.

Selfishness

George, the screenplay writer, comments, "Film writers, as do other authors, need blocks of time to drift with possibilities— testing ideas, mentally viewing actions, reactions and conversations. This 'other world' is best visited alone, and can easily add to writers' loneliness because it excludes friends and lovers.

"Dedicated writers very often seem selfish, and sometimes it's an accurate label, particularly about the use of time.

"In the past, I used to hole up for days, devoting myself to a screenplay, only hazily aware of my family, except when they dared to interrupt me. During an obsessive writing spree, I existed on very little food and two or three hours of sleep whenever I was exhausted. Emerging from a creative splurge, I would expect instant attention, as if I had been on a long trip. My wife has business interests, friends and hobbies of her own. She would not be demurely sitting, waiting for me to rejoin life. Abandoned, I would sulk—the unappreciated genius.

"Experience and maturity have taught me that the world does not revolve around me, waiting to celebrate and play at my convenience. My inner clock does not tick in tune with my family's normal schedule—they are sleeping while I'm writing, pacing, and mumbling lines. Sometimes I do feel lonely, but I understand it comes with the territory of my chosen craft.

"Since I'm being so honest, my fantasy is to have total silence while I'm working, no emotional demands placed on me, and then when I'm finished, walk into an expectant and affectionate family group who will slather praise on my overworked head. We all have our daydreams!"

Have you been called selfish or inconsiderate because you expect your friends and family to plan around your writing schedule and to empathize with your frustrations, but discount their problems because they are not creative? Authors who hope to enjoy friendships and love must grow to appreciate the value of everyone's life and talents. As authors we are not ex-

cused from the give-and-take of relationships just because we
are blessed with special gifts.

Like George, writers can and must learn to laugh at their self-
centered wishes for the ideal life in which devotion to writing
takes precedence over all other responsibilities. Loneliness occurs when people neglect to learn the art of sharing feelings,
time, and consideration. Very few friends will remain loving
and supportive just to be in the presence of a talented person.
One aspect of maturity is the realization that we must earn love
and respect and that they are not automatically given without a
mutual exchange of attention and affection.

Alienation

Writers require solitude in order to be productive, yet many
complain of loneliness, creating for themselves an emotional
paradox.

Solitude is positive, a chosen activity necessary to the job of
writing. Loneliness is negative and passive, a feeling of despair
that, even if one desired company, there is no one who cares.

Chronic loneliness—an ongoing sense of abject loneliness
pervading a person's entire life—is widespread in our society.
The chronically lonely individual feels invisible. Depression,
linked with loneliness, further prevents people from seeking
solutions to their predicament. Physicians state that the majority of patients with psychosomatic disorders have a history of
loneliness. They seek the "kindly doctor's" attention to briefly
remove their feeling that "nobody cares."

Authors must defend against falling into the trap of loneliness because that state can erode one's enthusiasm for writing
and for seeking validation through publication. If you allow the
negative thought that "nobody cares" to enter into your philosophy, the next pervading thought is usually, "Why bother?"

Our society has formed a definite attitude toward loneliness.
From early infancy, a person is trained to be a part of the
group—any group, just so long as he is not found alone. The
emphasis on group interaction can be traced to the early history
of our society, when people had to work together and stay
closely connected in order to survive. To this day people identify themselves with groups whether political parties, religious
affiliations, unions, hobbies or groups that gather for learning
to deal with divorce, death, single parenting, or dieting. Where-

as most people socialize with those involved in similar businesses or professions, creative people often take such enormous pride in their individuality that they shun groups, taking a chance on dealing with loneliness and society's attitudes. When you recorded your personal psychogram, the questions make it apparent that many of your attitudes and reactions are formed by the treatment and opinions of the adults around you. Children take their cues from parents and other adults, and if those authority figures give the impression that being alone is strange, perhaps even bad, a child can grow to adulthood unconsciously believing that solitude is undesirable.

Writers learn early in their careers that they must develop discipline and self-motivation alone, without a manual to teach them these necessary skills for a productive career. It follows then that one must grow to value and prize being alone in order to fulfill one's creative goals.

If you have achieved the state of enjoying solitude for creative contemplation and work and yet suffer from loneliness in the other aspects of your life, consider your options. You can remain in a state of alienation or change your attitude and actions to promote friendship and interaction with other people.

The antidote for loneliness has always been involvement with others. This requires the lonely person's taking the first step, since most people are too busy to spend much time with a passive, self-pitying person. To receive companionship and the delights of friendship, you must extend yourself. Examine your secret expectations about relationships. Are you looking for instant acceptance without a mutual exchange of caring and sharing? Do you really care about others, or do you just want someone to care about you? What do you do to make yourself interesting or attractive to other people? When you reach beyond the negative, self-centered dreams of acceptance without sharing personal commitment, you will make the first and most vital step toward overcoming loneliness. Self-determination, a quality consciously employed in the writing field, can also be used to cope with problems which affect your daily living.

Julie, the confessions writer, admits to a "cascading loneliness" when completing a story. "Sometimes I work on a piece for a month and feel a sudden rush of loss when typing the final draft; the characters so vibrant and alive in my thoughts for such a long time are suddenly gone. I lose another set of companions even though they are all imaginary. I force myself outside to become part of society again. I love being around people when I'm not working, so I visit the local nursing home, filled with older citizens eager for affection and company, or drop by a nearby child-care center and read stories to the kids. I have coffee at the city university's crowded snack shop where conditions force strangers to share tables. Being an extrovert, I find it easy to begin conversations with students about their courses and dreams. Even a shy person can almost infallibly start an exchange by asking any young person, 'What is your major?'

"Of course, no writer who reads need ever be lonely. Good books are like friends, always there when you need them.

"Loneliness shouldn't be allowed to overcome a writer's spirits, because it can be a trap, stunting your creativity, and drawing a vicious, self-pitying circle around all of you and life. You have to make yourself mingle and join groups to ward off that sense of seclusion. You have to search out good companions with the same determination you use to research ideas."

Loneliness caused by external situations can also affect a writer's sense of well being. The person residing where there are few kindred souls regularly suffers feelings of alienation. Company and conversation shared with other working artists lessens spiritual loneliness. But one cannot always choose a conducive, artistic environment where it is a simple matter to meet new friends or join societies dedicated to the encouragement of the arts.

"I live in a remote corner of Wyoming," writes Frederika, an author of radio plays. "My husband works for the Forest Service and we live where they send us, always rural. When I fell in love I did not think I would be lonely for other writers or creative people. My husband's co-workers and their spouses love the outdoors. They aren't boring, but their life direction is outward-bound and their avocations are sports, survival techniques, botany, and animal life. They cannot fathom my writing career and are constantly amazed that anyone would stay cooped up inside inventing imaginary situations when there is so much excitement outdoors. They inquire politely about my work and expect the briefest answer. After a year or so of exasperation, lack of stimulation and just plain feeling like an alien, I realized I have a strong need to talk with other writers, that I felt lonely for other creative people who thought about ideas, plots, and characters. The one writing conference I attend yearly is like a mouthful of cool water given to a lost desert hiker—it quenches immediate thirst but doesn't begin to satisfy the need for liquids.

"I began connecting with other writers—far-flung creative brothers and sisters. I subscribe to ten diversified magazines, writers' journals, and two newsletters for playwrights. My address book contains names and notations of fellow writers met and admired at writing conferences. Writing letters in my spare time keeps me in touch with many friends who are involved with the world of ideas.

"When a letter to the editor appears in a magazine, revealing similar interests or opinions, I write the person and suggest corresponding. If I am entertained by an article or story in a magazine, I send a grateful note to the author, in care of the magazine. Novelists and nonfiction authors alike receive appreciative letters. Extremely busy writers usually send a hastily written thank you, obviously too involved with careers for new acquaintances. Many others have responded positively and we maintain contact, sharing the peaks and valleys of freelancing. We add to each other's lives by exchanging encouragement and giving advice. Since I live in a tourist area, pen pals have visited, adding to our friendship bonds."

Preoccupations with Ideas

I become obsessed with my characters during the writing of a screenplay," reports Brandy. "Each person in the film is a part of myself. I switch identities with every change in dialogue. Unintentionally, I form favorites and invest my people with real life—they are truly alive inside my imagination. I even get sad when it's time to kill a character. I've learned to plan deaths on Saturdays, because I need the next day to grieve.

"I tried explaining to an acquaintance the total engrossment with my characters' lives, only to receive a leery glance, obviously categorizing me as a certified looney. Fortunately, I live in Los Angeles, where several acting friends understand my identification with fictionalized characters, a necessity in their own careers.

"I live in two mental worlds—reality and film plots—and often they are not complementary. I have been called forgetful and distracted because I daydream about screenplay action while I should be dealing with the real world. I strive to keep the worlds of fact and fiction in their separate compartments, but it isn't easy."

The creative unconscious steams along even during dreams, planning the next day's sequences. An example of dreams' influence on creativity was reported by Margaret, a poet and short story writer.

"I grew up in Detroit and attended Wayne State, a nonprejudiced oasis within the city. The multiracial student body had little interest in the issue of color, so strong were the bonds of poverty and intense desire for upward mobility. I had many Black friends but never realized the depth of their cultural loss and sorrow until I read *Crisis in Black and White*, an extremely comprehensive and emotionally wrenching book on American slavery. I wept when I finished, once again astounded by man's inhumanity to his brothers.

"A normal person would probably feel depressed and sad for a while and then forget the book's message. That very night, I dreamt myself an African man in Dahomey, dancing in a tribal celebration, proud of myself, my woman and my sons. I was captured and, during quick scenes of dehumanizing slavery, lost my sense of strong masculine identity as I bowed and followed orders of white bosses. At the end of the dream I was a sophisticated, prideless, lonely jazz musician, without family, love, or home.

"The next morning I leapt out of bed, and, as if my hand were guided by another spirit, wrote a poem entitled, "The Way It Was," incorporating my intense dream experience into a minihistory of an African's spiritual transformation into a faceless Black American. The poem was written totally inspired and needed no revision. It found easy acceptance in a literary journal and was eventually published as a single-poem chapbook. Someone (I'll never know who) sent the poem to the Detroit *Free Press*. They ran it—even paying me $25—as an example of contemporary Black poetry. I felt silly trying to explain that I was white, so I kept quiet, hoping the published poem would spur on young Black writers.

"All my life I felt burdened by the insistent, never-ending flights of ideas, story lines, and poetic phrases in my head, the persistent, vivid dreams, forever on my mind—distractions from reality. The dream-inspired poem jolted me into an appreciation of the creative unconscious. I cherish the bubbling stream of ideas and pray it never diminishes."

Jennie, the novelist, concurred, but felt a tendency to abstract ruminations even invading normal, everyday thinking, to the point where it was often an encumbrance to her sense of orderliness. "I have a very active mind and am always mulling details. I often catch myself mentally reviewing the most trivial matters of the day. I can't escape pondering. A superficial remark on television, a friend's political observations, or overheard gossip—all get the same attention as creative moilings. I know it's ridiculous to review and rewrite my arguments with my teenagers! My husband warns of brain burn-out from excessive brooding. A part of me yearns to be able to concentrate on one idea at a time, before exhaustion sets in!

"A group of writing friends meets for a weekly confab, kidding ourselves about our strange thinking, to purposely inject a little levity into our serious natures. We offer support to each other, accept our literary madness, and temporarily ease our 'Martian' feelings.

"Hal writes animated films, popular because of their funny dialogue and the inventive, improbable antics of his anthropomorphic creatures. Everyone assumes that Hal himself is carefree, witty, and full of elan. In actuality, Hal is morose, pessimistic, and always worrying about his hypochondriacal symptoms. He faithfully attends our 'therapy' sessions, counting on us to tease away his gloom.

"Hal contracts a new physical complaint monthly, has himself whisked to the doctor, and hopes for immediate hospital admittance. He's actually disappointed when lab tests fail to show that he has diabetes, high blood pressure, or some other exotic disease he plucked straight from the Merck Manual (his leisure reading!) Last week, while finishing an assignment, Hal knew he was having a heart attack and made his wife drive him to the emergency room. The attending physician diagnosed an acute anxiety attack, but no cardiac disorder. His wife, also a busy writer, refuses to offer any more sympathy and laughs when he whines about sudden aches and pains. She said her doctor insists that attention to Hal's excessive worries only encourages further imagined illnesses.

"Hal has read about hypochondriasis and knows he's seeking attention. But he refuses to consult a psychiatrist because he's afraid that digging into his neurosis will sap his creative flow. He's unhappy but productive, believing artists are meant to suffer. I disagree but know special gifts can exact a psychological price. Creative people are usually dissatisfied, demanding better and better personal performance and appearing egocentric and internally preoccupied. Most people forget their work when they leave the office, but writers are always thinking about present assignments or new ideas. You can't expect total psychological serenity when you are creative—the two just don't seem to go together."

Psychosomatic Disorders

A successful mystery writer consulted us after his physician could find no physical cause for his headaches and stiff, painful neck muscles. He reported thought patterns filled with intrigue, devious villains, plots and plans, bizarre murder methods, and anxiety-producing chase scenes involving the book's hero. "When writing, I'm in a sadistic, macho-mania world," reported the client. "I must be alert, keeping the story gripping and action-packed. I can't concentrate with persistent headaches and neck pain."

After a few sessions, the writer came to understand that even though he emptied his mind daily of adventures, via writing, he refilled the void with further conflict, subconsciously preparing for the next day's writing. This, added to the "average" person's share of psychological conflicts, was overloading his system and contributing to psychosomatic symptoms.

He viewed himself as gentle and was surprised he wrote only gruesome and violent stories. He envisioned the hero as distinctly separate from his quiet, unassuming personality and denied any aggressiveness.

We asked this writer to fantasize himself as the heartless detective, at ease with rough language and tough actions. The exercise caused unpleasant anxiety and a sharp increase in head and neck pains. He had a memory of his family's expressing horror when he behaved cruelly, was disrespectful, swore, or "beat up" his siblings. They programmed him to deny normal aggressive thoughts and actions. The writer suddenly realized that he had been using psychic energies to deny his own repressed "mean" streak.

Through free association, the writer discovered that the attempt to suppress aggression had caused him to adopt the rigid body carriage of a righteous, stalwart deacon above vicious thought. The head and neck pain that resulted was self-inflicted punishment for unconscious revelry in the detective's dirty tricks.

Admitting that he identified with the detective's mayhem and accepting his inner satisfaction at thinking "horrid" thoughts allowed his headaches and neck pain to disappear.

Shortly thereafter he lectured at a mystery writer's convention on the topic of "Getting in Touch with Your Id." In the speech he shared his history of psychological repression and the external, physical outcome. He told his audience how, when he accepted his primitive, instinctual thoughts as normal aggression and no longer needed to censor them, they added to his scary plots, gory murder methods, and authentic solutions. He said, "Accept your primitive, nasty thoughts as normal and you'll be a freer writer. You'll have a creative advantage when you explore the darker side of your mind. Readers of mysteries enjoy aggressive action vicariously. As mystery writers, we gleefully plug into the reader's submerged id, have the supreme luxury of self-employment, financial gain, and the chance to satisfy our readers' need to read about evil deeds which they would never do."

Hiding Behind Work

"My personality was very similar to my mother's," relates Sheila, a journalist. "I identified with her inquisitive nature, always searching for truths. Unfortunately, I also began to mirror my mother's obviously critical, doubting, and tactless approach to other people. My inability to accept anyone at face value made me appear paranoid. Interviewees commented that my questions seemed more like interrogations than a genuine quest for honest information. My mannerisms put people on the defensive, even though I thought of myself as an objective reporter. The boss loved my assertive approach because it made excellent copy, as people often become flustered when under fire and unintentionally blurt out more than they intended to say.

"My assertive approach worked well on the job, but didn't help my social life. I never learned to turn off my invasiveness after work and, as a result, I alienated acquaintances. I rationalized my lack of friends by boasting that writing was my reason for living. You can actually fool yourself into believing that you don't need friends.

"One man I interviewed pierced my intellectual armor. The piece was about a ghetto gang who gave up violence, now lending their time and talents to preventing violence between the ghetto's youth and police. Their active anti-drug campaign, aimed at the killer drug PCP (angel dust) was meeting with great success, because the young toughs respected the older and wiser gang members.

"The headquarters was located in a run-down building with scary-looking punks hanging around outside. Super-confident vibes protect me from urban hassles and I breezed into the building to talk with the director. He was a huge, intimidating fellow, dressed in blue jeans, heavy-duty motorcycle boots, a leather vest barely concealing a knife and snakes tattooed on his massive chest. My background research had prepared me for his habit of dressing and talking like his street-wise clients as well as the fact of his advanced degrees in psychology.

"My customary line of questioning began with more than a hint of cynicism (what's his power and financial gain?). After answering a few questions he turned his charismatic gaze on me and asked me some personal questions about poverty, drugs, and crime. I quickly turned the conversation back to him, wanting the interview to remain professional. The aloof approach had always worked in the past, but he kept staring at me, waiting for my answers. When it was obvious I had no intention of talking about myself, he said, 'I like to "read" people, you know, figure them out by the way they talk and look into my eyes. You think you're pretty smooth but. . . .Sister, you're just like these punks, you're all spikey on the outside— pretty hard to warm up to. Your questions are too fierce and insistent—like I'm the enemy when you don't even know me. I'd tell you lots more about my life and give you a better story if you were really interested in me instead of treating this operation like some scam. You should learn to like yourself and be kinder or you'll end up alone and bitter. Just a little free advice. I wouldn't bother except you're a gifted lady.' He smiled and smoothly moved me toward the door, directing another counselor to take 'the lady' to her car. I felt like a scolded child, slapped across the face. He had invaded my defenses, leaving me speechless.

"Back at the office, I turned on the automatic writing pilot and completed the investigative report, hitting all the salient points of victims, villains, and rescuers. But his remarks kept replaying in my mind during the following weeks.

"I took some vacation time and applied to a southwestern re treat community whose members fasted, meditated, and took an oath of silence. A week of introspection, reading, communing with nature and my long-forgotten softer side gave me some insights. I really didn't like myself. I avoided personal growth by being a writing machine, rolling over people, zeroing in on success. In the background was an unconscious belief that fame and riches would someday bring me love and adoration. I had a fantasy of me presenting Mother with a long list of achievement awards and plaques for outstanding writing and showing off a briefcase bulging with stock certificates, and basking in her pride and pleasure. This breakthrough insight showed a life pattern of intellectual pursuits hiding unmet childhood needs for affection and acceptance. As a child I only knew I wanted hugs and kisses and didn't get them. I thought there was something wrong with me. I remembered being jealous when I would go to a girlfriend's home and see her parents put their arms around her and say that they loved her. As an adult I knew my mother was incapable of physically demonstrating her love, having been reared in a family of brainy nontouchers.

"I laid by a mountain stream and had a good, long cry, seeing the little girl I once was, longing for love and growing into an obnoxious, always-on-the-attack journalist. It was a relief allowing myself to grieve for a thwarted childhood, almost like a funeral. I felt refreshed and like I could begin life anew. I would still be an effective reporter, but vowed to improve my personality.

"I couldn't expect others to find me pleasant or attractive when I didn't like myself. I tackled my negative traits one at a time, gradually reducing my abrasiveness. The first was my overall critical attitude. It was masking a fear that people would scrutinize my flaws (just like at home)—attack first, before the enemy nails you!

"I signed up for a photography class and willed myself to relax, instead of spouting brilliant cutting observations. Every time sharply pointed comments came to mind, I smiled instead. After class discussions, my jaws ached from clamping them shut, thinking of tactful remarks and then pleasantly contributing them in place of the harsh cynicism of my 'former' self.

"I was invited to a party one evening by the husband and wife sitting next to me. Most people might consider the invitation at best a minor victory, but it was a rarity for me. I'm a prime example that being attractive has no social advantage if a person is disagreeable.

"Before venturing to the party, I concocted a mental movie of myself, making all the past social gaffes, ending the evening alone and unhappy. I locked that brash person in the closet. Admitting vulnerability, I approached the party as a new beginning, since my classmates never knew 'the bully.' The fun-loving group enjoyed talking about different creative interests, with no attempts at one-upmanship. I was able to restrain the grating voice and superior attitude and have fun.

"A year has passed since the ex-gang leader shook my iron-clad, nonsensical defenses. I joined a therapy group to understand more about my abrasive approach to people. I learned to give up childhood dreams of fame and concentrate on being a likable person to myself and others, without a loss of creative energy. I've changed jobs because the boss kept complaining that my 'fire' was gone. Still a journalist, I now cover stories which don't require manipulating people and enjoy writing even more because I'm relaxed and that attitude flows over into my prose."

Like Sheila, we all have psychological identifications, positive and negative, which form our adult make-up, our personalities resulting from programming, defenses against psychic pain, and coping devices that we learned to help deal with the vicissitudes of life. In your psychogram, you may have pinpointed events which caused emotional problems. Consider the defenses you may have erected to protect yourself from future stress.

Common Defenses of Writers

A defense is a psychological device which begins in childhood, becomes strengthened and fortified during adolescence, and is solidified in adulthood. A defense can appear to be a natural part of an adult's personality since its inception and growth occurred over a long period of time. A defense, however, is only a mechanism to avoid pain, a sophisticated form of protection, to be sure, but one which requires considerable psychological energy to maintain. When a defense is given up, the energy formerly required to nurture it flows into one's sense of well-being and creativity. We have discussed the defense mechanism of repression to block out memories and associated feelings. The defense of rationalization is also used when an author can view rejection of a manuscript only as an editor's stupidity rather than examining the faults in his writing style. These defenses reduce tension and internal discomfort, but they sidestep a realistic exploration of deeper problems. The personality is drained of spontaneity and openness with the self and others when energies are used to cover up real feelings. It is healthier in the long run to admit feeling frail and vulnerable and fearful of rejection, thus allowing yourself to evaluate just how necessary a defense is to living life well.

Another common self-defeating defense is being a braggart. Bragging about or exaggerating one's achievements is self-flattery. Its underlying purpose is to provide a sense of worth in one's own eyes and the eyes of others.

Gilda, the novelist, told us about an acquaintance of hers who was a songwriter. "Jay was always boasting to people that he had sold songs to several famous country and western singers, when in fact his lyrics were continually rejected. Jay bragged so much that he came across as if he wanted to make others feel inferior. He didn't know that he was making a fool of himself and that people saw through his exaggerations. He would have received more sympathy and maybe even offers to help him improve his lyrics if he had been able to tell people about his rejections and the fact that they made him feel like a failure."

Bragging to cover up lack of self-esteem is a costly defense because people tend to ignore the boasting after a while and eventually shun the braggart. The problem of low self-esteem is then compounded since the braggart feels like a failure in work and personal relationships, all the time denying his real feelings of worthlessness. To combat the defense of bragging, one must admit feeling like a failure, then direct attention to becoming a better writer and establishing higher self-esteem by trying to improve instead of telling stories about imaginary successes. Save your story-telling ability for your work.

Another sophisticated defense against inner pain is to become super critical, always finding fault with others' works (and then pointing out those faults without being asked). The writer who cannot deal with the frustration of repeated rejection may read the creative works of others solely for mistakes. He wants to feel that no one's writing skills can match his own, and protects this feeling by appearing to be an idealistic reader. Creative people who come in contact with a highly critical person do not appreciate his superior attitude and shun further confrontations.

The defenses of bragging about oneself and criticizing everyone else are extremely harmful protections for the writer because they cause others to distance themselves from the defensive personality. This, in turn, adds to the feelings of alienation which afflict many authors.

Another self-defeating defense is an obsession with perfection. The perfectionist feels that everything must be done with meticulous care, and so every act takes on crucial importance. When this defense extends to writing, the perfectionist can never find satisfaction or fulfillment in his work and spends countless hours rewriting beyond necessity.

Marcia, an articles writer, commented, "I found myself becoming more and more demanding of my work—so caught up in my need to be the perfect writer that I lost the spontaneity that makes for good reading. I was so serious in my approach to writing an article that the words came out boring—precise but boring. Before, when I had a full-time job and writing was a part-time endeavor, I rarely worried about being perfect; I revelled in thinking up ideas and writing interesting pieces. The need for perfection became apparent when I decided to make my living as a freelancer. My dependency on the income from magazines caused me considerable stress and a fear that I would have to go back to a daily job. Instead of facing my feelings of self-doubt and worry, I became frantic about being perfect—and wrote boring prose.

"I looked back at my psychogram and saw repeated incidences of my family's doling out praise only if something was perfect. My parents were always talking about the perfect report card, and if I got five A's and one B, I was an inferior person. Their high expectations and giving affection only if I performed perfectly were imprinted on my unconscious tape. "I decided that I wasn't a perfect person and didn't have to be one in order to love myself and to produce good writing. The release from the judgmont of my inner critics relaxed me, allowed me to look at my freelancing assignments in a realistic manner and to enjoy writing to the best of my abilities."

Perfectionism can drive a person to distraction and covers up the fear that, no matter how hard you try, nothing will ever match up to the harsh taskmaster inside who withholds the feeling of satisfaction for doing one's best.

Several editors have mentioned to us that some writers send with their manuscripts letters that try to induce a sale by eliciting pity. This maneuver does not work and immediately turns off the experienced editor, who considers it unprofessional to make appeals such as, "I know you will read this with a positive attitude because I have worked so hard on this story and although I have little talent and don't understand grammar too well, I deserve a little kindness."

Self-depreciation is a defense with which the person paints a depressing picture of his situation, hoping that others will accordingly not expect too much, will refrain from criticizing the "poor" person, and perhaps give some sympathy. This defense against being exposed as an inferior person has little room in the world of writing, because those who read and buy manuscripts are only interested in content and writing styles, not the author's personal condition.

Anger, unassociated with specific events, is another defense against internal pain. The angry person feels worthless, inadequate and futile but avoids facing those feelings and turns his wrath toward others, ventilating his own rage through temper tantrums and offensive behavior. Anger is a normal emotion, but it must be expressed in mature ways instead of becoming self-indulgent and childish by spewing accusations, hurling threats and yelling at those who frustrate one's goals. The writer who is angry at the world and reacts to rejections with hatred does little to help his career and drains his creative energies.

"I had a defense which looked good to the outside world, but was actually a rigid way of dealing with people, and it stagnated my career," shares Jennifer, a novelist. "I was an example of absolute agreeability, never wanting to offend anyone, agreeing with all opinions in order to gain approval. Whenever I spoke to an editor about an advance, I never stood up for myself, or bargained for a better deal, but always complied with a charming voice. I thought if I was the all-time nice person, then people would accept me, something I learned as a little girl.

"While I was bartering for recognition as the wonderful, sweet person I completely lost touch with my real reactions and responses. I was not a genuine person and neither was my writing, because I was always worried about distressing some imaginary reader. I presented myself to the world as compliant, and always agreeable. It was like living in a constricted space, and wearing a mask to hide my real feelings from the world and myself.

"I didn't know that the role I had adopted was harmful to me until I developed ulcers and was referred to a psychiatrist. In therapy I learned that I had a lot of anger at being treated like a doormat, something I encouraged with my defense mechanism of being so agreeable. I had to face the fact that I was afraid of everyone and that, whether they were threatening or not, I cajoled them into thinking I was harmless and nonaggressive, someone nobody would criticize or reject. I was also lonely because the defense appeared to be my total personality and stopped people from knowing the real me.

"These insights and the release of feelings in therapy cleared up my ulcers and gave me the courage to drop the smiling mask and be myself. That doesn't mean I became an irritable or unkindly person, but I let myself experience normal reactions to situations and people."

Jennifer's defense against her fear of being unacceptable is called a reaction formation. This defense denies forbidden feelings or impulses and converts those reactions into their opposites. Another example of this defense is sometimes apparent in people who are horrified by explicit sexual scenes in novels and seek to ban them from the adult reading public. These righteous critics often deny any normal interest in sexuality and defend their own secret curiosity by appearing to be more moral than the rest of us.

One of the lessons learned during the complex journey toward adulthood is that we cannot trust everyone. We learn to use common sense, intuition and past experiences to judge the trustworthiness of those we deal with personally and in business. We have trust and faith that a publication will pay us when we submit an acceptable piece of writing. Contracts are necessary when selling books, screenplays, plays, and songs because of the complex financial and copyright laws, but they are still based on trust that the publisher will fulfill the agreement.

The person who has no trust in others has magnified healthy suspicion into total cynicism. This defense colors all of life with a persistent pessimism and a belief that everyone is out to trick the cynical disbeliever. The cynical person defends himself against extremely low self-esteem, projects the feelings of having no value onto the rest of the world, and in the process of exuding suspicion, becomes a shunned person.

Authors who suffer from cynicism destroy any chance of success because the negative attitude infects their writing. The characters in such authors' stories are apt to be unlikable, and they quickly turn off editors who understand that characters must be multi-dimensional in order for the reader to identify and care about them.

A person can be afflicted with one or several of these defenses which buffer him from feelings of fear, rejection, aggression, or low self-esteem. Whether the defenses protect the bearer or are meant to impress others, they are all self-defeating because they either exact a psychological price which interferes with full creative expression or offend others.

If you are determined to reach for your full potential as a creative artist, examine the pros and cons of continuing to maintain a defensive posture, and make a decision to remove the protective device and face the buried feelings.

Personality problems which affect relating and writing can be dealt with calmly and effectively to increase creativity. No one should passively accept unpleasant symptoms without a struggle toward solutions.

Anxiety and Depression

Anxiety and depression are two debilitating emotions which cause creative stagnation. Both can be overcome by personal insight or psychotherapy.

Anxiety

Normal anxiety, experienced as sudden fear and physical alertness, is manifested in response to real danger. The body automatically increases its adrenaline flow to quicken a frightened person's flight-or-fight response. We need normal anxiety when faced with danger in order to take appropriate action. When the danger and response have passed, anxiety subsides and a person gradually calms down, eventually regaining physical and mental composure.

Writers often complain of body tension or feel edgy and uncomfortable sitting at the desk thinking, writing, or daydreaming for an hour or more. Body anxiety can be relieved by getting away from the working area for a ten-minute spurt of exercise, taking a brisk walk around the block or jumping rope. Writers discharge intellectual energy while working, but the body is sedentary and requires regular physical activity.

In unpredicted anxiety an unexplained apprehension takes over all feelings, targeting on unknown impending doom or injury. An anxiety attack can cause overwhelming dread, panic, tension and fatigue, often accompanied by profuse sweating, heart palpitations, hyperventilation and chest constriction. These sensations may last for only a few minutes, but in chronic cases, they are persistent.

When people are anxious, they usually make everyone else nervous too. They are usually in constant movement, attempting to discharge uncomfortable physical and psychic panic sensations. They sigh, jiggle their feet, eat too much, twist their hands, tap their fingers, talk incessantly, interrupt others, and jump at the slightest noise.

Children react to anxiety by yelling, screaming, and hyperactivity. Adolescents cope with internal tensions by impulsively destroying things, fighting, and yelling. Adults often develop drug dependencies to dampen anxiety's shrill pain.

Unpredictable anxiety, unattached to realistic dangers, can ruin creative thought and even the ability to write at all.

Phobias

Some people, in an attempt to avoid the "unknown" quality of unpredictable anxiety, displace the fear onto specific objects or situations, providing a tangible, external reason for morbid panic. This unconscious displacement is called a phobic reaction.

Some helpless, dependent children, unable to deal with insecurities caused by abusive parents, will develop phobias for animals, becoming terrified to leave the house, fearing that a dog will devour them. Small children, overly anxious about parental separations, often develop bath water phobias, convincing themselves that they will be sucked down the drain, never to see parents again.

The list of possible phobias is long and often appears humorous to those who never experience such compulsive terrors.

"I thought of myself as normal, although I knew I was over-conscientious and worried about making mistakes," shares Theresa, a part-time writer. "I dreamed of the day when all my kids would be in school. With three preschoolers the only opportunities I had for writing were late at night or before dawn. I rejoiced the first free September, and every day I spent four happy hours writing and sending queries.

"For no understandable reason, a silent, creeping fear of going outdoors began to filter into my life. At first, I explained it away by a busy schedule. I began asking my husband to pick up groceries on the way home, pleading deadline preoccupations. Taking the children to the park suddenly became too much.

"One day, I forced myself to make a trip to the post office to buy stamps. While standing in line I became paralyzed, felt faint and breathless, and broke out in a cold sweat. Quaking and shaking, I managed to stumble to my car. People looked away as if I were drunk.

"In six months my life was reduced to a shambles. My husband's patience was strained to the breaking point, and my children were angry and confused over my refusal to leave home. The friends I would not meet for lunch or visit in their homes melted away.

"My embarrassment, which resulted from a phobia, eroded my self-esteem. I derided myself as cowardly and began doubting my writing aptitude. How could I write nonfiction when I was a virtual prisoner of irrational fears? My insecurities about my creativity finally frightened me into therapy. I couldn't bear to think of hiding inside without at least my work to sustain me.

"I called a community mental health clinic and described my problem to a counselor. When she volunteered to make a house call, gratitude swept through me. 'If you have agoraphobia, there's no sense in forcing you to the office. By the time you get here, if you even make it, you'll be too upset for an interview,' she explained. She came to the house the following day and we talked for two hours. She set up connections with cured phobics who became supportive companions: holding hands while stepping outside (first down the sidewalk and back, then around the block, etc.), exchanging fearful experiences, and lending strength and nonhumiliating encouragement. They'd been phobic themselves and deeply sympathized with my unfounded dreads and self-imposed restrictions.

"Over the months it became clear that my phobia grew out of unconscious guilt associated with my freedom from children and the chance to enjoy my writing. My work ethic, child-oriented unconscious was in a rage when I turned attentions to selfish pursuits. I was stunned that internal forces could actually control my consciousness in such an exaggerated form.

"I'm a phobia-helper now and have written articles on overcoming phobias. I have listened to many wretched tales of exaggerated and paralyzing fears of disease, eating, infinity, insanity, thunderstorms, sleeping, the opposite sex, germs—anything you can imagine."

Obsessions

Another method of deflecting anxiety occurs with idea obsessions; repetition of trivial phrases, words, or songs; peculiar rituals, or a compulsive need to perform magical ceremonies to ward off imagined danger.

Sometimes obsessions become so ingrained in a person's daily routine that one can be unaware of habits which are considered peculiar by others. Some of these rituals include checking the time every few minutes, looking in the mirror compulsively, counting aloud while slicing foods, stepping over lines on the sidewalk, dressing and undressing in a prescribed, rigid routine, wiping all silverware before use, answering the phone only after a definite number of rings, repeated washing of the hands, or counting steps while climbing stairs. The list of compulsive actions is as long as man is complex. However, most obsessively compelled people are aware that their persistent compulsive acts are silly, needless, and without purpose, but they experience intolerable tension if they do not carry the thought or ceremony through to a conclusion.

"I diagnosed insanity," reports Ted, a children's story writer, "when, before I could allow myself to sleep, I had to recite the states of the Union in alphabetical order. If I left one out, I had to start again from the beginning. After several nights of this nutty ritual, I decided something really strange was happening to my head. I was embarrassed to ask my friends, 'Say, do you make up word games to torture yourself?'

"I reviewed my situation. My work hours at the restaurant had increased. My sister was calling every other night, dumping her divorce problems in my ear. But my quota for daily word output was the same, and I had stopped getting regular exercise on the handball courts. It was obvious I was draining my inner resources with too many demands. I was denying irritations and using the obsessive word litany to avoid facing feelings.

"I took active steps against daily pressures. Writing came first. I worked out a trade-off arrangement with my co-workers for a saner job schedule. I insisted my sister talk to a trained therapist instead of me. Her repetitious story was more upsetting than I realized, when she stopped calling I felt great relief. I had been too fatigued for exercise, but the change in work hours and my sister's respect for my sanity soon got me back in the groove. The weird ritual of repeating the names of the states stopped tormenting me and I resumed my normal life."

Compromise Emotion

Anxiety dissipates energy and eventually interferes with creativity. Anxiety is a symptom of inner psychic conflict, just as a toothache is symptomatic of decay or an abscess.

Undesirable thoughts or feelings occur in the unconscious, primitive id. When the unconscious ego refuses to deal with the forbidden material, the outcome is a compromise directed by the unconscious superego of anxiousness—the person suffers discomfort but is unaware of the underlying source or internal restrictions. Anxiety, then, is a compromise emotion, even though the bargain is a painful one.

No repressed memory, feeling or thought can be more unpleasant to face than living with anxiety. In past generations, sexual repressions caused anxiety when people denied their forbidden thoughts and feelings. Today, because sex is considered a normal appetite and is accepted instead of repressed, the most common prohibited or frightening memories and ideas causing anxiety are aggressive, or murderous impulses. Lifting the lid and exposing one's aggressive feelings and revengeful fantasies can quickly ease anxiousness. Many people have trepidations about an honest exploration into primitive fantasies, but none of the material will be self-destructive. Uncontrolled anxiety, however, eventually deadens the spirit and dries up creative flow.

Transforming Anxiety

Some authors manage anxiety by transforming their restlessness into productivity. This eases body discomfort and directs concentration away from internal distress. Although it does not solve or uncover the unconscious factors, it is better than unhappy inactivity.

"I get anxious after silly fights with my spouse," explains Helen, an article writer and aspiring novelist. "We never reach an intelligent conclusion because our vituperations bring forth ear-splitting accusations. Our method of simmering down is to avoid each other for a couple of hours. Even though I know the truce is inevitable (our basic love is deep and will eventually pull us back to normal), panic convinces me that he'll leave and disappear forever, making me a deserted-mate statistic. I'm too angry to confess these childish fears and sputter off to the den. He usually reads, probably having fantasies of escape or abandonment.

"I fill pages of legal pads, describing our disagreement—how right I am, how very wrong he is, his unfairness and obstinacy and the weapons I'd use to scare him into begging forgiveness. Writing out my feelings assuages my anxiety, controlling my childish impulses to keep on fighting and saying vindictive things I'll regret later on. Thus purged, I can work on articles or novels instead of stewing over our clash. The writing I produce under this stress always needs extensive revisions, but I've at least composed *something.*

"I've also saved 'fight narration' pages, since they're good for future laughs and useful when describing highly emotional responses in my novels. As writers we can always use our neurotic reactions for describing characters and their reactions."

Free Association

The internal factors causing your anxiety when no obvious external event prompts panic can be discovered through free association.

Find a quiet spot, lie down, and close your eyes. Visualize a blank screen and let your thoughts flow, saying aloud anything that comes to mind no matter how trivial or silly it may be. Think of yourself as a curious detective, searching for clues. Ask yourself, "What feeling or memory am I avoiding?" Pinpoint a person, situation, or thought that incited anxiousness. Answers will occur if you stick with the process long enough. You must excuse and forgive any nonsocial thoughts or fantasized actions erupting from probing your unconscious. They are only thoughts and not deeds.

You may become alarmed if a picture of violence against a helpless victim pops into your mind's eye, but this would only be a signal that you may be angry at someone and are denying the aggression.

Free association is a simple and effective psychological tool that can be used to quickly discover the primitive feelings that exist in all of us. The id's reactions, which remain self-centered throughout life and are impulsive and immune from social judgments, become covered over with a learned sense of right and wrong. Our conscience sifts through the selfish demands and the quick revengeful reactions of the primitive id and either represses the original thought or reduces its intensity so that your reactions are smoothed out into acceptable behavior. During free association excuse these "unacceptable" thoughts, because they are a part of normal mental activity and an aid to uncover honest feelings. Finding anxiety's root and facing the denied feelings frees the "forbidden" thoughts from the judgment of the superego.

The anxiety you have experienced will be greatly reduced because your bargain with your superego will have been broken. You will have confronted the unconscious factors which cause internal distress, freeing up the psychological energies deployed to maintain the compromise. Whenever you overcome anxiety, the feelings which are freed from their repressive cage will be converted into well-being. Unhampered by unpredictable anxiety you will naturally have a clearer mind to bring to writing.

"I went to a movie as a break from working on a delicate love story that required sensual prose to arouse sexual tension in the reader," shares Mark. "I had no idea *Who's Afraid of Virginia Woolf?* was a film about a sado-masochistic marriage. Halfway through a violent scene of a shrieking husband and wife, I was gripped by a viselike pressure across my chest. I became breathless and fidgety. I rushed outside the theater as though escaping some catastrophe. At home, the discomfort persisted as I paced around the room, unable to sit still, let alone write.

"Lying on the floor, I recreated the scene in the movie that had caused my anxiety. I had a flash memory of my parents' yelling at each other, with me cowering in the corner, a helpless child. I had forgotten the apprehensions of my youth caused by my parents' threatening to divorce each other every time they fought. Replaying the family quarrels, I felt the old fears rise and relived my worries of being abandoned as the raging adults departed, forgetting their helpless little son.

"During this reconstruction I realized that in my love relationships, I placated women to avoid unpleasant arguments— to my unconscious *all* disagreements led to hateful acrimony. I was afraid confrontations would engulf me in childhood terrors of being alone. I've since learned that while the unconscious may convince a person that he will be as emotionally destroyed as he was in childhood, as adults, we have learned and developed methods of coping to defend ourselves against emotional devastation.

"My overpowering anxiety vanished in the light of my memories and insight and my writing improved. In the original draft of my love scene, the way the starry-eyed lovers had worked through problems was to gloss over them to avoid angering each other. The revised story dealt honestly with normal lovers' hostilities, resolved without either of them collapsing. My romantic scenes were more realistic when presented within an authentic male-female relationship."

Psychotherapy

Psychotherapy should be considered if you cannot overcome the cause of anxiety that disrupts your creativity. Therapy is an option when you feel blocked by unconscious forces that inhibit your enjoyment of life, your ability to maintain relationships, or if you are experiencing chronic loneliness and depression. Sometimes it is too difficult to work through problems alone and it is only sensible to visit a specialist. No one should feel he will be labeled weak or crazy if he seeks the help of a trained professional. Some creative people enter analysis because of an interest in exploring their lives in order to grow to their full potential.

A competent psychotherapist is trained to ask pertinent questions that aid unconscious recall and help clients gradually gain insight into their personalities.

Therapists are not magicians with instant cures for long-standing problems. They are emotional detectives who, with the client's cooperation, fit together the pieces of each person's unique psychological puzzle.

After talking freely to a therapist, clients can expect interpretations of their thoughts, feelings, dreams, and behavior. Eventually, clients are able to shed defenses and develop mature and workable coping skills to handle life situations.

Defenses which have become entrenched over many years take time to dissolve because many clients unconsciously fear that if they give up defenses they will face a void inside of themselves. A client may feel consciously motivated to change but unconsciously resist remembering in order to defend the self against the possibility of emptiness when defenses are stripped of their powers. The psychotherapist helps the client realize that selfhood and personal esteem grow during the process of therapy, and psychological energies shift from defenses against pain to an enjoyment of life and increased creativity.

Clients often feel dependent upon the therapist, particularly during the beginning of treatment when a person feels helpless in the face of debilitating problems. The goal of therapy is to help clients become strong and independent, and the feelings of vulnerability associated with dependency on the therapist lessen as clients begin taking responsibility for their own happiness.

Competent therapists have a relaxed, self-confident attitude which puts prospective clients at ease. Most people are nervous about coming to discuss their problems with a stranger and feel grateful to be met by an understanding and empathetic professional. If you experience the therapist as cold and lacking in kindliness, you will be uncomfortable and unable to enter into the essentially intimate relationship necessary for trusting another individual with your most private thoughts and feelings. The therapist who suggests medication as the *answer* to your problems may be offering you a pill to relieve symptoms but will do nothing to resolve the underlying problems which cause psychological distress—that is, a tranquilizer can effectively calm anxiety but does not deal with the cause of mental pain.

It is important to ask a therapist if he or she understands creative people and their special problems. If a therapist talks about the importance of adjusting to society and settling down by becoming like everyone else, the creative person is in the wrong office.

You have the right to ask the therapist what kind of treatment he or she offers. Consider if you will be comfortable with his or her approach. Some therapists sit behind a desk with clients facing them; others prefer that their patients lie on a couch with the therapist sitting alongside or behind. Some therapists don't care whether the client sits, stands or paces around the room. You may have a preference of gender when looking for a therapist. Stick with your inclination in order to begin therapy on a positive note.

The main ingredient for a successful alliance between therapist and client is that the distressed person feel comfortable, accepted and trusting. Without these essential components, the client will be too nervous and wary to concentrate on the work at hand.

Many therapists develop a warm and friendly relationship with their clients, intuitively understanding that "partnership" aids in the quick resolution of problems. When this occurs patients often ask aloud, "If you like me so much, why do I have to pay?" and have the feeling they are paying for a friendship. The therapist must be paid because he or she has invested years of time and money in becoming a trained professional. The patient is paying for the experience and wisdom of the analyst, and the friendly feelings are free.

Depression

Freelancing includes predictable depressions. It would be abnormal to remain cheerful when receiving the usual number of rejections, delays, broken promises, negative reviews, frustration with writing problems and the juggling of time, relationships and work a writing career entails.

When depressions occur, the goal is to regain emotional equilibrium as quickly as possible. Each of us experiences various depressive symptoms, depending on our personalities and the events which cause the problem. Usually, depression is characterized by a profound sadness, discouragement, pessimism, and low self-esteem accompanied by feelings of hopelessness about recovering and social withdrawal. Physical symptoms are a mixture of weariness, irritability, headaches, insomnia, and loss of appetite. The depressed person becomes disinterested in his appearance and cannot concentrate. The wounded state, if left to fester, can lead to melancholia, an exaggerated, apathetic dejection so painful that suicide becomes an option.

Events causing normal emotional lows are loss of love through dissension, divorce, or death; a sudden change in lifestyle; financial difficulties; injury; aging (even at thirty!); continual frustrations; and unexpected bad news. It is normal to experience depression when experiencing a blow that changes our lives and forces us to realize that life is not crisis-free. Ideally, we should expect some misfortunes and inevitable changes, but they usually come as a surprise to the majority of people, because we are conditioned to believe that we are capable of coping with shock without an emotional cost or that "nothing can happen to us." The longevity of our depression depends on the inner resources we have to help us to bounce back.

Writers receive unexpected bad news each time the mail contains rejections. High hopes are dashed when material is turned down. A sudden plunge in artistic self-esteem opens the gates to depression. Depression can also descend when writers feel blocked and unable to think with originality. Indulging in depression must be brief because despondency wastes emotional energy and provides no tangible side benefits.

No creative project should carry such an exorbitant emotional investment that problems with its writing or rejection could cause a long-lasting sorrow.

Restricting Creativity

Scott, a successful poet and sport columnist and frustrated novelist, has been writing for fifteen years. "I allowed depression to interfere with creativity for two long years. My first completed work exposed academic corruption and transcript manipulations to assist athletes on college campuses. The first editor who read the manuscript wrote back full of excitement and publishing possibilities. I naively assumed guaranteed success and became lost in daydreams of riches and fame. Anticipating a large advance, I quit my job on the local newspaper. My wife and friends gladly celebrated my good fortune. Euphorically, I began another book.

"I received an apologetic letter a month later. The editor explained that three out of five editors were required to pass on manuscripts before contracts were awarded. Only he and another editor found merit in my story. Disbelieving, I pestered the poor fellow by telephone. He sympathized, offering to review any further projects.

"Fifteen years ago, I knew nothing, judged the manuscript unsalable and sadly filed it. Resubmission never crossed my mind. I reapplied to the paper, thankful I hadn't spouted off, telling the boss my opinion of his intellect. I lost interest in my new story and sank into a lethargy, listlessly going to work, avoiding old friends and functioning only on a superficial level. Time passed and I eventually forgot my brief foray into creative enthusiasm.

"Two years later, a co-worker helped me. She had attended a writers' conference and related a lecture on handling rejections, suggesting quick submission to other markets. She inquired about my dusty manuscript and made an offer which changed my life. She said, 'You've never recovered from that original experience and I think you've lost your nerve. I'll send out sample chapters and won't tell you about rejects. You'll have to promise not to ask.' A few months after making our deal she showed me a letter from a publisher. They liked my style and, although not interested in the book, sought permission to send the chapters to a sports magazine that specialized in investigative reporting. I quickly sent approval and the magazine ran an updated series of articles.

"The dull and cheerless spot in my heart catapulted away. My forte, honed by my journalistic experience, was articles and I soon made sales to several magazines. My success lifted the depression and induced the beginning of another book. The new book is as yet unpublished, but I have realistic hopes. I wish I had been wiser when first rejected. I could have dealt with my sinking spirits had I known that one rejection doesn't mean anything except send it out again to another publisher."

Scott's depression could have lingered without his friend's

aid. Fortunate writers experience only temporary depressions, lasting a few hours or days, and then jump back into the literary fray, their spirits back to normal.

If you cannot shake a depression and begin to feel helpless and without hope for the future, find a therapist to help you overcome the despondency. We think life is too precious and too short to remain unhappy and nonproductive for more than a month. Others may live in a depressed state, only existing and functioning at minimal levels, but talented people have a responsibility to themselves and their craft to take care of emotional problems.

Remission Techniques

Active measures for remission are necessary if depression settles in after many setbacks and frustrations.

Depression very often results from unexpressed anger. When denied an outlet, anger turns against the host, expressing itself as spiritual dejection. The deeper the rage and the longer it is denied, the more it contributes to despair and inadequacy.

In our society many people are taught by parents and teachers during childhood that anger is abnormal. Well-adjusted individuals learn to be "good sports," hiding anger and disappointment when losing and never expressing their fury toward winning opponents. Women, because they are taught that angry displays are unfeminine, develop mannerisms which hide virulence. However, anger is a normal emotion, a sudden response to feeling wronged or mistreated, and it demands verbal or physical action.

Unexpressed anger can be transformed into physical ailments—headaches, ulcers, high blood pressure. Psychological indications can be seen in passive anger—setting up situations that make others explode while the emotional manipulator appears blameless. For example, passive anger can be manifested in forgetting promises and appointments, habitual tardiness, repeating boring trivia, and not being attentive when listening to others.

Writers are rightfully angry when work is rejected. There are several methods of releasing anger when lacking opportunities to confront rejecting editors. Talking about indignation with sympathetic friends releases pent-up tension. A good listener will not dissuade you from anger or instill guilt about vindictive thoughts, but will allow you the catharsis experienced with uninterrupted ranting.

"My rejections arrive, via the mail, at ten in the morning," recounts Maurice, a cookbook writer. "My friends are working either in their offices or busy with their own creative pursuits at home. I can't bother them, but I know that I need immediate release to avoid gloom and doom. So I play Beethoven's highly emotional Fifth Symphony to heighten my dour mood and then I draw scenes of rejecting editors with daggers in their hearts on a large sketch pad and swear aloud to vent my spleen. I'm back to normal after only twenty minutes of private anger. No one sees, hears, or judges my outburst and it has proven effective over the years, since I have no symptoms of depression. If I pretended I wasn't angry, I know I would stew about the rejection, and my preoccupation could inhibit writing for a day or more.

"I cannot imagine accepting frustrations without a reaction and purging. I have no time for prolonged sadness or self-pity because I am making a living. People care little about your failures and don't enjoy the company of a depressoid. You must rely on yourself to invent your own effective discharge for anger."

Fantasies are an excellent outlet for discontent. Creative people are at an advantage and can employ their rich imaginations to construct scenes of torture and mayhem with the "uncaring" publishers, thus getting rid of aggravations while inflicting only conjectured pain.

Fatigue often accompanies depression, promoting physical inactivity, and compounding despondency. Exercise releases body tensions, rejuvenates the mind and depletes anger. Brisk walking, swimming, tennis, running, chopping wood, or any exertion appropriate to your physical condition helps discharge antagonisms.

"I have a punching bag in the basement," shares Sally, a songwriter. "When one of my songs is turned down I put on the gloves, picture a crass, cigar-smoking music producer's face on the cover, and beat the hell out of the bag. The longer I exercise, the better I feel."

The solution to depression is finding the anger source, accepting negative feelings as normal and healthy, and talking or physically working it off.

Unconscious Factors

Another cause for depression can be unconscious mental activity.

A respected and successful author became increasingly depressed and was unable to continue his craft. When consulting us, his history revealed an inability to mourn his own father's death. His ranching family reared "strong men" who did not cry or expose their vulnerability. Even though one of his westerns became a much-admired film about a boy's longing for a father, he thought it was a sign of weakness to feel tearful over his long-dead parent. When he understood the necessity to mourn with tears, he remarked, "I've pulled tears from my readers and movie audiences when I'm the one needing to cry." He also learned about survivor's anger—abandonment and rage toward the deceased for giving up life and leaving behind bereft loved ones. His melancholy dissipated after expressing his denied sorrow and anger.

"Why do I get unexplainably depressed while in the middle of a project?" wrote Robert. "I will be immersed in an advertising campaign, brimming with ideas, my mind blazing ahead of my typewriter. Suddenly, I clutch, a black cloud moves across my heart, eclipsing my excitement and productivity. I morosely prowl around the office. I might as well go home instead of picking on my secretary and the layout artists. They've learned to look very busy when glimpsing my drawn face. I'm not angry at anyone, so why the swift and unexpected depression?"

Robert's depressions occur only at the height of creative inspiration. Investigation into Robert's unconscious tape recording revealed family jealousies about his talents. In his childhood, his parents and older siblings attempted to convince him that his creativity was meaningless and even "wrong." They earnestly believed writing and drawing were linked to homosexuality. The family was ashamed of their son's gifts. His unconscious voice confirmed that he deserved punishing depressions because he had rebelled against his family's notions of masculinity.

Robert took control over his own unconscious intent to destroy his ebullient creative moods. Before undertaking a project, he sat at his desk, cleared his mind and called a fantasy meeting of the family. Speaking to them through a loudspeaker while they sat bound and gagged on straight-backed chairs, he shouted at them to mind their own business and told them they were no longer allowed to judge him. He yelled that he deserved freedom to work to full capacity.

"My old imprinted message cannot be altered, but I can change its effect. Every day I perform the exercise against mental forces and my routine has stopped the sudden depressions. The proof that this technique works for me is that the stultifying emptiness returns if I forget to fantasize the envious family group and berate them for their stupidity. I have implicit trust in this method and recommend it to other creative people who courageously went against family pressures."

Writer's Block

Depression is an unwelcome companion to writer's block. The treadmill trek begins when writers emotionally step onto the creative block mechanism. Fear of failure, self doubts and depression become heavy loads, effectively stopping all forward movement.

In the mythical ideal, productive writers consistently labor at their work, completing daily quotas with ease. Many authors, comparing their habits to this myth, assume they suffer from writer's paralysis if they fail to perform like well-oiled machines.

There are periods in every artist's career when creativity peaks out. Sometimes ideas dry up in the middle of an assignment, convincing a writer they are gone forever or that inspiration has flown away to live with other more deserving writers.

The cessation of ideation can often be a positive unconscious signal, suggesting time to break off and relax. Authors who pay attention to this signal quit without alarm. They take off a few restorative days and let their subconscious ruminations sift and rearrange ideas.

You must expect dry periods—an experience shared by all gifted people. Painters know a canvas is rarely finished in one smooth session; they often leave it to rest before taking up the brushes again.

Self-condemnation over a writing stoppage misdirects energy. If you can't write for a while, attend to neglected chores, socialize, read, or concentrate on exercise. You don't have to write every day to prove your worth.

"I had seven completed chapters of a twelve-chapter book

about adoptions," remembers Bill, the psychologist. "After I finished making revisions, I was sure there was not another word to say on the subject. My mind was a blank. The next morning, I read over my manuscript and continued to be stymied. I felt washed up—the book wasn't feasible with just 120 pages. In desperation, I called my editor, a man with thirty years' experience. I confessed my inability to complete the project. He calmly said, 'You've been working too long on the same idea. Set the pages aside for a week, avoid thinking about it and take a vacation from writing. Go for walks, see some movies, visit the gym, play cards—anything, as long as it's unrelated to adoptions. Call me after your week's rest.' His reassurance and vacation prescription surprised me. I had expected him to be disgusted with me.

"I covered my typewriter reluctantly and shoved the manuscript in my desk. The following week I drove to Santa Fe, New Mexico, home of many writers and artists. I enjoyed the opera, visited museums and trooped through countless art galleries. Many shopkeepers are artists, potters and craftsmen and very receptive to questions about creativity. In talking with a variety of artists, I learned my experience was not freakish, because, to a person, they spoke about having spurts of creative ideas followed by total drought.

"Upon my return, my mail contained a large package from the editor filled with articles concerning adoption; a note attached said, 'This should spark your brain.' The next day I was back to work, amazed at how much material I had overlooked.

"Now, I plan a writing break somewhere in the middle of a manuscript, even if things are going well. My so-called writer's block was actually a signal to take a refreshing trip away from the material."

Many writers feel frustrated and angry with themselves when they procrastinate even though a part of them wants to get down to business. Freelancers lack familiar authority figures—mother, babysitter, schoolteachers, drill sergeant, professors and bosses. Self-employed artists do not hear, "Get moving," "Do this right now," and "Start work at nine," so must train themselves to be disciplined and to keep a reasonable work schedule. Most writers evolve ritualistic working warm ups like sharpening pencils, getting out paper clips, emptying the wastepaper basket, meditating or staring at the typewriter. Enjoy your diversions instead of fearing an irreversible skid down the writer's block abyss.

"I save the evening paper for leisurely morning reading," reports Gene, the gag writer. "My wife laughs at me, calling me obsessive. The paper projects me into the world of words and kindles comedy ideas. If I don't have a paper, I read something else. I feel more content and ready to work after my reading needs are satisfied."

"I feel ready to tackle writing after I've straightened the apartment," says Jeffrey. "I like an uncluttered visual environment. I'm not avoiding writing, but setting the mood."

"I gaze out the window for ten or fifteen minutes, watching the people parade," says David. "I'm fascinated by different mannerisms, postures and peculiar behavior prevalent on my city street. My viewing psyches me up for writing."

Writer's block has received a great deal of attention, causing many authors to fear its sudden onset. Like sexual performance fears, the more one worries, the more the self-prophecy tends to come true.

Consider yourself on a temporary recess if you are really stuck and unable to finish a project or to even move the pen across the page.

Some established techniques to ignite the mind again include writing free associations about writing fears, perfectionist first draft expectations, thoughts about your personal and business relationships, frustrations of freelancing, what you ate the last few days or dreams you've remembered. These ideas are easily recalled and take little effort to scribble or type. You're writing something again.

You can also ask your unconscious voice what trickery it has in mind, diverting energies away from writing.

Rewrite a sentence or paragraph from a random source, using *Roget's Thesaurus* to find other words. This marvelous writer's aid will suggest numerous possibilities for alternate expressions and, with everyday use, you will find that your working vocabulary increases along with your self-esteem. Many authors have said that they routinely glance through a thesaurus, idly looking at words and synonyms to jolt creative thinking.

"I felt blocked in the beginning of a children's story," relates Margaret. "An exciting way to grab interest eluded me and I couldn't continue without a magic opening. I stewed and fretted, jumped up and drank coffee, paid some bills and called my mother. I surprised her with my gregarious interest in her activities. Usually, she calls and I talk grudgingly, eager to get back to work. I took a walk, feeling inferior and depressed. What was wrong with my brain? I passed a schoolyard and watched children running and playing. It dawned on me that I was trying to please an editor instead of my actual audience—children.

"I rushed home and imagined a circle of little people sitting with myself in the center, telling them a story. The first lines came easily as I charmed my fantasized group. My writer's block was blasted away by getting out in the world and seeing my potential readers.

"I've discussed the invisible audience technique with other writers. A successful greeting card writer said she has used the same device for years. Whenever she feels dry she envisions a mother waiting for a card from a traveling daughter or son, a hospitalized patient opening a get-well card, or a child receiving a birthday greeting from grandparents."

If you still feel gripped by the inability to write, consider the affliction similar to a phobia. Why are you targeting on writing as a forbidden activity? Since you can form words, move a pen across the page and operate a typewriter, some unconscious force must be operating to freeze your actions. Maybe it's time to wander into free associations about creative restrictions, fears of competition, expectations of failure or exposing vulnerabilities.

Meditation

Over the years we have discovered a preventive measure against writer's block or creative plateaus.

Many people shy away from learning the art of meditation because they assume it is connected with difficult intellectual activity, related to mysterious religious cults or merely another gimmick for "quick solutions" to psychological problems. Meditation is none of the above, requiring no advanced education, particular religious rituals or belief in any psychological system.

Meditation in its simplest form is a type of relaxation of the mind which allows the thinking, plotting, planning, worrying, ruminating part of your busy brain to rest. The mind, which continues activity even when sleeping, in the form of dreams, needs quiet periods to refresh itself. As an extra benefit, meditation reduces tensions and gives a lift to your spirits. And it is one of the rare forms of personal improvement that doesn't cost any money.

Many authors who have meditated daily for some time notice that they have increased energy, don't get as upset over minor irritations, and find an enhancement in work, play, and creativity. They are usually surprised and pleased with these enrichments because they have been taught that increased enjoyments involve hard work, dedication, and sacrifice, none of which is demanded by meditation.

To begin, find yourself a quiet spot where you will be uninterrupted for twenty minutes. Sit in a comfortable position so that you don't have to think about your body. Rest your hands on your thighs and place your feet flat on the floor. If this is not comfortable, you can lie down. The main point is to be at ease.

Choose a simple word, perhaps one which brings to mind peace and tranquility ("river," "meadow," "sunshine," "love"), or one that has no emotional connection, such as "one." It is not necessary to attend costly seminars and buy yourself a word or mantra, because the word you choose is only a vehicle to shut out other thoughts. By repeating the same word you will prevent the continuity of thought—like dwelling on one or several ideas and considering their implications.

Breathe through your nose, being aware of your breathing. Inhale and exhale deeply. With every inhalation, say your word to yourself and repeat it again when you exhale. Continue breathing in and out for approximately twenty minutes while staying with the word. If you decide you don't like the word your originally chose, change it. The word itself is unimportant, but the repetition of the same sound is valuable to blocking off the normal stream of conscious thought patterns.

It is only natural that stray thoughts will pop into your mind as the brain is unaccustomed to being turned off. The thinking part of the brain is not used to all that quiet and tries to interfere with grocery lists, old grudges, and mundane concerns. Don't waste time thinking you are failing at meditation when you discover that you have strayed from repeating the word. Simply note that you are not saying the word and return to concentrating on breathing and repeating the word even if you have to pull yourself back into breathing and saying the word several times during a meditation. Meditation is most useful when done every day, and whenever you feel you are procrastinating and wasting precious time by daydreaming, use the time for meditation in order to feel you are doing something worthwhile.

When you finish meditating, sit quietly for a few minutes and then gradually open your eyes. Don't expect instant energy, just continue to meditate every day and eventually you will reap the benefits of less tension, more creative energy, and a brighter outlook on life.

Experienced meditators are able to practice this technique without closing their eyes and sometimes in trying or tense situations—from boring social events to being subjected to noise pollution—they simply turn off for a few seconds and mentally say their word a few times, bringing a sense of peace and mellowness at uncomfortable moments.

When you have grown comfortable with daily meditation, you can direct energies toward specific tasks. Meditate on the word for five minutes. Then, say the word on inhalation and give a short directive on exhalation. For example, inhale (word), exhale (write the best with confidence).

"I meditate before any writing, even if I'm only sending queries," said Helen. "It refreshes me and I feel a sharpened sense of purpose. I also experience a delightful physical sensation, which feels like a rush of ecstasy throughout my chest. It's like a soothing wave of good feelings. I teach meditation to new friends and urge them to pass it on."

Can something so simple and easy actually work? Shouldn't it cause some pain to be useful? What's the catch? Is it magic? It works, it's painless, and there's no hidden secret. We have meditated for the last fifteen years and feel it is as important to creativity as understanding unconscious forces.

Alcohol and Drugs

Alcohol

Alcohol is a serious problem when it negatively affects work or relationships.

Many famous authors, illuminated by celebrity's spotlight, have been exposed as alcoholics. Some have admitted in magazine and talk show interviews that they have struggled with drinking too much and being too hung over to work. A psychiatric colleague once exclaimed that he didn't understand why all writers were not alcoholics, considering the constant impediments to success, the isolation of the writing life and the frustrations and worries about talent, creativity and income.

Chronic over-indulgence in alcohol eventually harms physical and mental health. Hung over writers have a difficult time thinking or composing. The brain cannot concentrate when mired in thick fuzz and the body feels depleted of vitality.

One writer confessed that he wrote in the late afternoon because of regular morning hangovers. "It was not a choice, but a condition forced by regular nightly drinking. Like other alcoholics, I lied when my doctor questioned my drinking habits. I said, 'Oh, just a couple of cocktails before dinner and a brandy later in the evening.' This was true, but the cocktails were drunk from a huge water glass filled three quarters with Scotch, and my brandy was quaffed from the same generous container. I drank the same large quantity nightly for at least ten years, using unhappiness as an excuse—I was a lonely bachelor and an unsuccessful writer.

"I went to my teaching job in a fog and my head didn't clear until around two in the afternoon. I feel guilty about those students who received minimal attention. No one reprimanded me and I felt safe. I wrote for two or three hours in the afternoon and started boozing at six, escaping into an unthreatening drunken haze.

"With the help of group therapy, I've reduced my drinking to a 'real' cocktail or two and feel much better. The writing I did while under the influence was atrocious. Even the work done between intoxications was not good enough for acceptance.

"Members of my therapy group share similar experiences. We all drifted into alcoholism, unaware of the encroachment on our skills."

Some writers drink too much to sedate overactive minds or to blot out frustrations and disappointments. Occasional bouts of self-pity are to be expected, but dependence on alcohol to eradicate the disappointment results in the loss of precious time and productivity.

If you suffer from alcoholism, decide your priorities—creative pursuits or continued escape into alcoholic stupor. If you cannot overcome obsessive drinking alone, seek professional help from your physician. Alcoholics Anonymous, an organization of former drinkers, offers family solicitude and a highly successful program. Members come from all walks of life and accept anyone willing to break the dependency on alcohol.

Drugs

Legal and illegal drugs are available to anyone interested in obtaining them.

Some writers have explained a dependence on drugs as a writing necessity. They cannot imagine attempting to write without the drug crutch. Some artists convince themselves the drug does the work, not understanding that intuition and perceptions are the results of their talents and efforts.

Medical research has only scratched the surface on the subject of the effects of drugs. Until there is conclusive information, users of drugs—from tranquilizers to speed—take chances with their health.

The current drug scene involves a wide choice of mind-altering chemicals. When drugs are used to escape from life rather than to enhance good feelings, they will perpetuate problems. Learning to handle tension, conflicts, and challenges is a normal part of living and eventually adds to one's self-esteem. Most drugs tend to isolate a person rather than stimulate involvement with others. The writer who must learn to deal with isolation as a part of his craft does himself little good when using drugs to buffer his pain.

Some of the most popular drugs available belong to the amphetamine family. These drugs lift the mood, speed up thought processes, increase physical energy, quicken speech, and heighten sensory awareness. Also known as "speed," amphetamines are available in several forms: Dexedrine, Benzedrine (or "bennies"), and diet pills. Cocaine is also an "upper" that gives the user a quick rush or high which lasts for a few minutes.

The "downers," barbiturates or sleeping pills, are found in the medicine cabinets of many homes. They are sedatives that induce drowsiness and sleep and may be physically addicting as well as extremely dangerous when combined with alcohol.

Tranquilizers are used to reduce excessive anxiety and can be as addicting as barbiturates. Many people take tranquilizers on their doctor's orders, and since the prescription comes from a physician, they are convinced that it must be harmless. However, dependence on tranquilizers can erode one's sense of organization and determination to work and grow as a person and an artist.

Narcotics are derivates of the opium poppy. Narcotics relieve pain and induce sleep. Heroin is the strongest illegal drug and produces a relaxed, highly pleasurable, dreamlike state.

Hallucinogenic drugs alter the consciousness of the mind and its visual, auditory, sensual or emotional perceptions. Marijuana induces a dreamlike, passive state of pleasure wherein nothing seems of great significance. Mescaline from the peyote cactus, psilocybin from the Mexican mushroom, and the most powerful, LSD (lysergic acid), alter the user's perception of reality. Depending upon the person's emotional stability, the environment, and the dosage, an LSD trip can range from pleasant imagery accompanied by delightful feelings of well-being to overwhelming dread and panic stimulated by frightening hallucinations.

Experimentation does not necessarily lead to abuse, as many curious writers have discovered. A drug abuser is one who uses drugs excessively as a crutch to avoid reality. Writers who must deal with the reality of creative concentration and the very real world of business cannot afford to depend on drugs for inspiration, motivation, or discipline. If you have drifted into the belief that you cannot be creative without drugs, then you are fooling yourself into believing that your creativity rests outside of yourself and inside of a chemical.

Anyone wishing to reduce or quit drug consumption should consult a physician in order to avoid withdrawal complications.

Active Health

Dedicated writers take the active approach to problem solving. You are totally responsible for your sound mental health. The benefit of challenging psychological problems is increased joy in creativity—something we can always add to our lives.

Chapter Seven

Developing a Productive Lifestyle

DO YOU EVER find yourself wishing you were more productive? Do you ever rationalize your meager output by blaming external pressures that interfere with creativity? Do you ever feel that if you only had the perfect creative environment, writing would be easier for you?

We all occasionally find ourselves looking for excuses to explain why we don't fit into that mythical image of the disciplined, calm, self-assured writer who produces his masterpieces in a comfortable writing room undisturbed by everyday responsibilities.

Instead of dreaming about the perfect setting for writing, or comparing ourselves to an unrealistic ideal, we can learn to manipulate our environments to our own advantage. As a freelancer you must become your own boss and recognize that only you can arrange your life in such a way that you will be more productive.

First, you must evaluate your unique circumstances and then consider the options open to you. Taking charge requires discipline: You must control how you spend your time, consider and prioritize your other commitments, set up a daily health program, and construct an atmosphere conducive to writing. You can become more productive and experience the glow of higher self-esteem which comes with a workable regime.

Time Management

One of the shocks of life is the deeply felt insight that time cannot be recaptured except in memory. The ability to use time well, whether for work or relaxation, is a sign of maturity. Time can be wasted in endless pondering over rejected creations or used productively to rework or resubmit manuscripts.

Do you have a clear picture of how you spend your precious gift of time? Do you feel guilty when you relax, or do you feel worthwhile only when you are working? The time you devote to activities that are unrelated to writing may be a form of rejuvenation that adds to your enthusiasm for your work. Authors who manage to balance their work and leisure time bring a healthier perspective to the craft of writing than those who continually waste time berating themselves for not meeting a schedule.

If you are a full-time freelancer, you are fortunate to have available hours of the day or night to arrange a writing routine. If you are a job-holding, part-time freelancer, you might use up ten or more hours a day working and commuting. You will have to consciously budget the few available hours left to squeeze in time to write. Have you considered if there are any sections of your working day which could be used for creative endeavors?

"As a poet, I'm always on the lookout for material," says Jamie. "My job as an air conditioner and furnace repairman offers a wonderful variety of experiences and encounters. The business conversations that take place in the presence of repairmen would amaze you. People act as if we were deaf and therefore inconsequential.

"The homes I enter are grist for my poetic mill. They're filled with a fascinating array of people, unusual family situations, animals, and decorating schemes. One lady insisted her parrot had to 'read' my 'vibes' before I could clean her furnace. The bird passed on me as an 'OK guy.' I briefly touch my customers' lives as the rescuer when they endure the stress caused by broken machinery. Everyone reacts differently. The children and retirees who hang around watching, forever curious and eager to exchange opinions, add to my storehouse of possible poetic subjects.

"Job-holding writers should pay acute attention to their surroundings and keep a notebook to record ideas, settings, characterizations, snips of conversation and plots."

Marcia, an articles writer, rearranged her work day to increase productivity and cash flow. "I am a bank teller with no time during the hectic day to ponder about my writing. I needed a plan to make use of free daytime hours to move toward my goal of a full-time writing career. On the hour's bus ride to and from work I jot quick descriptions of fellow travelers. It's an exercise in concise description of personality types, faces, dress, and responses as well as a catalogue for future use. I stopped going out to lunch, brown-bagging a homemade diet meal which takes five minutes to eat in the employee lounge. In the remaining time, I sketch queries, talk to co-workers about what's happening in their lives, and browse through magazines for ideas. I work on three or more article concepts each day, then refine and write query letters in the evening. I haven't sacrificed anything, but I have lost weight, and my career has benefited from the increase in my submissions and assignments."

"I am a full-time freelancer," reports bachelor Maurice, a cookbook specialist. "I assiduously fight against my lazy character. I can too easily become absorbed in leisure reading and waste valuable working hours. My writing schedule must take precedence, since my livelihood and freedom depend on my productivity. My work and relaxation list (which I post) keeps me in line—a persistent reminder to be businesslike. I get up at six, and by seven-thirty I have showered, exercised, dressed and eaten. I think self-employed writers should keep up appearances even if they don't see anyone. It makes you more alert if you're dressed and presentable, even if your clothes are old and comfortable.

"I watch a news program on TV until eight and then begin the day's routine. Much of my work involves researching old recipes, for which I have amassed a large reference library. I keep my desk uncluttered because it makes me feel tidy and virtuous.

"After each hour's work I take a ten-minute break away from my writing den. My telephone is in the living room for a special reason. It's important when writing to get up and move around to keep your circulation active. The walk to answer the phone forces me into some physical activity, and I don't mind a few minutes' interruption.

"My continued success as a freelance writer rests squarely on finely tuned physical and mental health. At eleven, I jog for half an hour. It's absolutely necessary to get outdoors and away from the writing environment. Otherwise you can start to feel like a mole. After a quick shower I have lunch. I have several food and restaurant critic friends who meet regularly for lunch, gossip, and discussions about new recipes. These interesting companions add to a well-rounded day.

"I continue writing, with a few breaks, until five o'clock. If I have wandered too far from my program, I make up the time in the evening. It is a form of self-discipline. No one else will prod me to good time-management."

Lauri, the playwright, adds, "My life is full of time-consuming demands. I am a medical receptionist in the morning. Previously, my afternoons were fragmented by errands, volunteer work, housework and cooking, then chauffeuring my school-aged kids to gymnastic and dance classes. The evening hours seemed like the only available time to write. The children respected my creative privacy, but missed my company.

"I consulted a novelist friend who had the same family responsibilities but seemed to be better organized. She helped me rearrange my schedule, chiding me as a 'Superlady.' 'The kids are old enough to handle more responsibilities. Superladies don't like to delegate authority and duties because that makes them feel nonessential.' She explained how to switch errands to coincide with the children's extracurricular classes and how to use afternoons to write. We talked about a priority list. The children and creative time are my life's loves. The kids would soon be independent teenagers, their growing years never to be replayed. I was missing their company in the evening, locked away like a recluse. I could always scribble down ideas during the evening and work on them the next day.

"Volunteer work drained my overextended energies and so I gave it up as part of relinquishing the Superlady role. The sensible reorganization of my day affords me three blissfully uninterrupted writing hours. The children soon learned to help with housework and meal preparation. They had to adjust to the new me and look at themselves as partners in our operation instead of children to be waited on. They don't miss Ms. Dynamo and say I'm more relaxed since the change. My creative needs are satisfied before they arrive home and we can enjoy sharing our time together."

List your community involvements, family responsibilities, recreational interests, and club memberships, and evaluate them in terms of self-fulfillment, and enjoyability. Writers who find enrichment and stimulation in committee or club memberships can consider the activities worthwhile. If your participation is based on perceived duty or your inability to decline requests, it is actually a disservice to yourself. Activities founded on "shoulds" cause hostility and boredom. It is not selfish to choose writing time over nonconstructive affiliations.

"I stopped attending a weekly bridge game," confided Katherine, a speech writer, "because the players' competition was too fierce, too tense, and overly invested with seriousness. Partners made snide jibes, glaring over wrong bids as if the game involved life and death. I was depleted after an evening of this. Now that I've stopped going, I'm either at the library or writing lectures for clients. How I spend my leisure time affects my creative energies. I realized this when I felt more carefree away from the grim-faced card players."

"The amount of time I spend socializing depends on my current assignments," says Joanne, an author of nonfiction books. "My family and friends understand that after I sign a contract I turn into a hermit. They accept my absences from social events as commonplace. I write full steam ahead for at least five hours a day, and I'm tired when evening comes. I don't feel conversational, because I am preoccupied with the unfolding book. Luckily, my husband and teenage children pitch in and take over all the household chores. They concur that my financial contribution warrants a release from homemaking.

"I spend evenings rewriting the day's rough draft and then listen to music to gear down.

"My investment in a telephone answering service is invaluable. When I am obsessed with writing, the telephone breaks my concentration. Now the service handles incoming calls, and my family has a coded emergency ring so I don't miss anything important."

The need to create forces one to plan writing spans. Sometimes the responsibilities of jobs, child care, and family illness require stealing away for late night or early morning writing.

We all juggle and trade off activities depending on personal ambition, ingenuity, and the priority we give to writing in our lives.

Even with the best intentions many writers find themselves procrastinating about getting to work.

Jason, the columnist, says, "I have a deadline to meet, and yet I often postpone writing by thinking up little chores, dawdling over coffee or looking blankly out the window. Of course, I feel guilty, but I continue to meander around the house, getting in my wife's way. Soon I start hating myself, which is not the right attitude to bring to work. Finally, I invented a trick to break up the tendency to avoid writing. I force myself to read over my last several columns, and even start retyping one of them. At least I'm at my desk. The act of reading and typing jolts me out of my procrastination and I can begin."

Other writers say they think the fear of writing leads them to put off getting started. They write a letter or make an outline to get them off and running. Since we writers must be responsible for our own work schedule, only we can admit that we are avoiding our work and then, like Jason, consciously develop tricks to overcome laziness.

Active Health Programs

Although we have stressed the need for psychological balance for productivity, physical fitness is just as vital. No one performs at full capacity when his or her attention is distracted by illness or chronic discomfort. We are ultimately answerable for our own physical vitality.

Writing is sedentary and must be balanced by regular exercise. Physicians, during the yearly check up, can give information about the most beneficial and appropriate exercise program for you as an individual. People who have lapsed into inactivity are ill advised to begin strenuous jogging.

Jed, the retired doctor turned novelist, comments, "Like many physicians, I was a terrible patient, too busy to follow a fitness program. My stamina was poor and muscle tonus flabby. After checking with an internist, I began taking an hour's brisk walk each morning with my wife. Now we enjoy close-up appreciation of the changing seasons, and we take advantage of the time to converse about current events, story ideas, and plans for the day. After a few months, I added an afternoon swim at the local university's pool—an excellent exercise, which uses all the body's muscles. I do facial exercises while I write and have worked up to forty sit-ups before bedtime. I feel more vigorous than I did twenty years ago. I continually pester and annoy inactive acquaintances who rationalize that there is no time for exercise because of writing tasks. No one can possibly write all day, so they are deluding themselves, cutting years off their lives by avoiding physical exertion. Using medical examples, I describe the internal breakdowns that occur in unused bodies. I try to scare them into taking care of themselves. I am convinced that a lot of senility results from lack of exercise, starving the brain of oxygen."

Obesity

Gifted people are not immune from obesity—excessive fat (from 15 to 150 pounds) stored in various sites of the body.

Even ten or fifteen extra pounds add stress to the body's delicate mechanisms. The body's capacity to store protein and carbohydrates is strictly limited, and excess food in any form is converted into and stored as fat. Any caloric intake persistently exceeding caloric output leads to obesity.

Being overweight contributes to a number of life-shortening illnesses: diabetes, high blood pressure, heart disease, arthritis, strokes, post-operative complications, pneumonia, and cirrhosis of the liver. The likelihood of complications accompanying pregnancy and childbirth is enhanced by being overweight. Even death from accidents is considerably more common among the obese, because their reflex time is slowed by their corpulence.

As with exercise, wise nutritional habits practiced during youth and midlife improve the quality of later life. Crash and fad diets, popular bestsellers, skirt the issue by promising a magical weight loss.

Home-bound authors must resist the temptation of easily available food, which can quickly become a balm to ease frustrations and tensions. The momentary pleasure of constant snacking exacts the price of the accumulation of ugly fat that only increases unhappiness. The majority of overweight people spend a great deal of time thinking about how unappealing they look, silently berating themselves for their food indulgences and making plans to "really start on a new diet"—on

Monday, the first of the year, or after everyone's birthdays are over, but not today.

If you have a weight problem, understanding why you overeat can possibly help you control the urge to stuff yourself. Very few people can get away with the rationalization that their "glands" cause them to look like a blimp. Eating more calories than your body requires is the main cause of being fat. The first step in losing weight is to stop blaming external situations for your problem since no one but yourself moves the food from plate to mouth.

Using self-motivation, insight, and will power, anyone can change the bad habit of overeating into sensible eating practices.

If you are forty or over, you probably remember that in your childhood everyone expected and accepted the so-called fact of "middle-age spread" as an inevitable part of life. And it is inevitable if you think you can eat as much in the middle years as you did when you were a growing teenager. In addition to this fallacy, World War II rationing and the financial depression before that caused food to become equated with security for many people. Emphasis was placed on eating and being able to afford to buy food. Children were taught to eat everything on their plates because of the "starving children elsewhere in the world." To eat a lot made you a "good" child. During those years it was also thought that a fat child was a healthy child. Many people were made to feel guilty if they did not eat the great quantities that their mothers had slaved to cook for the family. These food and eating myths have long since been medically disproved, but not to the people who grew up during those times.

Many people also relate food to love and feel a warm pleasure in eating. It is true that food is one of the first expressions of love that we receive as infants. We all begin life as oral people. This means that all of the infant's needs, drives, and wants center around and in the mouth. This is nature's way of insuring the survival of the little human body. The baby must be fed often in order to grow and will immediately cry and scream if not fed when hungry. As the infant is governed by the id or self-centered survival mechanism, he is unable to handle any frustrations of the need to be nurtured. The infant has no sense of patience or idea of the concept of concern for others, but only feels great discomfort when hungry. The overweight person experiences that same sense of haste and impatience when reaching for food to relieve anxieties or tensions.

Along with this oral drive in infancy is the need for mothering in the form of cuddling, rocking, and cooing that makes the child feel loved and secure. If the mother or substitute is of a giving nature, the baby's needs will be satisfied and this sense of being cared for and loved enables the little being to begin to grow a sense of self-worth in the world that appears to be a pleasant and giving place. It is the only time in life when a person receives free love just because he is alive and needs it in order to grow.

When this oral stage of life is happy, the child easily moves on in his development. Although we all retain the pleasures of the oral period in our enjoyment of eating, drinking, smoking, kissing, and talking, those pleasures are only one part of life, not the center of existence, for the mature person. Those who cannot control their eating habits are actually returning to that oral phase of life, regressing back to original enjoyments instead of seeking adult solutions to the daily problems of living.

If the oral period was one of deprivation for you or if food was forced upon you, the unconscious voice will promise you that only food will make you feel better. Your unconscious tape recording will be imprinted with the message that food really is love and mothering and that only food will solve your immediate problems. As a thinking person you can understand that eating does not resolve anything, but emotionally you may continue to believe that it is a source of love.

Since we cannot go back and relive the oral period, an overweight person must accept the fact that something was not right during that crucial period of life and move on from the position. If you admit that you use food to comfort yourself, then you can make plans for different, less self-destructive ways of dealing with distress. There are other means of mothering oneself besides eating and drinking. We can take a hot oil bath and luxuriate in the sensual delights of a long soak. We can treat ourselves to a massage which reduces physical tension, but also can be experienced as an entire body caress. A visit to the hairdresser can be thought of as a mothering experience when the operator washes, cuts and dries your hair for you. Giving oneself a manicure or a pedicure can be a form of self-mother-

ing as you pay special attention to your hands and feet. Some
people feel cozy and mothered by wrapping up in a warm af-
ghan and snuggling down with a good book. When you devise
other means to receive comfort besides food, you will be exchanging a bad habit for a good one.

Most overweight people know how to diet, because they
have been on many different regimes during their battle with
the bulge. Sticking with a sensible eating plan requires that you
accept the fact that realistic food intake must be a lifelong practice, not a temporary sacrifice to be discarded when completing
an instant loss program. In order to begin and stick with a
weight loss diet, assume that you will devote six months or a
year of your life to getting back in shape instead of hoping for a
miracle.

The same dedication that you depend on for the discipline to
continue writing can be used to maintain a diet and stay a
healthy person. As a gifted person, you owe it to yourself to live
inside of a trim body for a joyful, zesty, and productive life.

Jason, the columnist, recalled, "I gained twenty-five pounds
in my first year of freelancing. The lifestyle—sitting, reading,
or writing—was opposite from my previous teaching position,
where I was always moving, settling fights, and often physically defending myself.

"I snacked on delicious, easy-to-prepare sweet rolls when I
took coffee breaks, rationalizing overeating as a treat to calm
my anxiety about the stack of unpaid bills. I felt righteous about
my eating habits; I had earned my treats with arduous work. It's
easy to convince yourself that you deserve extra food. I became
intrigued with different kinds of ice cream and always had
some on hand.

"The extra weight made me sluggish and my brain languid,
but I could not resist the hypnotic pull to the kitchen. I responded to it like a robot.

"A toothache forced me to the dentist, who lectured me on
poor oral hygiene and, peering at my enlarged stomach, inquired about a physical check-up. I invented imaginary rebut-
tals for the doctor about a gland problem, but was dismayed to
see a poster over the weight scale—a midnight sneak, stuffing a
huge sandwich in his mouth, his deed illuminated by the re-
frigerator's light. The caption read, 'But, Doctor! It's my
glands!'

"The doctor, an old friend, wasted no words, saying a jump in blood pressure, shortness of breath, and an increase in colds in the last year were all related to my being overweight. He outlined a bleak future with a decreased life expectancy if I chose to continue indulging in food binges. He said, 'Your creative spirit does not excuse your obligations to your health. Next time you need a treat, take a walk or a bubble bath, get a massage, or call an old friend in place of gorging. No amount of food will permanently soothe your tensions over the future.' He advised a reasonable diet regime with moderate exercise. After six months I was trim again. He made me realize that good health is vital to my career, let alone life itself."

Sally, the songwriter, works at home, usually two or three hours a day, collaborating with several composers. "I need to be sharp and alert to match lyrics with tunes, and I owe my creative partners my full cooperation. Physical fitness is a must—sometimes we work without a break for several hours. Along with regular workouts on a punching bag, I skip rope, lift light weights, do isometrics, swim laps at a local health club and attend a twice-a-week dancercise class. I cannot afford to be ill. I eat correctly and sleep seven hours a night—enough for my constitution. Too much sleep makes me dull. I also meditate twice a day—one session of creative concentration centering, and the second session directing a message of continued dynamism to my whole being. The concentrated psychological energy directed to physical vitality stimulates my life-drive force. The combination of exercise and my other programs has resulted in perfect health for the last three years. I haven't even had a cold."

Sally's philosophy mirrors our belief in applied, preventive personal health habits. Too many people have developed a passive approach to body functioning and healing, depending on medical care for cures after disease has already invaded their neglected bodies.

Physicians have recently turned their attention to the combined efforts of both patient and doctor in the healing process. The passive patient who ignores symptoms until a disease progresses to the need for hospitalization lacks a strong will to live and a sense of control over his body. This dependent attitude fosters panic and impairs the healing process. Active, strong-willed individuals turn their psychological energies inward to heal themselves, whereas passive patients burn up energies with panic responses.

The blend of exercise, proper sleep, moderation in food and drink intake, emotional equilibrium and meditation on excellent health can add years to your life.

The Creative Arena

Our children grew up thinking that eating meals in the living room was normal, because the dining area is our writing room.

The old oval table's center contains a hodgepodge of materials: pens, pencils, ink pad and stamp, stapler, postage scale, paper clip holder, scissors, rubber bands, magnifying glass, ashtrays, stamps and address labels. The typewriter sits on one side, facing the room and back-lighted by a large window. Across from the machine and on both ends, space is left for writing, with legal pads, scraps of paper, a dictionary and thesaurus strewn around. An old, adjustable piano stool suffices as a typing chair, and a thick atlas is a sturdy foot rest. The chairs around the table are old dining room chairs, comfortable, but not cozy enough to cause sleepiness.

Shelves around the room hold our psychological reference books. A telephone—which we sometimes disconnect—sits on a small table with a wicker chair beside it. The walls have a couple of paintings and a calendar. A fireplace with a heat-blowing apparatus warms the room in the winter. A closet-size room next to the writing area houses a real desk, with drawers, file cabinets, and a blackboard listing book proposal whereabouts and assignments. It looks messy, occupied, and visitors comment on the creative ambiance. Things have remained in place over the years because of the authors' minimal skills in decorating. ("Let's stick this here; looks okay to me." "Sure, fine.")

Our writing space is the most positive aspect of our arrangement. We share an inability to write with noise distractions. Neither of us can write when the children are home because of our sensitivity to sound—neither a positive nor a negative trait, but a fact. As collaborators, we discuss subjects and work on outlines together but respect each other's need for quiet when it's time to write.

Our son, Aaron, composes poems and novels accompanied by favorite jazz or rock selections, unbothered by the traffic's roar, his roommates' activities, or the telephone's ring. Everyone has unique requirements for concentration and productivity, and these should be followed without comparative judgments.

"Visual harmony is indispensable for my creative flow," responds novelist Jennie. "I enter a spiritual province when moving from reality to imagination's sphere, and I want the room to match my frame of mind. The walls of my haven are painted a pleasing light lilac, graced by a portrait of my husband. Two African violets in porcelain planters sit on the window ledge, reminding me of nature's exquisite gifts. I found my pecan desk at a barn sale and refinished it. Writing pads and my favorite pens are on the desk, with all the business papers filed away in an old wooden cabinet. I type completed manuscripts in the kitchen, separating the creative atmosphere from the mundane typing jobs.

"A friend who writes poetry, screenplays, short stories, and greeting cards laughs at my 'obsessive need for order and beauty.' She writes anywhere. Her den is scattered with piles of scripts and half-finished stories. Ideas are tacked on the wall, and several neglected plants add to the disarray. She works in the den, but also in the living room with the noise of the television, kids banging around, her husband chatting on the phone, and a couple of snoring and wheezing dogs lying about. She can write at meetings, riding the commuter train, and even during meals. She is successful, so her method is right for her highly tuned concentration level. She advised learning to produce in the middle of any commotion as a form of self-discipline. It just doesn't work for me: I'm too easily distracted by confusions."

Thomas, another writer, relates, "I'm poor. I sleep and work in one room of a rented house I share with four roommates. I found a sturdy table in the garage that is fine for typing and my file cabinets are old copy paper boxes. There's just space enough for a bed and a chair. Cramped though it is, I feel good working here, but I have fantasized about how much more creative I would be in a luxurious office. I see myself, all tweedy and confident, working at a leather-topped desk, a mellow fire casting its glow around my sound-proof study.

"In the last two years I have finished four screenplays, two novels, and approximately fifty poems. After a great deal of hustling, I was invited to Los Angeles to negotiate a script sale. I was surprised and delighted by the producer's special and respectful treatment. He was awed by writers' talents and was very complimentary. Even though the sale didn't materialize, he encouraged me to submit future concepts. I had a viable contact!

"While I was in Hollywood, I renewed my acquaintance with a well-known actor whom I had worked with—as errand boy and general gofer—several years ago. After lunch at his home, I was shown his writing studio. It was a spacious, wood-paneled room, with expensive furniture, plush carpeting, and original art on the walls. During our conversation he mentioned a five-year writing drought. He had all the trappings, but no creative motivation. My envy evaporated as I compared our productiveness."

Your writing space should consist of a place to sit and compose with comfort. The chair must be adjusted to the table's height, with a sturdy back placed correctly to avoid neck, shoulder, and back problems. Proper lighting and adequate ventilation are necessary for concentration. The remaining equipment is personal choice. Some authors have radios or television sets as companions and to keep up-to-date with world events. Many writers decorate the walls with rejection slips, although these negative reminders seem torturous to us. Most writers collect eye-pleasing pictures or posters to look at while contemplating the next line.

"There was no room in my house for a writing room," revealed short story writer Marilyn. "My three children had their own bedrooms and I didn't want to usurp their privacy. I partitioned a section of the basement, found some used carpeting in a thrift shop, scrounged a flat door from a friend and laid it across two filing cabinets bought at auction. It's not fancy, but it's all mine. I enjoy my cat's company when I'm writing, and he's content to curl up by my feet, oblivious to my mumbling and sighing."

Make your work area comfortable and well enough organized to stimulate good work habits. It is a space where you will spend many hours, thinking, researching, and writing.

Between Times

You can't count on inspiration to keep you writing. This intense, charmed excitement in which phrases flow easily from a cascade of images happens infrequently. The magical moments of inspiration are a minute respite from writers' everyday plodding and self-discipline. There will always be periods when neither inspiration nor desire to write will occur naturally. No one writes all the time—that is an impossible accomplishment.

In fact, you may find that you become a better writer if you force yourself to set aside a day or two not to write. Mini-vacations are a psychological plus for all freelancers. Some authors never work on weekends, even if they are "on a good roll."

"The two-day weekend break from assignments and research is imperative to a balanced, enjoyable life," comments Grace, a writer for a weekly financial newsletter. "I work with a deadline which seems to gallop toward me. The office atmosphere is barely contained hysteria. Weekends are a reprieve from the high-stress work week, and I detach myself completely from national and international finances. I play the flute with a quartet, escaping into a musical world that is devoid of words. I visit art galleries and museums and attend movies. By Monday morning I am refreshed, prepared to join the fray, studying often-conflicting information, unraveling financial predictions, and interviewing economists."

Bill, the psychological writer, arranges three-day weekends away from his combined clinical and writing career. "I'm so wrapped up in my patients' difficulties and in writing practical advice about personal problems, that I must replenish my soul every week by doing something totally unrelated to being a therapist.

"I'm a bird watcher and take two- and three-day outings with other watchers. The birds' behavior and songs are exciting, fascinating, and totally different from listening to patients. The group I travel with never talks about psychological matters, so I'm never drawn into professional discussions. When I go back to work, I feel restored, ready to empathize with my clients' emotional pain.

"Many authors castigate themselves when they take vacation time or even when they relax from a regular writing schedule for a week. But a pause from thinking and planning usually opens new doors. A self-employed friend writes computer programming textbooks—very demanding and precise writing. Her mornings are set aside to care for her flock of racing pigeons. She blocks her writing out of her mind and devotedly feeds the flock, cleans their compartments, checks their health, and lays back to glory in their flights. She says the diversion keeps her sane."

The children's story writer says, "Both my creativity and my relaxation revolve around words. If I'm not writing, I'm reading. A co-worker defined me as a cereal box reader. I avidly read anything which passes my visual field whether it's an editorial, a label on a can of okra, match-book covers, the tiny print on the back of tickets, want ads, old letters or a novel. The written word calms me down. Of course, I also eat, sleep, exercise and make love! I'm often in the library's juvenile section, keeping in touch with children's interests, and joining kids' groups at the story hour. I can't afford vacations, but I travel in time and space every time I pick up a book. My horizons are stretched with each new book, and, ultimately, my reading vacations improve my vocabulary, my style and my ideas."

Skills expand with the freedom to relax and the pursuit of interests which rest one's creative "muscles." We can manipulate time to our creative advantage, rigorously monitor our physical fitness, and arrange a pleasing work environment. Freelancers, taking premature and intuitive excursions into areas without established pathways, have limitless boundaries to explore. Every effort you make to balance and control your lifestyle will make your journey more fruitful.

Chapter Eight

Developing an Emotional Support System

WE ALL NEED loving relationships in order to feel valued and emotionally connected. Understanding support from friends and relatives eases the strain and frustration of writing, and affection and reassurance can rescue a pessimistic writer from doubts and discouragement. We need others to celebrate with, talk to, love, and grow with. We also learn during our development that in order to enjoy genuine relationships, we must be willing to extend ourselves and contribute to others' needs.

The joy of living is continually rejuvenated by those whom we love and who love us. A parent's pride in our determination or accomplishments makes us feel valued. Friends or lovers who delight in our creativity give us courage to continue during the times of struggle for publication. Other creative friends who spark ideas and enjoy our company add to the structure of our emotional support system.

Those with whom we share bonds make up our emotional support system. A psychological bond between people involves a sense of trust and dependability which grows from repeated experiences, both positive and negative. You know that you can count on a person's continued love when you share the bonds of affection. Without intimate emotional connections, we feel adrift and incomplete, often unable to concentrate or work up to par.

We first experience emotional bonding during infancy, when we are totally dependent on the love and care of our parents to feel safe and secure in the world. While children are growing toward adolescence, the rituals, memories, and learning experiences in the home build a sense of bonded family security. When juveniles enter the wider world of playmates and school, they become attached to friends and other adults, forming new bonded relationships.

By the time a person reaches adulthood, he learns that the joy of being emotionally connected with others can only be attained through mutual caring and sharing. We learn that we cannot expect the total acceptance and love from others which we received from our parents during childhood. Authentic bonding with friends and lovers requires us to earn respect, affection, and loyalty by learning the arts of communication, compromise, compassion, and developing empathy and dependability.

Many creative people feel an instant sense of family when they first meet each other and realize that they share an unspoken understanding of the unique qualities of being creative. The pleasure of feeling accepted sets the groundwork for a strong bond and for deeper intimacy, exchanging personal information and opinions, and sharing experiences. The less defensive people are, the quicker a sense of authentic bonding can flourish and grow.

Our bonds—blood family ties as well as psychological family ties with our friends and lovers—are the anchors in our lives.

"I expanded my psychological family and sense of belonging when I joined a barter club," reports Peter, an articles writer. "I met several writers, two inventors, and a houseperson who concocts the most delectable chocolate desserts I've ever tasted. Our interest in bartering was a starting point for sharing tricks and techniques and for evolving new friendships.

"I'm also a member of a gleaners' society—people who travel to the countryside and pick the imperfect produce the farmers leave after the harvest. They are generally retired people who are eager to pass on tricks such as drying fruit and canning. The out-of-doors trek is a healthy break from indoor writing, but the most beneficial aspect is the opportunity to construct new emotional bonds. Being with people much older than myself has also added new dimensions to my work. Because of the stories I have heard, I now regularly sell articles to retirement magazines, a market I had never considered."

Friendship Bonds

One of the great pleasures in life is having friends who are loyal, trustworthy, and a constant presence in one's heart. Friends differ from acquaintances, for their knowledge of you goes far beyond the superficial exchanges which pass for socializing. Friends love and accept you and stand by you in times of stress, and they expect the same support from you.

We should be open to friendships throughout our entire lifetime, even though many people stop making new friends after college. Creative people, to continue growing and learning, should have friends in a variety of ages and occupations.

Several years ago a movie company came to our city and hired many locals as extras. We had small speaking parts and enjoyed the experience greatly both as writers and for the opportunity to take part in and learn about something different.

One lesson we learned is that waiting is the primary activity of actors and actresses. The crew must set up the scene and light the set before the director calls for action. During the long periods between scenes we talked with the stars and heard great stories about their struggles and successes.

During lunch one day we sat with the casting director, a young man of twenty-two. He had just finished writing his first screenplay and planned to return to Los Angeles to sell the script. During the conversation we talked about our writing careers, and he suggested that we expand our writing into screenplays. He even offered to stay in town for a few weeks to teach us the mechanics of filmwriting. The young man is now twenty-five and never left our area—we three formed a screenplay-writing partnership and have just recently established our own movie production company. Our friendship bond started because of the creative interests we shared, but during the years we have grown to love him as a dear companion. If he had had arbitrary opinions about people who were twenty and thirty years older than himself or if we had discounted him because of his youth, we all would have missed the opportunity for friendship and the creative growth which we have all stimulated in each other.

Any place you live, work, or play may be the starting place for friendships. Most people are attracted to one another by common interests that open the door for conversations and the beginnings of friendships. As adults we know that instant companionship is impossible, but the time and feelings we invest in relationships can grow into the deep bonds of care and trust that develop into intimate emotional connections.

Friends trust and accept each other, perceiving strengths and weaknesses, and appreciating each other as multidimensional. Friends give support through attention and affection when you are down and vulnerable—a regular experience in writers' lives. They share happiness and dreams, celebrating successes without jealousy. Dependability is a cornerstone of being and having a friend. You feel assured that if you need advice, hugs, favors, or companionship, your friend will deliver. Mutual friends are nonjudgmental, they don't try to hurt each others' feelings intentionally, but they reserve the right to point out foolish or self-defeating behavior.

You can relax and be yourself with a friend, neither posing nor trying to impress. Confidences are easy between comrades because of mutual trust and the unspoken ethic which respects privacy and avoids gossip.

Friends play together, comfortable enough with each other to act silly if they feel like it—something creative people should regularly do, because much of their work is serious and demanding. Just because you are a dedicated artist does not mean you must always be serious. The ability to feel silly means you are still in touch with the carefree, creative child within you, able to enjoy frivolous behavior in the service of relaxation.

Teasing between pals is another affectionate expression; friends intuitively know what areas are open to satire.

A staunch friend likes to give compliments, just to watch your grateful smile.

Friends understand that differences in tastes, opinions, and reactions make for entertaining conversations, and instead of demanding agreement, they give each other room to be individual.

Gene, the gag writer, states, "My circle of close friends includes two writers, a painter, and a garage mechanic. They all have a lively curiosity and are interested in people, concepts, and originality. We always feel uplifted after getting together, whether as a group of five or as a twosome.

"A very special friend who adds much to my life's elan is a woman I have known for twenty years. She's like a sister to me and has the best common sense of anyone I've ever known. She can pierce through situations, providing solutions to seemingly formidable dilemmas. I'm lucky that my wife isn't one of those 'Nervous Nellies' who neurotically think all women are predators. She accepts friendship with another woman as normal."

Companion Sex Friendships

Writers in particular should consciously seek out friendship with the companion sex. A good author should be able to write from both sexes' viewpoint and being comfortable with the other gender helps achieve an internal balance. This can be accomplished only when you really understand the other sex. Many people relate as if men and women were separate species.

John, a real estate broker and part-time freelancer, was asked by his young sons, "Who is your best friend?"

Without hesitation, he replied, "Mary Lou."

"No, no. She's your business partner. Who's really your best friend in the whole world?"

"It's Mary Lou."

"But, she's a lady!"

This conversation was repeated in various forms for several days. John said that his boys, aged seven and nine, kept pestering him because they were in the "boys only" stage and could not comprehend how their idealized father would want a woman as a best friend.

"They'll absorb my attitude as they grow older and learn that men and women are all just 'people.' "

He candidly admitted that his views about himself and women had changed dramatically over the last ten years.

He was influenced by his family and culture, growing up in a devout Catholic home—his mother a housewife and his father the traditional, bread-winning patriarch. Coupled with his religious schooling of twenty-five years ago, John and his peers had a rigid view of femininity. Women were regarded as "saints or bad girls."

John related, "We were taught that women were fragile, good mothers and homemakers, but inferior in intellect, and most of all, mysteriously emotional. Men, of course, were strong, smart, and the great protectors. I had a completely romanticized view of women. I was involved with 'the boys' all through my schooling and during the Vietnam War. When I fell in love, married, and had children, I still didn't perceive my wife as an equal, even though she was smarter than I.

"My narrow view of the sexes affected my writing, and a relative suggested I enter analysis. The therapy helped me grasp the fact that my self-view was limited to a half a person—that I must accept my own inner femaleness in order to be a total, loving person, able to write from a broad spectrum of emotions. My analyst was a woman who was very 'whole.' She was the first female I knew who enjoyed her own aggressiveness, was brilliant (and didn't apologize for it), intuitive, sexual—a combination of personality traits I thought was strictly divided between the sexes.

"My friendship with Mary Lou began on a professional basis. She was a supervisor for my group in some advanced real estate classes. Later, we worked in the same office and often had coffee together. Our relationship grew into a deep bond when I went through a devastating divorce. The strengths which had seen me through wartime vanished when I lost my sense of identity as a husband.

"Mary Lou was sympathetic and often listened to my ridiculous rantings when I was bogged down in my feelings of failure during my divorce. She and her husband invited me to dinner often and we would eat and watch television—nothing spectacular, just people accepting me into their family circle, knowing I was mourning the loss of my own. Being a friend isn't always listening to problems, but often just being emotionally present. She knew I needed a lot of reassuring affection. During those stressful months, Mary Lou gave me uncounted pats and hugs. It was the first time in my adult life that a woman touched me without sexual overtones.

"When I recovered from my divorce, our friendship grew into mutuality. When talking about how healing her support and affection had been, I asked Mary Lou why she had extended herself to me. Her answer stunned me. She said, 'I always thought you were a special person.'

"Women can more easily handle this up-front acceptance, because they learn to evaluate others on a right-to-the-core basis. We men are taught to judge ourselves on performance, and I thought she must have liked me because I was a good trainee and assertive salesman—never because of my essence."

John and Mary Lou ended up with a joint brokerage firm which was professionally pleasant, but the main reason they

work together is because they enjoy mutual support and respect. They both expressed gratitude that Mary Lou's husband
and John's second wife take their friendship as a matter of
course.

Because of their age and upbringing, both of these people had
to overcome an overlay of cultural attitudes about men and
women as romantic figures rather than platonic friends.

Many young adults (fifteen through the early twenties) have
benefited by the social changes in the last fifteen years and
would wonder what the fuss is all about. They have had the advantage of growing up more equally, without so much murky
distance between the sexes.

Dedra, twenty-one, an aspiring novelist, has been traveling
around the country since she was seventeen. She wanted to
travel and meet all kinds of people, so she moved in stages from
Maine to California and now lives in Colorado. She has recorded her impressions in a journal and plans to write a book one
day about how different personalities are attracted to different
states. She presently works as a police dispatcher and enjoys
dealing with all the crises. Her roommate, Andy, works odd
jobs and spends a lot of time at his typewriter, working on a
novel. They met through an ad Dedra placed for a roomie, and
don't consider it odd that they are a man and a woman sharing
living space. Their main concern is learning how to live together—cleaning, cooking, shopping, paying bills—each taking responsibility in order to make their apartment comfortable.
They fight about long distance phone charges and emptying the
cat's litter box, just like all roommates.

"We liked each other from the start. Andy's kind of a quiet
observer and I'm an extrovert. We talk about everything from
finding love to our writing dreams and exchange tales about
our adventures. We've seen each other naked—can't help that
when you live together—but having sex with each other isn't
an issue."

Andy commented, "I've learned a great deal about women's
feelings and about myself since I started living with Dedra. I've
learned that most people have the same emotional needs, and
Dedra has helped me learn about my soft side. I can actually explain a woman's feelings much better when I'm writing a male-
female scene because of what my roommate has shared with
me."

You can form friendships with the "other" sex and overcome

the entrenched cultural-social systems of expected behavior between the sexes. You must first accept the fact that all humans require acceptance, understanding, support, affection, love, sexual satisfaction, and empathy. We all have a yearning to be known—not our facade, but for our inner selves. But we hide (protect) that inner self with defenses—sophistication, intellectual performance, casual and laid-back attitudes, the clown, the loner, the superperson. Underneath these veneers we present to the world, we all share the same personal emotional requirements.

Male-female friendships will add to your life. Examine your views about sex-related behavior. After you accept the complementary side of your personality you will relate to your companion sex with a "whole" view. When you begin an opposite sex friendship patience is the first priority. Many people who have had negative experiences may be leery of offered intimacy, fearing that others might be trying to get something from them. Some people will not believe that you are looking for companionship rather than romance and love commitments.

Jan invited Tim for a drink after a hectic day of copy presentations at their advertising firm. After they sat down and ordered, Jan noticed Tim's nervousness. Instead of ignoring his discomfort, she plunged in and said, "Let's just relax. I didn't invite you to start a romance. I just admire your way with words and how beautifully they match the layouts." He was suspicious, but he calmed down while they chatted about office gossip, their writing careers, and ideas for future copy. They ended the evening making dinner and sharing life stories.

"That was three years ago," said Tim. "I'd always assumed that I couldn't be just friends with a lady. Sex and love had to happen. Love did occur, but it is a 'comrade's' love—a helping love. We have coauthored three plays and are working on a children's story about boys and girls learning to be friends.

"When I got married last year, Jan was my 'best man' (we changed the title to 'best person.') My old jock pals were incredulous, but I figure they don't know what they're missing."

Jan said she had always longed for a brother, and Tim met that deep need. "He's not my big brother/protector. I don't need protection. He's a dependable pal, affectionate, teasing, sympathetic when I have problems, and he shares in my creative endeavors."

The psychological family feeling which grows between men- and women-friends gives a sense of belonging in this often de- humanizing world. Family bonds make you feel someone real- ly cares about your well-being.

Tim volunteered, "When you feel like a brother and sister, the same incest barrier is present as if you are blood relatives. We don't think of each other as possible sexual partners even when we are sitting side-by-side working on a writing project. We may be sensual with each other, like taking turns giving massages after long hours at the typewriter, but it's done with the intention of giving a present rather than trying to arouse each other.

"I had learned enough about myself from sharing feelings with Jan—my sweet, cuddly, hidden little boy who cries when he is moved and needs to talk about fears—so that when I fell in love with Bette I was prepared for a friendship with romance. She had some difficulty accepting my 'buddy' love for Jan, but not anymore. She thinks my 'best person' is a leveling and har- monious factor in my emotional state."

Bette related that she felt twinges of jealousy in the begin- ning, not because Jan and Tim loved each other but because, "they were so comfortable together. I had to accept that they had a longer history than Tim and I did, just like any close friends. Their creative arrangement was so rewarding and pro- ductive, I realized that it would be childish to feel left out. I re- membered a boy in college who was a soul mate, who wrote poetry with me. We had drifted apart after leaving school. I found his address and wrote to him. The feelings we share back and forth in our letters are the same as those shared by Jan and Tim. We truly are 'deeply in like' with each other."

Robert, a columnist who is a forty-year-old bachelor, decided that life was too short to limit himself to having only male friends, saying, "Once you start revealing yourself and realize that you want to get close to a woman as a friend, the going is easy."

The benefits of male-female friendships are a feeling of being in harmony with the human race, a comfort and easiness with one's responses after accepting shared needs, affection which blends the different joys of male and female touch, discovering (and writing from) the viewpoint of someone brought up differ- ently because of gender, and a rise in self-esteem as a result of having overcome cultural programming and limitations.

The People Around You

Realistic Expectations

Drew is a young man who traveled for two years after high school and then attended college. After graduation he worked for a couple of years with Hollywood film crews here and abroad until he acquired enough money to support himself while writing a novel.

Drew moved to a small mountain town in Wyoming that was quiet and fairly inexpensive—a place he imagined would be the perfect writing atmosphere. He wrote diligently, three to five hours a day, six days a week, relaxed evenings and Sundays, and vacationed one week out of five to rest his mind and review the novel's progress. He dated a girl who seemed awed that he was a novelist, which he admitted appealed to his dramatic view of himself as the struggling artist.

The community consisted mainly of ski bums (ski instructors during the winter who worked odd jobs during the off season), people who worked in the tourist area, ranching families, and others who operated businesses catering to the local needs. Most of the people said they lived there to escape from the big city life and were looking for peace and quiet.

Whenever Drew attempted interesting conversations with his girlfriend or acquaintances, they had nothing to contribute and often responded to his comments about a book, movie, or current events with a shrug: "I don't get into anything heavy. Don't dig reading, man. I'm laid back, ya know?"

Drew's previous experiences made him an anomaly in the small town. He came from an intelligent, politically active family, and was educated at a highly competitive university with stimulating instructors and participating, committed students. He had taken for granted the creative excitement generated on movie sets by imaginative actors, directors, and the stage crews. In the small town environment Drew stood out like a proclaimed atheist at a prayer meeting. He was accepted at parties but was ignored if he sought meaningful dialogue—the ingroup was disquieted by his penetrating questions. His girlfriend did not understand why Drew felt irritated and complained that he had no one to talk to. She preferred the passive entertainment of TV to reading books. The need for companionship kept Drew attached to her, although he was unpleasantly aware that his blathering bored her.

When he completed the first draft of his novel, Drew announced the achievement to several of his acquaintances in town. Everyone congratulated him, saying, "That's great," and changed the subject. His girlfriend was pleased, and bought him lunch but had no further interest in his accomplishment. Seeking solace, Drew telephoned his family and college friends who responded to his excitment, sharing in the celebration.

A novelist-aunt suggested his complaints about feeling isolated were invalid. "Stop expecting people who aren't creative to understand or care about your work. You picked a town of happy-go-lucky, normal people who just want to enjoy life. You have to live where creative people gather and work if you want scintillating discussions. You're impatient and want the best of everything."

Drew's creative loneliness stayed with him throughout the novel's three rewrites and his search for a publisher, but when he returned to his film job, he re-experienced the familiar artistic bond with his co-workers. "I was naive, expecting from regular people stimulation that was way beyond their interests and capabilities and thinking I could excite them into thinking about ideas when they just wanted to work and play. I'm in a quandary, searching for a place which doesn't kill your spirit like the big cities, but isn't an intellectual wasteland.

"I felt as if I was living in a community of 'pod people' like the creatures in the classic horror film, *Invasion of the Body Snatchers*. The humans were murdered in their sleep and replaced by twin images of themselves who hatched out of giant, viscous pods. These 'twins' were vegetable zombies who spoke, ate, and moved like humans but had no soul."

People who seem like the pod people from outer space have a dull look in their eyes and speak without enthusiasm. They float through life rather than participating or contributing, unlike artists who feel compelled to be involved and to challenge the status quo through their crafts. Because these life-evaders remain aloof from intimacy or close interaction with others, they most often look upon writers as a nuisance. They don't want to be bothered by questions and care little for the exchange of ideas about current events, books, or human nature. This behavior is often shocking to the ever-curious writer who cannot believe that everyone isn't as fascinated with life as he is himself.

The sensitive artist whose feelings are easily hurt may take the reaction of "pod people" as a personal rejection, but that is a narcissistic stance. To assume that the disinterested are conspiring to put down your creative spirit will only make you feel paranoid. It is better to understand that they are unable to care much about anything and lack the capacity to form meaningful relationships or to become involved with issues. Psychologically, these people feel worthless and have developed the defense of noncaring to avoid looking into their personal voids. Continuing attempts to wake them up to life's possibilities will only have a deadening effect on the artist's soul.

Although these people are essentially passive and can do little harm when we accept the fact that they are unable to live a full life, it is best for the writer to avoid them. We all have enough problems as freelancers without having to deal with disinterested, uninvolved individuals.

Those people who *actively* demean writers' talents or aspirations should also be considered a negative force.

Jealousy

Many noncreative people have an unresolvable jealousy toward gifted individuals. The creative person, striving for recognition, often has a difficult time comprehending why anyone would be envious of his talents and is hurt by the disguised put-downs of the jealous adversary.

Our society teaches, at home and at school, that jealousy is a mean and childish response toward others. The jealous adult may initially feel guilty when he feels spiteful toward those with special gifts and then may repress his most obvious jealous reactions. The repressed feelings become unconscious to the jealous person, who expresses envy through different channels—disdain, disbelief, mocking, or devaluing special people as dreamers fleeing reality. As with any psychological defense the jealous person comes to believe that his reactions against gifted people are accurate and have nothing to do with jealousy. He is actually unaware that creative peoples' special perceptiveness, curiosity, and intense drive to communicate are threats to his own self-esteem.

The writer need not confront the defensive, jealous person with his unconscious envy, but understanding its roots can be a great protection against feeling rejected when such a person throws barbs your way.

"Many people become instantly leery when they hear I'm a writer," shares Margaret, a short story writer. "They try to put me on the defensive by asking who my publisher is and wondering outloud about my financial success—two status symbols which supposedly make you a worthwhile citizen. When I hear those questions, I know I am dealing with an adversary. They are nervous in a writer's presence, fearing we will observe and record their faults. They are correct, of course, but I'd never tell them how authors subliminally file people's peculiar traits. I can't explain that perhaps one of their mannerisms may surface in a character who won't resemble their entire personality, since it would only make them more nervous.

"A well-established author once told me that even though he has published over thirty books, envious and threatened people still ask him the same veiled, vindictive questions about his craft. He recommended that I take these kinds of comments lightly. He felt that envy was predictable because the voids inside of some people's constricted lives were made glaringly apparent by creative people's glow and sparkle. He said it is unimportant to impress others with your chosen career, that a writer must feel his own sense of value. I have learned to gracefully change the subject and remove myself from the company of those threatened by my work."

It would be ideal if we only had to deal with people who thought our gifts were wonderful and if those "others" would disappear. There will always be situations when you will be forced to deal with noncreative people, when you have no choice, such as business, social, and family gatherings.

You do have options when you choose your closest friends. You can choose dynamic companions who are not jealous of a writer's talents and who will enrich your life.

Arthur, a screenplay writer, explains, "My best friend is miles away from anything to do with writing. Ben runs a gas station and thinks of his clients as a giant movie passing through his business. I met him when I took my car in for repairs. I'm a dunce around anything mechanical and feel really proud when I can put a carbon ribbon in my typewriter without messing something up.

"I was fascinated with Ben's quick diagnosis and his creative repair of my car. He improvised a part on the spot that would have cost me a small fortune at a dealer. While he works he tells stories about his customers and weaves in tales about his other inventions for solar projects, superefficient engines and even board games for his kids. His stories about people have given me ideas for characters and he's just as interested in my plots and fantasies as I am in his inventions and stories."

Arthur has learned that his creative friends do not have to be only other writers. Many people are interesting companions (and aren't threatened by writers) who find satisfaction is creative cooking, healing, mechanics, painting, carpentry, or any activity which advances beyond the "norm."

Creative peers usually experience normal professional envy if you are successful in publishing your work and they are not, but they rarely treat your writing career with disdain or force you to defend your identity as a writer.

Specific Problems. Jealous people on the periphery of your life can be easily evaded—co-workers scornful of writers can be related to in a businesslike fashion, snide remarks from strangers can be sloughed off, and writers who suffer professional jealousy can be explained away by putting yourself in their predicament. However, relatives, mates, or close friends who maliciously envy the energy, time, and love invested in writing create a paradox—how can they love us and yet envy our work?

Writers are confused when an intimate, claiming to love them, turns sarcastic and bitter about their "other" love.

"When my first poem was published," relates Shirley, "I proudly showed my husband the journal it appeared in. After a cursory glance he looked up with a strange expression, and said, 'I never did understand poetry.' It was like being slapped across the face with a dead fish. As he was well educated and had minored in English during college, I knew he was deliberately being rude and cruel.

"One evening I wrote several poems and was typing them. He stood over me and said, 'If you would only give me the same attention, we could be happy.' I could no longer shrug off his jealous attitude toward my writing. He had subtly alienated most of my friends and had watched me carefully at social events, acting as if I were going to run away with any man who paid me attention. I had laughed away his suspicions because I had no interest in flirting or adultery. His consuming possessiveness caused him to view poetry as a living thing, seducing me away from him. It was incredible. I spend an average of only five hours a week writing. The problem climaxed when I was invited to give a one-person reading at the local university. The event was a success, and afterwards some students complimented me and asked for advice. I was edgy because my husband was standing nearby, glowering darkly at every man who approached me. On the way home he accused me of being a misfit, demanding I renounce writing. The whole scene took on an aura of unreality. He refused marriage counseling, leading to a stormy divorce complete with detectives following my movements—they must have been totally bored.

After I recovered from the trauma of the divorce, I could look at my ex-mate's behavior as if he were a character in a bad novel. Although he was accomplished in his field and financially secure, his self-esteem was extremely low. He thought of me as a possession to be controlled, as if my devotion to him would prove he was a valuable person. The crazy thing is that I did love him before he started to treat me like a piece of property. His obsession turned him into a frightening, menacing tyrant. He seemed to be slowly strangling my creative enthusiasm and joy of life. He just wanted to own me.

"Currently, I am a therapist and often deal with mates' jealousies—a widespread problem. Whenever I detect exaggerated envy targeted on a spouse's gifts, bells start ringing. Of course, a jealous spouse doesn't automatically mean divorce, but it's an issue that must be resolved."

Jealousy is not an expression of love, even though the recipient may be flattered when a lover or mate first displays possessive symptoms. Jealousy is a normal, although immature, emotional reaction when someone is more attractive/successful/happy/cherished than we are.

Children are jealous of their siblings and their parents' interests because they are self-centered and want exclusive attention, still believing the world revolves around them instead of understanding that love can be shared. As we grow up, most of us learn to give up childish envy. Hopefully we direct energies to improve skills to increase our self-esteem. A person who feels good about himself and strives toward goals is usually too busy to become preoccupied with jealousy.

Jealous mates should be tactfully confronted and, if feasible, assisted in overcoming this ultimately destructive affliction. It isn't always easy to be tactful when bringing up the subject of jealousy because possessiveness makes one feel persecuted and, eventually, vindictive. Name calling, accusations of childishness, threats, or sarcasm only make the jealous person feel defensive and widen the gap in communications. The person with a valid complaint should, if possible, calmly try to express the worry that jealousy may be a problem and ask the envious partner to listen to how one feels when that person is jealous. Most jealous people are unaware of the discomfort their resentful attitude causes. If you explain that you feel unjustly accused it may lead the jealous person to think about the consequences of his or her behavior.

Jealous mates should be given the opportunity to ventilate their feelings without interruption or censure. The listener has the responsibility to concentrate on the emotional content of the message without yawning, looking superior, or thinking of rejoinders. Perhaps the jealous mate has some realistic points for you to consider. Admitting that the other person is right does not mean that you lose face. You won't collapse from admitting you are less than perfect, but you will establish an atmosphere of mature compromise. It may appear to be jealousy if a mate becomes angry when a writer spouse comes home, mumbles a greeting, gulps dinner and rushes off to a writing sanctuary without a thought or care for the other person's feelings. But in this case the writer is just plain selfish and should consider making some changes if he or she plans to continue the relationship.

If the complaining partner has no concrete basis to explain the feelings of jealousy and admits that writing is perceived of as a competitor for love, the writer should try to be sympathetic. The confrontation's goal is to understand and attempt to elicit change, not to win an argument. Jealous people often feel ashamed and embarrassed by their childish reactions, and a sympathetic partner can often help them overcome jealousy just by listening with a spirit of generosity and love.

Next, the reality that each of us must find areas of work which makes us feel meaningful and valued for ourselves must be discussed. We cannot expect self-esteem to grow by demanding another person pay total attention to our needs. If emotions are too high and couples feel they cannot work out the negative feelings surrounding jealousy, counseling should be considered before the green monster invades every aspect of the relationship.

"My wife concealed her jealousy about my writing but always picked a fight just before she left for work," relates Reg, another writer. "I was working on a play that required my total concentration. My wife would begin a tirade while she made her breakfast, criticizing me because I wasn't dressed, didn't mail a letter or run an errand or any other excuse to begin bickering. We usually ended with a shouting match. Sometimes the subject was simply differing opinions about a news item or the weather. A pattern was established with her storming from the house, leaving me distraught, vulnerable, and unable to write. She wasn't angry about having to work, because she liked her job, and I was contributing a steady cash flow from articles.

"I was too caught up in my misery to understand her strange behavior—nasty in the morning and cheerful at night. I was spending the time I should have spent writing trying to figure out her awful attitude and thinking of ways to avoid her. I talked the problem over with my mother-in-law. She concluded, 'As stupid and senseless as it sounds, my daughter is just plain jealous of your writing. Tell her how upset you become after she leaves and see what happens.'

"After several evenings talking about ourselves, my wife admitted that she resented my freedom to stay home and write. Embarrassed, she confessed to a perverse glee when disrupting my work.

"Talking about our feelings quieted down our household. She even learned to joke about her envy and stopped acting so hateful. Other writers discussed their mate's jealousy with me, saying it could be impossible to overcome and sometimes resulted in breaking up the marriage."

Jealous mates, relatives, or close friends are people who look for happiness outside of themselves, putting the gifted person in a no-win position. Their unspoken request is for the artist to somehow fulfill them by devoting his or her exclusive love and attention to them. Even if the artist complies the jealous one would still be unhappy, because of their basic self-esteem problems.

Appropriate self-satisfaction comes from accomplishments, thoughtfulness, caring and sharing, and genuine wishes for a loved one's good fortune. Unsatisfactory reactions come from harboring passive expectations for happiness through another's attainments—pouting for attention and holding grudges when one's emotional needs are not met.

No writer can afford to be tortured by jealousy, because it impedes work and causes unnecessary personal conflicts. A successful, envious manipulator can cause inappropriate guilt and even convince the author to sacrifice talents in the service of peace and quiet. This always leads to bad feelings, because the writer will feel like a possession instead of a person.

Make a resolution to avoid involvement in the jealousy-baiting game. Love of work is different from love for another person, just as romantic feelings are distinctly separate from parent-child attachments. Turn the psychological tables on a jealous person by asking him to talk about his expectations of perfect harmony (often a daydream of being loved without earning it through mutual caring). Do not accept the position of a selfish person who steals time from a mate to pursue writing tasks. A loving partner delights in a mate's accomplishments and creative involvements. We are not talking about some "writer's right" to withdraw from the responsibilities of relationships, but about the freelancer who loves his mate and is bewildered by unfounded accusations of "loving your work more than me."

Other Disruptive Relationships

Ideally, emotional connections should be based on mutual care, respect, and affection, and creative expression would be governed purely by self-motivation, uninterrupted by discord or unhappiness. Few are so fortunate to live and work with completely healthy and satisfying relationships.

Evaluating your current emotional attachments will illuminate their positive and negative effects on your creativity.

Outline the characteristics of the people having an impact on your emotional equilibrium, and describe your major reactions to these important figures.

Bruce, the novelist, reports, "My lovely, well-balanced wife shares her love generously and is always quick to help me with my work. My daughters are basically delightful, and my irritation with their normal, adolescent excitements is my own fault. My family adds to my feeling of being loved and admired.

"But my relationship with a writer-friend was negative. He

was continually courting depression. He couldn't believe his good fortune if he sold an article. He borrowed trouble, fretting about whether or not editors would ever buy another piece even though his writing is excellent. He called weekly, infecting me with his gloomy attitude. I'm so easily distressed that I would believe his dire predictions and feel weighted down, unable to produce. He brought nothing positive to my life, and yet I continued putting up with his pessimism out of duty and habit.

"My wife suggested that he represented a childhood vestige of someone in my family who was always available to dampen creative enthusiasm. She said, 'Examine what he gives to you. Shouldn't friendship involve some gaiety? You can't lift his depression, and he just uses you as a sympathetic ear. If he wanted to change, he would be paying a therapist. I'll bet he has a list of people to call and you're just another of his pseudo-psychiatrists.'

"I experimented the next time he called, perfunctorily inquiring about my writing. Instead of casually dismissing my work and asking about his, I talked about myself, my family, my work in progress, and how wonderful it was to be alive. My effusiveness made him hostile, as if my happiness were a personal affront to his imagined suffering. As my wife predicted, he stopped calling. It was unnecessary to reject him, since I was no longer a useful tool. I vowed never to put myself in that position again, because his need for reassurance was a bottomless pit."

Sensitive people feel bound by duty and allow themselves to be manipulated into maintaining one-way relationships. It is not friendship if you extend the majority of the support, advice, and affection and aren't cared for in return.

"I had to face my neurotic need to be a rescuer," states Judith, a novelist. "My list of kindred spirits was top-heavy with people in continual upheaval with creative work, love quarrels or job problems. I was the strong, serene, 'together' friend who patched them up, actually unconsciously encouraging their dependency. Why should they overcome their hysterical indulgences when I was always available for calming them and salving their wounds? What was I getting out of it?

"During a session of free association, I discovered a need to feel superior, always strong and wise. Also, I was doing little creative work when the phone was ringing frequently or people felt free to drop by the house. I suspected my rescue work was a ruse to avoid writing.

"Discovering the unconscious motivation made it clear that I had to extricate myself from the nursemaid role. I began telling all the emotionally crippled invaders that I was involved with a project and couldn't help them right away. The angry, bewildered reactions shouldn't have been surprising, since I had set them up to expect reliable, instant mothering. Later I took a more honest, fair approach, telling my 'patients' that it was unhealthy for me to coddle them, only encouraging dependence.

"They all drifted away when I gave up my role of the comforting mother. After giving up my unconscious need to be superior, I invested more energy into writing."

When outlining your relationships, consider the repetition compulsion, the unconscious need to repeat childhood feelings. Attachments are negative if the main element of a relationship mirrors hurtful early family experiences. A conscious decision can be made to weed out or wean yourself from connections that add no creative stimulation or enjoyment to daily life.

Building a solid emotional support system does not mean relating only to bland, nondisruptive individuals, but rather choosing friends who genuinely wish you well and understand the complexities of freelancing.

Chapter Nine

You Are in Business

MOST WRITERS—without an agent to represent them—must handle the business aspects of their careers themselves. Yet many writers are struck with sudden shyness when faced with the business side of writing. They may have great confidence in their talents when they are working, they may even understand the need to compete against other worthwhile freelancers, but when faced with writing to or talking with an editor about fees, confidence and assertiveness vanish. Some authors even feel that their creativity and talent might be tainted when spoken of in the same breath as *business*. These blocks to handling your writing as a valuable product can drastically cut your income.

You will not diminish your creativity or artistic identity when you learn to professionally transact business. In fact, your self-esteem will increase when you take an active role in selling your product. You must consider yourself as a unique person with a special product, not a romantic figure who hopes for discovery and quick riches.

Your Business Responsibilities

Creative people must learn the skills of business which include negotiation for fees, understanding contracts, collecting accounts receivable, and developing a businesslike approach in letter writing and verbal communications.

Realize that you must hustle your own material. No one is

searching to discover you. The outcome of your career rests squarely on your shoulders.

Organize your time to study the markets, write intelligent and interesting letters, and submit material in professional form. Resubmit elsewhere if rejected.

Know what to ask for—down-to-earth financial expectations are essential. The best way to gain perspective on the market is by reading about what various publishers pay in the latest *Writer's Market*.

Educate yourself about the various publishing rights so that you can make the best deal and resell material later.

Develop assurance in your ability to talk about fees with editors. When editors say "no" you are not defeated but must try again.

Relate to the buyer as a business person, not as an authority figure. This puts you on an equal plane. An understanding that business arrangements are conducted impersonally will buffer your emotions when you're negotiating for fees.

Avoid the stance of the sensitive artist who is above discussing money. This will gain you the respect of editors.

Keep a level head about earnings and refuse to live on "projected" income. This will help make you a practical, realistic, and solvent business person.

All of these skills can be learned. But you must devote your time and energies toward learning them just as you did becoming a freelancer. As with any new skill, repeated experiences add to your confidence—eventually business can actually be enjoyable.

Respect Your Product

Lillian, a nurse and beginning writer, received a check for her first article, fifty dollars for a three-hundred word piece on the importance of fathers' participation during childbirth. "I felt guilty about receiving money for a piece which only took an hour to write. I thought I had cheated the newspaper which ran the article. I had written it as an inspiration for young couples and taking money seemed to taint the poetics of my message. I know this is a paradox because I knew newspapers paid writers. I told an artist-friend about this reaction and he burst into laughter. He said it takes him a few hours to complete a painting, and when people ask him how much time he devotes to his pictures, he answers, 'Thirty years'—each painting was the result of three decades of his training and experience. In the same manner, my article was a culmination of many years of nursing care and observing patients' needs. He taught me to respect the worth of my special knowledge and my years of experience.

"Back then I had the business side of writing confused with the joy of passing on my wisdom. I now see myself as a specialty writer and a smart business lady and I don't feel squeamish about discussing fees before I begin a piece. I also feel confident enough to request appropriate increases in payments after I have proved my reliability by turning in assignments on time."

Some writers shy away from accepting their business responsibilities because of romantic notions—the preoccupied dedicated author devoting his time exclusively to creative work while a selfless companion does the boring, mundane chores of typing final drafts, reading about potential markets, and sending queries. It's a lovely fantasy, but not realistic.

Talking About Money

As with any skill, the more you practice negotiating fees, the more comfortable and confident you will become. You have probably overcome the myth that good writing is a magical form of expression flowing smoothly from your pen and have accepted the hard work and difficulties of producing quality material. It is just as easy to push aside fears of being assertive about money and rights once you've learned to efficiently tackle the transactions of business.

"I used to be fearful about talking to editors on the phone or writing letters asking for reasonable fees," reports Jason, the columnist. "I realized one day when I was sweating over a letter to an editor complaining about his slow payment, that I was safe at home and he wouldn't come and attack me. Sounds cowardly, I know, but I'm afraid to offend people in positions of authority, especially those with control over my income. I had the insight that I was only asking for fair treatment, which I justly deserved, and that he didn't care if he offended me by not sending my money on time. Many other business people have to stand face-to-face and haggle. We writers are protected by distance—the phone or correspondence—so we shouldn't be afraid to demand a fair deal. It should be done pleasantly, but firmly.

"I've advised beginning writers to pretend they are going to bat for a friend instead of themselves when they are requesting good pay. This gives them more confidence and breaks down their fear of offending an editor or being rejected as pushy. It works when writers can set aside their personal desire to be liked and get in there and bargain.

"I tell young authors to look at the whole negotiating process as if it were a game: the rules are that they have to upgrade their finances by speaking clearly, giving the impression that they expect good wages, and not being intimidated. Then I tell them that editors are just people doing their jobs and part of that job is to buy material at a low price."

Most magazines and publishing houses have a low, moderate, and high payment scale for article fees and book advances, depending on such things as the writer's reputation and track record.

Uncredited authors are in the weakest position, because editors have no proof of their skills or reliability. You will most likely be forced to accept low fees in the beginning in order to build credentials. Unknown magazine writers are usually asked to submit articles on speculation with no definite promise of acceptance or payment.

An established writer—one who has published several pieces—should be given assignments, which means that the freelancer is hired to write on a specific subject and should be paid on acceptance. If editors do not use the assigned pieces, they should pay a kill fee to reimburse the writer for time and expenses. These arrangements should be clarified in advance and in writing.

To move from one level of assignment and payment to another you must learn to negotiate. If you don't ask for appropriate payment, no one else will do it for you.

Maurice, the cookbook author, says, "You have to convince yourself that bargaining for better money is worthwhile and realistic. In the past I was insecure and thought editors wouldn't like me if I requested a higher payment, even after having proved my writing abilities. Whether editors like you or not is immaterial. This is business. Writers have to ask assertively for higher payments as their writing credentials from previous sales accrue. Publishers will either say yes or no, but authors must stand up for their rights to be respected and treated fairly."

You are not compromising your artistic ethics when you discuss payment for creative work. Too many writers, afraid of never being published, accept the first offer without dreaming of asking for more. Even if it's your first sale and you think the offer is very low, you can still bargain for a higher fee. If the editor refuses, you can accept the offer but feel proud that you attempted to negotiate. You may have more success next time.

Jed states, "I had written articles about general health for several magazines before retiring from medicine. The payments were average. Now, when I query the same magazines, I say, 'I have become a full-time freelancer and would appreciate your highest fee. You know me to be dependable, and now that I am always available, I will add even more quality material to your magazine.' They consistently offer substantial increases. If I had felt it wasn't dignified to request better pay, nothing would have happened."

Reuben, a well-known nonfiction writer, states, "I hate to negotiate for advance money on a book but I have learned to be level-headed and can foretell the usual conversation between myself and a publisher. (I always seem to get a telephone call about advances instead of a letter. I wonder if publishers try to catch authors off guard.)

"The replay goes like this:

" 'Well, Reuben, how much did you have in mind for an advance?' (They never say what they have in mind.)

" 'The last book I wrote with another company received a fair price.' (It didn't but I can't confess to being a dolt.)

" 'Um. Well, we have to consider our rising expenses. What figure do you consider fair to complete this project?' (I'll have to suggest a price or we'll be here all day!)

" 'I think $10,000 would cover expenses.' (They'll never go for this but if I ask for twice what I hope for, perhaps. . . .)

" 'Of course, it's not my decision.' (Sure it isn't.) 'I'll have to take this up with the financial people and get back to you.'

" 'Thanks.' (Just give me the money you miser.)

"In the next phase the author waits, anxiously wondering just who these mysterious people are and what the outcome will be. (Tell this guy to forget ever submitting to us again. Who does he think he is anyway? What an outrageous demand!)

"Usually after a week of this kind of worrying I'll get a letter offering an advance which is half my asking price. Everyone's satisfied. The publisher thinks he's reasonable and the author has a workable income to begin the book. It's all so silly. I wish I could just say, 'I need $5,000 to write this book, take it or leave it,' but everyone has to act out their part in the game.''

Practical Attitudes About Sales

"I learned the hard way not to celebrate a sale until the check was in my hands," says George, the screenplay writer. "I gave my first script to an actor-friend of mine. He liked it and showed it to a director he trusted. They took it to a producer who thought it had great possibilities. We all met, and I was told everything was 'go,' and that the next step would be to have our attorneys work out contracts. It appeared I would make a great deal of money. I was on cloud nine for the next few days, lavishly using my credit card to pay for celebrations with my friends.

"Nothing happened. My attorney couldn't seem to get through to the producer or his lawyer. My actor-friend finally called the producer at home and was told the project was cancelled due to personal reasons. The story slowly emerged. The producer, even though he liked the script, decided he couldn't work with the director who, in turn, refused to let go of his 'found' script. The operation ground to a crushing halt. As a novice I had no knowledge of personality clashes in Hollywood or of how fragile promises could be. Luckily, the producer thought I was talented and asked to see other properties. I eventually sold him a treatment and did write a screenplay, carefully controlling my excitement until the papers were signed and I was paid."

"Use me as an example of a flight from reality," requests Reuben, the nonfiction writer. "The publisher heavily promoted my first book and I appeared on several network programs, including the *Tonight* show. The head of sales at the publishing company called, reporting that there was a flood of orders after my Carson appearance and that a paperback company expressed interest in reprint rights.

"I was seized by giddiness, foreseeing the end of financial woes and projecting myself into a millionaire. I thought a 'flood of orders' and a paperback sale were guarantees of riches. Looking back, I can't fathom why I believed this glamorous notion— perhaps from movies or starry-eyed naivete.

"Don't snicker at what I did next—this story could be told by many other authors. I bought a Lincoln Continental—a car I had secretly yearned to own since I had serviced and washed gangsters' Lincolns as a kid pumping gas in Chicago. I even special ordered a sinister-looking blue-black paint job with custom navy leather interior and seats. I selected new wardrobes for myself and my wife and bought expensive motorcycles for my two sons. They were swept up in the excitement and started making lists of things to buy when the money began rolling in. I grandly paid for all this ostentation, using precious savings, reasoning that in a few months I would be wealthy and luxuriating in security! A modicum of sanity prevailed—I did keep my job as a tax estate attorney, although I was frequently absent to promote the book.

"Eventually, the book went through six paperback printings and made approximately $30,000—certainly not enough to support a family of four. After the first year I sold the inappropriate automobile. I felt abashed and silly about my fancifulness. I also felt hostile to my editor for not tempering my unrealistic enthusiasm. This was also dumb—he wasn't my parent.

"Since then, I have published four books and have developed a sane attitude. Realizing that very few authors garner millions, even when they have a best seller, I now treat an advance as though it will be the total earnings, and I am pleasantly surprised when royalties begin to appear.

"Developing realistic expectations about the amount of money to be made hasn't dampened my creativity at all, but it has given an orderly manner to my enterprises. I no longer expect editors to calm down my behavior. Now I relate to them as literary helpmates."

When writing a book, an author usually receives half of the advance against future royalties after contracts are signed. The remainder is received when the book is ready for production—the manuscript completed, revisions made after the editor and copyeditor have gone over the material, and printer's galleys proofread. The first two royalty statements, usually sent twice a year, often show a deficit against the advance, and profits, if any, generally appear two years after publication. It is common sense to be conservative in your dreams if a book starts to catch on with the public.

Working with Editors

Editors dream of conducting business with the ideal author—one who brings original and salable ideas, responds promptly with quality copy, isn't petulant when corrections are necessary, and conducts business with a professional attitude.

The Need for Flexibility

A veteran producer of many popular television series invited a promising young scriptwriter to a meeting to discuss changes in her proposed television film. "She was brilliant and delighted me with her original concepts. Sometimes I read ideas for months without finding anything fresh. Too many writers develop Hollywood Incestu-itis, presenting only old, tried-and-true plots and characters. Her ideas and characters were well drawn but needed some slight changes. I explained some appropriate changes for her characters that would insure a sale and begin a solid reputation for her. The additions were minor and added depth to her original script. I know what can be sold to the network executives after working in the business for twenty years. She turned out to be a writer who clung tenaciously to her ideas as if changes were a matter of personal pride. Even though I carefully explained the reality of business, she remained inflexible.

"In television, writers can't let their egos get too involved in their material, because the willingness to compromise increases the chances of a sale. The too proud writer fails. Ultimately, I rejected her work, because I have limited time to handle nonprofessionals."

Should the writer have given in and made modifications to please the experienced producer? She may have left the meeting feeling idealistic but in reality her chances for success were diminished. The grapevine in the small family of television producers would label her 'too rigid,' quickly closing doors.

Accepting Criticisms

Editors and their staffs will often make suggestions, request additional material, or delete deadwood in assigned material. Experienced writers in all areas assume that suggestions for alterations in their material are made to improve the work and are not personal attacks on the writer. Their remarks almost invariably improve the manuscript.

Both book and articles writers should expect criticism, suggestions, and corrections from editors who must please their increasingly well-informed audiences. True professionals accept editorial requests and try to improve the material. This does not mean writers must accept everything editors recommend, but disagreements can be intelligently discussed, untinged by emotions. As a part of the collaboration that occurs between writer and editor, we assume that both the editor and the author are well motivated, educated, and informed. The two must be able to argue, disagree, compromise, and produce a quality piece of writing that pleases both parties.

"I was writing a book on women's feelings," recounts Helen. "My editor was conscientious and meticulously edited every chapter, often telephoning for clarification. I submitted a chapter on orgasm during a time when medical and psychological experts disagreed about the different types of female sexual response. There were two opposing camps—one denying vaginal orgasm claiming that women experienced orgasm only clitorally and the other defending vaginal orgasms. My opinion, after lengthly research with women and men, sex therapists, and physicians, was that both types of release were possible and that women should enjoy whatever suited them. The editor, herself a psychology researcher, belonged to the 'no-such-thing-as-vaginal-orgasm' school and adamantly insisted I rewrite the chapter to correspond with her viewpoint concerning clitoral orgasms. Ethically, I could not comply, because it would be unjust to present an inaccurate theory. We argued, but to no avail.

"I made the difficult decision to break the contract and returned half the advance, a requirement stipulated in the agreement. It was tough keeping my emotions in a separate compartment during our dialogue, particularly since we were discussing a highly charged psychological subject. We maintained a professional stance and ended our literary partnership with mutual respect.

"My past experience with editing had been revising material for style or adding interesting anecdotes to material to make it less boring. This was the first time I had to deal with an ethical problem in editing. There will be incidents in every author's career when such a decision must be faced. I eventually found another publisher who thought my research was valid, but even if I had failed to find a like-minded editor, I would have stood by my principles."

Understanding Editors' Needs

"I purposefully state in writers' magazines and market guides that our staff deals with hundreds of unsolicited manuscripts every week and that writers must expect a three-month wait," complains Ethel, the publisher of a small fiction press. "Even with this clear warning my overworked secretary continually fields calls from irrational novelists, accusing us of everything from losing their work to plagiarism. Those who refuse to read my requirement and the reason for delays set themselves up for rejection, because I send their works back unread. Anyone who ignores the obvious and then bothers my secretary with ridiculous accusations is not being a smart business person. Their nonprofessional attitude portends future problems which I prefer to avoid. By necessity my press is very discriminating when choosing a novel, and my editors must be able to work harmoniously with writers to produce the best product. We have no time for writers who do not even read our policies, particularly when there are plenty of thoughtful, understanding authors whose writing I would enjoy publishing."

We all yearn to know exactly why a piece has been rejected, and if an editor would care enough to explain, we would gladly rewrite the manuscript. This is rarely possible because of the incredible volume of submissions passing over editors' desks. It is the business responsibility of authors to study the specific interests of editors and present only what might spark their interests.

Years ago we published a poetry journal which was listed as requesting social commentary verse. Our mailbox was filled every day with poetry submissions, the majority unsuited to our journal's format. After you've read thousands of poems, the first two lines of a poem are sufficient to judge its style, content, and impact. (An excellent poem had a way of jumping from the page, instantly grabbing our attention and acceptance.) There was no time to write and re-explain our little magazine's needs to those who insisted on sending us nature or love-lost poems. They were returned without comment. We also threw away submissions of inconsiderate writers (and their numbers were staggering) who neglected to include a self-addressed, stamped return envelope, as we could not possibly afford the additional mailing expense.

A discontented, rejected poet complained about our journal to the Better Business Bureau, because we didn't return her submission when she hadn't enclosed a return envelope. The representative of the bureau chuckled when we explained our lack of fraudulent intentions and said he was unused to dealing with "the crazy world that poets inhabit."

Donald, who juggles the editing of several books at a time, comments, "My workday is blocked out with little time for dalliance. When I have finished one extensive project and sent it along to the printer, I must move on to others. Many of my authors interrupt my busy schedule with trivial calls which are out of my jurisdiction. The publicity people are in charge of promotion, advertising, and travel arrangements, all of which has been explained to them. But they still call with questions that I can't answer. I often feel like a beleaguered parent, fending off querulous children."

Psychological Transference

Publishers and editors are loved when they accept authors' proposals and hated when they refuse them. They do not deserve either response. Book publishing is a serious, increasingly expensive operation. Sensible writers understand that editors are paid to select works that show the greatest potential profit for their companies. Even when an editor has presented a book idea to the marketing department, received an okay from the editorial board, and sent a contract to the author, it is still a serious gamble for the publishing company. Publishers depend on authors for profit but they still must review all proposals with business acumen, and make decisions from the reality principle of profit.

Most writers have exaggerated reactions, both positive and negative, to editors. The author presents his best effort to an editor who sits in judgment over his work. The editor and other executives make the final decision on the manuscript's acceptance or rejection and are in total control of the situation. This circumstance puts the author in a vulnerable position awaiting the company's answer. The self-employed, independent, free soul's fate is suddenly removed from his own control and is in the hands of an editor, often a person known only through correspondence.

This situation regularly stimulates a psychological phenomenon called *transference*—an unconscious tendency to relate to another person in terms of past childhood relationships. Transference can occur in any relationship, but it most often erupts when one is dependent upon another, just like in childhood when parents are in absolute control of their offspring's well being and security. Most people transpose their parents' attributes onto authority figures but it could be the attributes of whoever was responsible for childcare, i.e., a sibling or grandparent. Transferring the personality traits of one's parents onto current-day authority figures colors and obscures the character of that person. It is like putting a cardboard parental figure (with preordained reactions and feelings) in front of the dominant person (an editor), blocking his or her true self from view. The person who is transferring old feelings is unaware of what he is doing and is convinced that the distortion is accurate. An individual with kind and caring parents would transfer those qualities to the editor, but the person reared by unloving caretakers would attribute unpleasant characteristics.

Negative Transference. "I sent copies of a book proposal on children's fears to seventeen houses," recalls Joann, "and had already collected fourteen rejections. Then the phone rang and the publisher of a prestigious book company said she was very interested in the idea but was unfamiliar with my writing style. I gave her the title of my other published book and we discussed a possible advance if she found my writing acceptable. Her voice was clipped, businesslike, and abrupt, which unsettled me to some degree since I like to chat a little about the writing industry in general and then talk about the practical matters at hand.

"The following week I received a letter offering a compromise advance that I gleefully accepted, feeling honored to have a contract with a company so well thought of in the literary world. I devoted four months to writing a 350-page manuscript, confident that it covered all childhood and adolescent anxieties. I mailed it off and eagerly awaited the editor's response and the balance of the advance. Instead, the edited manuscript returned with a ten-page letter. My book's overall philosophy was honesty about feelings, and she embraced that credo, blasting my 'sloppy and often unintelligible writing, as if the typewriter wrote the work,' expressing disappointment and irritation over the loss of focus and 'lack of sufficient case histories and anecdotes.' She wrote a scathing—to me—critique of each chapter except the two that were 'very good.' I don't recall the compliment as having made any impression on me at the time. I thought that the letter's tone implied that she was uncertain about my abilities to submit an acceptable rewrite. Adding to my chagrin, she had the gall to ask for it in three weeks! The last line, 'looking forward to a magnificent rewrite,' passed by my eyes in a blur, utterly meaningless to me.

"My past experience with editors had been extremely pleasant. They had suggested improvements with sensitive remarks like, 'Perhaps this could be reworded to enhance clarity,' or 'Please take this suggestion for consideration,'—very personable and respectful comments.

"When I read this editor's letter again I felt like a failure and was full of self-pity. I had a foreboding that it would be impossible to gratify this stern, impersonal person: The proposed work seemed too massive to complete. I felt imprisoned, ordered to perform a grueling, punitive job. My daughter said, 'Just take it a page at a time and see what happens.' Children are so sensible!

"Beginning the laborious task, I sensed the publisher's imperious presence in the room, imagining that she was peering scornfully over my shoulder as I toiled over my typewriter. I thought, 'She hates me!' and I fantasized yelling at her, diminishing her self-esteem as she had mine.

"I would have laughed if someone had said that I was transferring the traits of my mother, who was never pleased with my creative or scholastic efforts, onto my editor. After all, didn't I have a letter that proved the editor's malevolence?

"I have since discovered that when a person is transferring parental traits to someone in authority, he relates as if in a trance, ignoring qualities which do not fit with the original parents' qualities. I had never considered the weeks of painstaking work the editor invested in the project or that her professionalism demanded the best possible book for a solid, commercial success.

"I finished the arduous task and, full of doubt, sent off my manuscript, sure of a final rejection. In a week's time I received a letter from my 'slave driver,' commenting very 'favorably' on the revised book and thanking me for my professional approach to her requests. I was flabbergasted! To prove how deeply transference can penetrate a relationship, I misread her sentence, 'The book will now go to the copy-editor for further suggestions, if any,' to read, 'The book will not go to the . . .'

"The book was improved immensely by her many sagacious suggestions and marginal notes. I was relieved that I had avoided making childish, nonproductive retaliations—refusing to cooperate, rewriting hastily, or telling off the 'nasty' lady—all things I dreamed about doing thoughout the revision period.

"Months later, after a psychiatrist-friend explained the power of transference reactions, I had an insight about my feelings toward that 'mean and cruel' editor. I reviewed her original letter and saw how I had read into it my mother's demeaning tone (in accordance with my childhood experiences) and disregarded her good comments. The letter was in fact quite businesslike, even when she expressed personal disapproval. I should have been prepared for this tone, since I had been made uneasy by her bluntness when we first spoke on the phone.

"The publisher had a perfect right to demand an unflawed manuscript. Her company was spending a large amount of money on the advance, production, and promotion.

"Our further communications were equally businesslike. I accepted her wish to relate professionally, and my writing skills improved remarkably from the experience. It was a big surprise to me to see how reality could be distorted because of transference."

Positive Transference. Arthur, the aspiring screenplay writer, has published poetry in many journals. "I was careful to submit my works to magazines with female editors, convinced they would appreciate my genius, much like my mother who bragged that Shakespeare would have had terrible competition if her son had lived in 'The Bard's' century. Being accustomed to the flattery, I believed her overblown evaluation.

"When a poem was accepted I would jot a too-personal note, share my innermost feelings, and hint at future romantic assignations. I assumed many female poet/editors are lonely (matching my mother's social isolation) and I played on this, secretly hoping the growth of intimacies would ensure further acceptances.

"One editor, Gale, returned my flowery note with a message that he was disinterested in homosexual liaisons. Mortification crept over me when he denounced me as a con man seducing lady poets to gain advantage. His last remark was 'Grow up. Serious poets will be published without promises of love.' I transferred onto him a jealous father, envious of my power over women. Actually, he was a dedicated editor tired of punks who tried to get published by devious means, and his admonitions did force me to look at my strange behavior.

"I already knew that my unconscious tape contained my mother's unrealistic opinion of the quality of my writing. It made sense that I projected those qualities on mother figures— women in control by virtue of their editorial positions. I was manipulating favors, just as I did with my mother. She was a sucker for any request, because I was her prince, and I assumed that all older women would find me equally delightful.

"My lesson learned, I now approach editors as people, not as fairytale mothers masked by transference. I battle my unconscious expectation that all women will instantly love me without doing anything to earn their respect maturely. The silly thing is that I am a good poet and didn't need to play games."

Discovering one's own transference behavior is always a shock, because people think their actions toward others are based on reality without recognizing the ongoing unconscious need to set up and repeat past emotional experiences.

A popular novelist commented, "Sometimes editors can become enmeshed in their own transference reactions, also. I switched book companies because I wanted to write two novels a year and my original publisher disagreed, fearing overexposure would hurt sales.

"My new editor was a fan and wrote a glowing note about his pleasure in working with me. The first manuscript I submitted was quickly returned with only four minor corrections. I was only momentarily flattered. My practicality swiftly took over. My old editor had been strict, found holes in my stories, pointed out weaknesses in character separation, and persistently called on me to stretch my talents. I wrote an inquiry, asking the new fellow if he was sure about the plot accuracy, characters, and tone. He replied, 'It's the best story by far.'

"Now, I enjoy a hero status with readers, and I understand that I am a fantasy figure to them, but I couldn't function with an editor who idolized me to the extent that his judgment was blinded. I requested a more experienced editor and was put in the hands of a hard-driving, super-critical, thirty-year veteran who made many acute suggestions. The young editor suffered from a worship transference that was of no benefit to my product. I teach a writing seminar and always tell students to suspect editors who cannot improve a manuscript. That's their job."

Catching Yourself. Both positive and negative transferences alter the emotional reactions in relationships that should be strictly professional. You may suspect that an unconscious transference has occurred when you experience intense feelings for an editor whom you really do not know, or assume the editor to be overly critical, incredibly sophisticated, cruel, kind, loving, or any other quality that you only learn about through experience.

List personality qualities which you automatically assume editors/readers/publishers exhibit, and compare them to your childhood authority figures. The editor is probably a recipient of your projections if most of these attributes overlap. This imbues the relationships with distortions, leading to disagreements, disappointments, and unpleasant surprises. When you, the artist, present material to a potential editor or buyer, your dealings should be done in a businesslike and realistic manner, unaffected by emotional baggage.

The Surprise of Transference. "I wrote a monthly column for an outdoor magazine," reports Lee, a sportswriter. "The editor seemed to be sharp and intelligent, an opinion I formed over two years of correspondence. He rarely commented on my work, but I assumed he approved since I was paid regularly. I viewed him as a casual, level-headed outdoorsman who would edit my efforts benignly and be 'my boss' forever. These are qualities of my father's personality. I later learned that even the belief in a permanent arrangement relates to childhood notions that protective, loving parents will always be there.

"On a New York business trip I impulsively visited the magazine's office. My hazy picture of an outdoor magazine office was that of easy-going employees working behind big desks, seated at leather chairs with a few trophy fish decorating the walls. I walked into pandemonium. The office was sparsely furnished with aluminum desks and chairs, outdated issues were stacked haphazardly, phones jangled and the staff moved around as if strangely agitated.

"I had arrived just before deadline. A frazzled secretary led me into the editor's office. He was yelling hysterically into the phone, and when he slammed it down, he muttered obscenities. He knocked over a coffee cup on his littered desk and absentmindedly mopped it up while tersely greeting me. Every time the phone interrupted our brief conversation he replied discourteously, and it became obvious he wished I would vanish. Making a hasty exit, I was sorry to have ventured into his insane realm. I'm sure other magazine's headquarters are different and perhaps I did intrude, but I still felt an enormous disillusionment.

"Writing my next column, I was inundated with visions of the editor's uncontrolled behavior. Disappointment disturbed my concentration and the enthusiasm I had experienced before was dampened. I felt strangely betrayed, fearful that the wrathful editor would eventually turn on me. I had a writing block for the first time in my five-year career. It was deeply upsetting because, as a full-time writer, I had no time to waste with neurotic reactions.

"I made an appointment with a therapist who specializes in creativity problems. She explained psychological transference, pointing out the shock of meeting the 'real' editor, who was the opposite of my father figure. The wide discrepancies in these characters were a severe blow that threatened my security. My therapist suggested viewing the editor as a business associate— neither kindly nor bombastic. 'Your professional relationship would not have altered without the meeting. Mentally, go back, checking how you built his serene character and you will discover the beginnings of your transference. Ask why you need an approving fantasy parent with your established career. Shouldn't success be sufficient validation?'

"She was correct. As I investigated my build-up of 'the boss,' I realized how much I missed my dead father's approval, which fed into the construction of a substitute. I accepted reality—no one will ever take my dad's place, regardless of my wishes for paternal praise and appreciation. I began writing my columns to please readers, not the editor 'endowed' with my father's characteristics. My writing block went away as soon as I was able to accept transference as an impediment to business dealings."

Transference interferes with realistic dealings between artists and editors, whichever disguise it wears. An honest examination of your reactions to those in control of accepting your articles can help dispense with transference and keep your relationships on a business level.

Chapter Ten

The Special Problems of Success

WRITERS LEARN to live with regular rejection. These periodic disappointments are made somewhat more tolerable by our realistic expectation of some rejections along the way to our goals of being published. Most of us do not foresee or expect the disappointments or complications that might arise from success.

Degrees of Achievement

Jamie, a successful poet, relates, "There are degrees of achievement. I don't think any serious freelancer can ever say, 'Well, I've made it!' There's always something more to create.

"I have been published regularly for many years now, but I still get excited when a poem is taken. Each success, whatever kind of writing you do, is just another plateau. Authors should continually seek personal growth, using new experiences as grist for our creative mills. You can become indolent if you neglect your curiosity or think you have written the ultimate message.

"My contacts with other writers have shown me that poets have the easiest time accepting success. Most of us find writing poetry a simple matter without magic, and feel normal pleasure when editors choose our work. I think it also relates to the prosodist's low-man-on-the-totem-pole status. When did you last see a poet on a talk show or a collection of verse become a bestseller? Few people enjoy reading verse. We rarely receive payment, and a scant number of poetry books see publication. A tiny family of dedicated editors encourages and respects poets' special visionary gifts. I enjoy my success because it's so keenly personal—a private joy shared with a small but appreciative audience."

Preparing for Success

In order to prepare for success, consider your fantasies about how it would alter your life. (Everyone has dreams!) What would you do if you received large sums of money? Do you believe that monetary gain would bring automatic happiness? Could you handle the emotional stress of becoming a celebrity? How does a successful author handle new friendships, lifestyle and romance? Do you think other people will be thrilled by your fame?

These questions should be answered and examined carefully. Even if you never receive acclaim, you will add to your understanding of yourself.

We are taught that wealth brings contentment and inner security, eliminating many of our daily frustrations. This myth is better overcome before you deal with the possibility of increased income.

Money can purchase things that contribute to a sense of well-being, such as good food, a comfortable home, and superior medical treatment. With more funds, perhaps you can buy a better typewriter and afford a quiet writing sanctuary, but the main benefit of sufficient funds is having the time and freedom to be even more creative.

Money does not satisfy one's innate inner needs for love, affection, friendship, security, and self-esteem. Financial success neither removes problems in relationships nor eases personal neurotic conflicts.

The Social Scene. "I was one of the very few authors with a bestselling novel," relates a well-known writer. "I was young and foolish, allowing myself to be caught up in a whirl of parties, autograph sessions, lectures and talk show appearances. It was a dream world—people offering instant friendships because of my rank as a celebrity. I overate and drank too much at too many lunches and cocktail parties. A year flew by and I didn't write a word. I was just basking in the limelight. Looking back, I understand the temptation to frolic was too seductive for someone so young.

"One morning, lonely and hung over, I realized no one would propel me to work except myself. I announced to the media, hostesses, and publicity people that I was leaving town to research a new book. I lived with an aunt in Canada for a month and worked on her dairy farm. I used the month to become myself again and think about my goals. I really didn't want the world of glitter and glamour. I wanted to write better novels and not be just another one-time novelist.

"Working on my behalf was the old maxim: Out-of-sight, out-of-mind. By the time I moved back to the city, I was just another person. I spent the next six months working on two novels without interruption. When my next book was published, I was extremely cautious about accepting social invitations and making appearances. I couldn't afford to ruin my creative energies again.

"The friends I have today are the same people I know and loved before all the hoopla began. My advice to authors who become famous is to consider carefully the consequences of socializing too much, as it surely interferes with productivity. Besides, a lot of noncreative people just want to know you so that they can drop your name. This really doesn't stretch your talents or give you the comforts of true friends."

Sudden Wealth. Thomas, a screenplay writer, comments, "In the movie industry, a writer can suddenly make a great deal of money. It's a heady feeling to be poor one day and be holding a big check the next. I had seen friends toss away their hard-earned money and then be broke for another year, so I prepared myself to deal with it.

"I refused to move to Los Angeles because I can't cope with urban insanity, the smog and the hassles which are part of city life. Even though people told me I would never make the grade unless I lived in L.A., I thought there had to be a better way. I found a receptive agent who thought my screenplays were well written. He showed them to a producer who agreed and asked to read additional concepts. I wrote ten original film ideas and presented them to the producer in Los Angeles. He liked two, and eventually I was paid handsomely for a screenplay that I wrote in a small Alabama town, conducting business by phone and a couple of trips to the city.

"My lifestyle didn't alter with an increase in funds. I ate better and felt secure that I had enough money to survive for four years—freedom to write. I had sense enough to avoid bragging to my friends and relatives about my financial gain—too many times people become jealous or demand loans. I made conservative investments and thought myself fortunate to be paid so well for doing something that is so much fun.

"Nobody wants to meet screenplay writers and I was never bothered with problems associated with fame, but I saw first-hand how rude and uncaring people can be around a famous person. I was involved in the production aspect of my screenplay, luckily shot in a small Western town instead of a city. Whenever I was eating lunch with the star, people came up to touch him and mumble stupid things. He was an exceptionally polite man and always responded, but he hated being touched by strangers. Who wants people pulling at your sleeve when you're trying to eat?"

Fan Mail. "After many rejections I finally began selling articles," remembers Jeffrey. "I was surprised when the magazines began forwarding long, rambling letters from readers, describing their complex problems and asking for solutions. It takes an hour to read a ten-page explanation of someone's life and I certainly didn't feel qualified to give advice. People must believe that if you can write a well-researched article, you are endowed with Godlike powers to solve their life-long problems. It was a side of success I had never thought about. I asked editors to stop forwarding fan mail. I didn't have the time to aid readers, because I am a part-time freelancer with an already overcrowded schedule."

You may receive fan mail and be complimented, but caution is imperative when responding to strangers. Many writers receive mail from prisoners, seeking correspondence or advice. A writer must weigh the possible results from a relationship with convicts. Some are sincere, but others are looking for future contacts for financial aid for themselves or friends soon to be released. Are you willing to follow through, adding complications to the lives of yourself, mate, and children?

You may also receive heart-wrenching letters from lonely people who write pathetic pleas for advice, friendship, or money. If you allow yourself to be drawn into this type of correspondence, you may find yourself overly involved and distracted from writing.

An overly flowery letter from an admirer can sometimes lead to bizarre consequences, as related by Jason, the columnist. "I received a rather gushy note from a lady in Florida. I responded, thanking her for her praise and writing on my personal stationery instead of using the newspaper's address of the syndicate that handled my column. Within a month she had written about twenty letters recounting intimate details of her life, loneliness, and search for a man 'just like you.' I wrote back explaining I had little time for lengthy letters but again thanking her for her comments.

"Some people refuse to accept reality—my brief notes were taken as romantic interest, and much to my shock and my wife's displeasure, the lady arrived in town, insisting on a meeting. Her voice was enticing and, truthfully, I was frightened by her strange behavior—a neurotic response on my part since I am in control of my life (I think). She suggested we meet at her motel. I quickly said I was very busy and hung up. I avoided her insistent calls, and my wife finally explained I was called out of town. (I am a coward.) She returned to Florida, thank heavens, but continued the barrage by mail. I returned the letters marked 'refused' and she finally gave up on me.

"I was foolish and acted unwisely, enjoying the attention at first. I should have paid attention to the obvious signals in her first fan letter—too personal, too suggestive, and too flattering. I promised myself not to get sucked in again by charming blarney."

Common sense can be applied when responding to fan mail. Experienced authors usually prefer writing a short thank-you note when a reader writes a complimentary letter. If you are disinterested in further contact, write without giving a return address. Our experience, even as psychological professionals, is to desist from offering advice and to suggest that readers consult a therapist in their community.

Reading Unsolicited Material. Several famous authors have confided that they cannot read the numerous novels, screenplays, or ideas aspiring young authors send to them. Some have been sued by malcontented, unpublished authors, accusing them of plagiarism when they may have invented a character or plot similiar to the aspiring author's story. The consensus is that, as much as established writers would like to extend friendly advice or help place material, they cannot take the chance of being tied up in litigation.

Gene, the gag writer, refuses to read others' material for the same reason, stating, "There are only so many ways to tell a joke and only so much topical material so gag writers are bound to overlap on ideas and content. I have a printed card explaining this and why the material is being returned unread. Writers must be careful when answering strangers, even though they may feel connected by mutual dedication to writing. You don't have to be paranoid, just use mature consideration."

Performance Fears. Margaret, a children's story writer, experienced a psychological undoing after the sale and publication of her first book. "I was deliriously happy to hold my precious book, and I kept looking at my name on the cover and my words actually bound and printed. All my dreams had come true after years of literary rebuff. Here was the product of my own creativity! My husband gave a big party and everyone congratulated me and brought copies for me to autograph. I felt like a star. One of the guests asked me what I was currently working on and I went blank, unable to recall any of the four stories I was outlining.

"The next morning when I sat down to write, I felt unpleasantly anxious and couldn't apply myself to the story line. I rationalized the trouble as overexcitement about my first book and stopped working for the day, but I kept making further excuses as the days went by until my husband said he thought I was reacting negatively to my success. 'You were full of vitality and determination during all those years of rejections. You learned to live and work under the umbrella of failure. Now you have to adjust to success and get on with your writing.'

"I sat down—with myself—to do some free association on my inability to concentrate. My internal conversation took an interesting turn, leading to an unconscious fear that I would never write anything better than the book that was already published. I was actually convinced that any rough draft had to be as polished as the finished version of my published book. I was thwarting my own efforts with my fear of not being able to perform.

"In order to fool my ridiculous, unconscious prophecy, I pretended that the book was never published and that I was once more a struggling, unheralded freelancer. I just blocked the success from my mind by meditating on myself as a novice writer. In a way this stance was accurate. My past work was finished and should never have been compared to fresh ideas and new material. Every new venture must stand alone. I started writing again, full of unique approaches."

Margaret's psychological undoing was brief, her recovery assisted by her spouse's interpretation and her own ability to delve into her unconscious motivations and quickly resolve the writing block that was her reaction to success.

Writers can encounter complex problems when coping with success and their own strange reactions. We are wise to constantly keep alert to our inner psychological world.

Hidden Fears. Jordon, an article writer who had written his first book, commented, "My difficulty was that I couldn't believe that readers actually respected what I said because of a mildly successful nonfiction book. Because I had such a difficult time writing it and I have the hangup of being a perfectionist, I'm never really satisfied with my writing, even when other people compliment me. I knew there were glaring faults in the style, and so I took absolutely no pleasure from the compliments and congratulations I received. I even developed an aversion to talking about the book, disappointing my publisher because I wouldn't give interviews or appear on several interested talk shows. I couldn't imagine that anyone would care to listen to me.

"The editor, who was very business-oriented, first became angry and accused me of reneging on my contract agreement for cooperation with publicity. He said I was failing to promote book sales by not granting personal appearances, which would create enthusiasm and impulse buying. He even admitted that one of the reasons I had been chosen to write the book was my good looks, amicability and speaking talents. His arguments only increased my timidity. The editor was so frustrated that he made an appointment with a therapist for me and offered to reimburse me out of his own pocket to insure I would keep it. The doctor was a well-known author, a regular television performer, and a lecturer on the college circuit.

"The first thing I learned was that by the time a book is

published most authors are totally bored with their creation's content. After all, we've read the damn thing countless times— in my case the first draft, three scrupulous rewrites, and a re-reading of preceding chapters before beginning a new one in order to maintain a consistent tone and style. Before typing the manuscript I read it again to check spelling and grammar and to improve wording with a thesaurus. Next, I clarified and tightened the text some more when typing the final version. Then the manuscript was returned by the editor with comments and suggestions and each page had to be re-examined so that any new paragraphs would flow smoothly into the existing text. After that job was completed, the copyeditor went over the book, and his comments required another perusal. Finally the galleys had to be carefully read to correct any misspellings or left-out words. I also prepared my index and bibliography—yet another pass through the text! Altogether I read the manuscript twelve times before the finished product arrived. The book sat on my desk for a week before I could stomach reading it again, and then I found the contents tedious and redundant and the style dull.

"I felt more than a little stupid when the therapist pointed out the obvious—the book is fresh and interesting to readers, since they haven't reviewed it a dozen times. He said, 'You're just seeing the flaws and projecting your own critical attitude onto your readers.' This information jolted me out of my recalcitrance, but I also had to overcome a deeper psychological problem before I was able to expose myself to the public as an expert.

"Many people erroneously believe that physically attractive folks have built-in self-esteem and confidence. It's just not true. My perception of myself was that I was still a chubby, clumsy little boy. I had an unconscious fear that if I gave interviews, I would be jeered at and teased just as the neighborhood kids had tortured me when I was fat.

"When I worked through my distorted view of myself and my irrational fears, I was able to get out and hustle my writing. I even learned to enjoy talking about the book, much to the amusement and happiness of my editor. The therapy was so beneficial that I declined the editor's generosity and paid my own bills. It was worth the money, because now I can handle the publicity work which comes with successful writing."

Expecting Reactions. Everyone reacts to change. If you expect a psychological response to success, you will be able to immediately recognize the symptoms for what they are and work on them without undue alarm. Subscribing to Jamie's attitude, that each success is just another step on the ladder of creativity instead of a goal, can help keep you level-headed and working.

In this vein, if you expect others' reactions to your success to be negative at times you can save yourself from confusion and surprise. Many people are childish, feeling envious when friends or acquaintances have the opportunity to be published. They may feign boredom when you share your good news, criticize your material harshly, or become derisive about the publisher. Understanding that these attitudes may spring from the murky pool of jealousy will help prevent you from feeling hurt or overly sensitive.

Mature friends will delight in your triumphs and be happy to celebrate your good fortune. Avoid obviously jealous people and share the happiness of your success with those who genuinely love you.

Celebrations

A sale is cause for celebration, an expression of the elation that floods the heart when rewards come in such a tangible way. Even if the payment will be used for living expenses, a portion should be spent on rejoicing.

When we edited a poetry journal, we were fortunate to have enough subscription revenue to enable us to send poets whose work we printed a few dollars. We received many effusive letters detailing expenditures of our small honoraria—a bottle of wine or a special, commemorative trinket.

"Whenever I receive checks for a short story," divulges Marilyn, "I take the family to dinner at a nice restaurant. We toast the editor's perceptiveness and get a big kick out of spending money earned from my gift with words."

Bill, the psychologist, remarks, "My wife and I have a ritual celebration since I began selling articles on a regular basis. We have lunch at our favorite restaurant. Coming from a poor family, eating out still feels like a great luxury. We don't gorge, but savor simple fare like salads and omelets, enjoying being together and being treated with good service. It may be a small thing to some people, but it's a big deal to me. Every time I pay the bill, I think about the writing that provides our meal."

Hopefully, you will participate in many celebrations over the sales and publications of your freelancing efforts. Very few people receive money earned through their imagination. You are one of the fortunate ones and should be as inventive in your celebrations as you are thinking up new ideas.

Chapter Eleven

The Psychology of Media Promotion

WHEN YOU BECOME a published writer there is always the possibility of media appearances. Television and radio usually look for nonfiction authors, because they can pass on information about their subject without giving away the story as a novelist would be tempted to do. Occasionally a novelist will be invited for an interview, usually to talk about how he or she became a writer rather than the book's plot. Sometimes a controversial article will spark excitement and more rarely, a screenplay writer whose script receives awards will be asked to appear on television or radio. No one seems too interested in lyricists, short story writers, or poets.

Public speaking does not have to be fraught with tension and nervousness. Being interviewed can actually be fun. It is an opportunity to share your knowledge with others, and meet many other creative people. But you must learn to develop an easy, relaxed presentation of yourself and your material. It's not as difficult as you may imagine. The majority of media people are thoughtful and kind to authors. And because they follow a set pattern in their questioning, you can make reasonable preparations.

A Common Rationalization

Many writers rationalize their fear of public speaking by ducking behind the old saw that authors express themselves via the written word better than they do with spoken language. This belief is comforting because presenting your ideas on paper is safer than talking about them with a stranger. Freelancers can rework, rearrange and hunt for the exact word when preparing a manuscript, with no one sitting across the table critically checking sentence construction or grammar. By the time material sees print, it has been scrutinized and honed by editors. Public speaking, however, whether in a lecture hall, a television studio, or in a radio broadcast booth, is immediate and irreversible—you can't stop the show to improve your presentation.

It is more difficult to speak about ideas in person than on paper, but the problem can be surmounted by learning a few simple skills before you are called upon for promotional appearances. When you gain confidence in your abilities to speak fluently and with enthusiasm fear can be dispensed with.

Know Your Audience

"I wrote for the extremely specialized dental audience," recounts Anthony. "My father had been a dentist, which gave me an insider's understanding of dentistry's special problems. It's the only profession whose practitioners are universally disliked by their clients because their work inflicts pain. Dentists work surrounded by daily patient anxiety and suffer stress from the invisible bombardment of fear vibrations.

"Using my family experiences plus psychological research on fear, I published a series of interesting, helpful articles for dental magazines—'How to Relax Your Patients,' 'Why People Fear Dentists,' 'Regression and Anxiety in the Dental Chair.' The articles were so popular that a state dental society invited me to give a sixty-minute presentation at their monthly meeting, for a handsome fee. Sixty minutes seemed really lengthy. I can't listen to anyone for more than fifteen minutes!

"I wrote a humorous, anecdotal speech, leaving room at the end for questions and answers. I put the salient points on 3 by 5 cards, because reading a prepared text takes away the spontaneous sound. Then I rehearsed and rehearsed some more in front of my uncomplaining wife, who judged me 'just fine.'

"The evening meeting began with an hour-long cocktail party. The doctors were hearty drinkers, obviously trying to relax after a hard day. When the multi-course dinner was served, along with accompanying wines, the members were in a bois-terous, garrulous mood. However, the heavy meal and rich dessert had a sedative effect, and when the official business had been concluded and I was introduced, some members of the audience were snoozing and the remainder looking glassy-eyed and lethargic—not an alert crowd!

"My delivery was bright and enthusiastic but the audience was tired, slightly inebriated and stuffed with food. Fifteen minutes into the talk I realized the sleepy dentists were ready to go home. I concluded with a statistic concerning the ex-tremely high suicide rate in dentistry and asked the audience for questions. Several younger men asked to have a few points about patient anxiety clarified, and then silence descended like a fog, interrupted with occasional snores. Everyone was re-lieved when the presiding officer adjourned the meeting—not one person complained that the hour speech had been short-ened to twenty minutes. I was given a generous check as the as-semblage shuffled out, and I left feeling foolish.

"I learned to accept only speaking engagements which run ten or twelve minutes. I also inquire if the audience will be drinking and eating before I begin and decline if this is the case.

"Know the conditions before accepting a speaking engage-ment."

Jed, the retired doctor, novelist, and essayist, reports, "I was invited to join a panel speaking to college students on 'The Mo-rality of Marijuana.' I had written an article that described how the daily smoking of marijuana dampens self-motivation and interferes with ambition.

"I assumed the audience would be hostile because I'm 'an-cient'—as my teenage grandchildren label me—and a member of the medical profession, which many young people suspect. I considered backing out from what I expected would be an in-tense barrage and then decided that would be cowardly. A dis-agreement in values should be a challenge and nothing to fear.

"The other panelists were an anthropologist, an ecology ma-jor, and a student who was a religious cult leader. We were giv-en three minutes to state our opinions, and then the audience was invited to enter a dialogue. The ecology major was ada-mantly opposed to ingesting any drug, considering them all physical pollutants. The cult leader demanded that his follow-ers abstain from alcohol, tobacco, sex, hallucinogens, singing, and any self-indulgences which 'distracted from spirituality.'

"I explained the medical aspects of marijuana as a mind-altering narcotic, noting that although research was incomplete, there was evidence of short- and long-term negative effects, just as there is with any drug taken over a long period of time. I did not negate or deny the pleasurable 'rush' which people receive from drugs, but suggested that the same 'high' could be attained through meditation. I concluded that everyone must make personal decisions about their one and only body. They could misuse drugs just as others consume excess food or drink or learn the art of moderation. If they used drugs as a crutch against emotional pain, frustration, or to avoid taking responsibility for their lives, they were immature.

"The anthropologist gave a brief talk about the historical uses of marijuana in different cultures and was of the opinion that drugs, used in moderation to celebrate life, were beneficial to mankind. No one discussed the illegality of marijuana because the public smokes it regardless of its legal status.

"The evening was stimulating and lovely. I spoke truthfully and had little difficulty defending my ideas. One student attacked my 'throwing the problem back on them,' and I responded that they should consider themselves adults instead of demanding strict rules from government or parents. They ignored the anthropologist and concentrated on their rigid pair of peers who denounced drugs without adequate information.

"We didn't change the world that night, but the exposure to a youthful, bright, inquiring audience was healthy for me and gave me several ideas for novels dealing with how this generation will handle the problems awaiting them in adulthood and the situation of a college student who cannot deal with homesickness and joins a charismatic student who begins a sect in order to have power over dependent types."

Overcoming Obstacles

Along with understanding who your audience is there are many preparations to take to be equipped to handle a book promotion tour or occasional interviews.

Overcoming the Fear of Public Speaking

Fear of public speaking is often disguised as shyness; but a bashful attitude can be a fear of saying the wrong thing and being judged inferior or stupid. Such timidity is excess baggage when you understand your topic. When you are well informed, you will say the correct words automatically. Most interviewers do not intend to trick you into appearing ridiculous; their job is to provide an entertaining, informative or helpful discussion for their particular audiences.

Practice Speaking Skills

You can learn to speak with enthusiasm. Take a speech class if you think your voice and presentation are monotonous. Talk in front of a mirror to develop pleasing facial expressions. Nothing turns off a viewing audience more than an overly serious demeanor. People like to see you smile at appropriate times, particularly—but not only—when you are introduced and say goodbye.

Speak into a tape recorder to learn the art of talking without phrases like "you know," "uh," "um," "well now." Learn to talk without wetting your lips or nervous gestures such as hair smoothing, beard patting, peering at nails, or blinking your eyes excessively. These skills can be acquired with patient practice.

Be prepared to explain the content of your book in one sentence. If the umbrella explanation describes the content adequately you will have a handy, condensed explanation to fall back on. ("Well, sir, just what is the book all about?" Gulp. "Well, you, um, ur, I guess it covers all the aspects of sailing." The author should be ready to give a thumbnail description— "The joys of sailing and the responsibilities and upkeep of all kinds of sailing vessels.")

Answer questions from family and friends about your subject. Make up controversial queries which you might expect from interviewers. Talking about the material in the comfort of your home, either with a recording device or understanding companions, reduces the fear of blurting out the wrong statement. Read your book (again!) and make up a card containing the major points.

The more you talk with others about your book, the easier it will become.

Speaking on television or radio is much less difficult than lecturing, because it does not involve voice projection. Technicians take a sound level reading of your voice and clip a tiny microphone on you so that you need use only normal conversational tones.

A solid foundation for speaking with ease can be built by giving talks to local organizations where you feel comfortable. Local programs, clubs, or radio and television shows are slower paced than the big-time productions in Los Angeles, New York, Chicago, or Cleveland. When the time arrives to promote a book on national television, confidence in your subject matter and yourself will be strong enough to override your nervousness. The best psychological stance to take is that book promotion is an enjoyable adventure and that you are building your credentials as an experienced book promoter. Publishers are quite impressed when you inform them of your promotional experience.

"I talked to many different groups during the research and writing of a book about single parenting," reports Peter. "I spoke to 'Parents Without Partners,' a group of divorced, widowed, and never-married parents who lend each other emotional support, discuss problems of rearing children alone, invite experts to share solutions, and socialize with their families. I attended many high school Family Living classes to get input from teenagers and also spoke at different churches whose members were concerned with single parenting.

"By the time the book was published I had plenty of experience in discussing my subject. I really wanted to promote the book and contacted the publicity department of my publisher to reaffirm my willingness to participate in promotion. They had sent out effective press material to the newspapers and media—an excellent summary of the subject, a biography which detailed my credentials, a photograph so that television producers would know my appearance was conducive for the camera's eye. The publishers also included the dates I would be available—anytime after the publication date. I was satisfied they were working on my behalf."

Not all publishers send out publicity material, because they cannot afford the promotional expenses on every book. A promotional tour can cost a publisher anywhere from $5,000 to $10,000 or more. This includes fees to publicity people in the various cities who contact producers, arrange appointments, and chauffeur the author to various appointments. Also included in these expenses are the author's travel fares, hotel, and food bills. The publisher must carefully consider an author's ability to make a good impression before spending the money. Sometimes publishers request the author to share expenses or wait to see if advance sales warrant the costs of promoting a book.

Presentation

Perhaps you will not be on a programmed tour, but a television show evinces interest in your book and requests your appearance. We will describe what you can expect whether performing for one show or many, because the format for writers is just about the same for local talk shows and major network productions.

Your Role

First, you are considered a performer, selling an expert's image on a particular subject. If you perform with genuine enthusiasm, people will purchase your book, in the same way that excellent singers stimulate sales of records when they appear over media. That's the cut and dried business side of promoting a book in the fiercely competitive publishing field. Performing does not diminish your status as a creative person but adds another accomplishment to your life skills. After you have enjoyed the excitement and fun of performing, you'll learn to look forward to getting in front of the television lights again.

Your male author, Jean, learned he was a performer several year ago. He had a book published on how personal habits and mannerisms reveal one's hidden personality. The publisher arranged a grueling tour—in three days in Los Angeles he was interviewed on thirty radio programs, talked with four newspaper reporters, performed five local television shows, and was on both Dinah Shore's program and *The Tonight Show*.

In the dressing room preceding the taping for *The Tonight Show*, a representative from AFTRA (American Federation of Television and Radio Artists) appeared with union papers for Jean's signature. He hesitated, saying, "But, I'm a doctor, not a performer." The representative politely insisted, explaining that after a specific number of appearances he was considered a performing artist by the industry. The message was plain: The "doctor" would not be a part of the show unless he signed the necessary membership cards. "I had a quick identity crisis," recalls Jean. "A great deal of self-esteem sprung from my 'doctor person' identity, and I felt ashamed to be labeled as a performer. Thinking it through, the AFTRA rep was correct. On the shows I was 'the understanding psychiatrist' selling a book. To the union I was just another participant on the show. I signed and no longer even think about my role as a performer, except to do the best possible job of entertaining the audience—getting across psychological advice as clearly and warmly as I can without talking down to the viewers or listeners."

Procedures

You may receive a call from a publicist working for your publisher or a call from your editor informing you that a producer will be placing a telephone call to inquire about your book and possible appearance on a show. Or, you may receive no warning at all and, while thinking about your child's report card, receive an unexpected call from a producer.

In order to react professionally, it is helpful to keep a card by the phone with a list of interesting points about your book. We have several books, and even though some are out of print, occasionally a producer will telephone to discuss the contents. Keep a card available for all books or controversial articles you have published.

The telephone call is frequently a crucial and decisive factor as to whether or not you will actually be invited on the show. As casual as the caller appears, he or she is conducting a pre-interview with two goals in mind: number one—do you speak articulately and enthusiastically about your subject, including illustrative anecdotes; and are you adept enough to quickly (and confidently, warmly and sincerely) answer questions and number two—can you explain why your book is different and interesting enough to appeal to a large viewing audience, or will they turn the dial when you come on?

Experienced authors assume the producer or assistant producer conducting the pre-interview will not have read the book. Producers do not have time to read all the books whose titles appeal to the show's researchers and depend on the author to explain its uniqueness. Authors must therefore present the book's concept with clarity and freshness.

If you pass the pre-interview test, another production staff member will call to decide on the appearance date and perhaps ask specific questions about the book. They may want to discuss only one aspect of your book—which is their prerogative. Seasoned authors accept the time restrictions of television shows and agree to whatever the producer requests.

This is the time to ask if the show will pay for travel and lodging expenses. (It's business, so don't be diffident.) If they do not include expenses, the author must get in touch with the publisher to request reimbursement for expenses before giving assent to appear on the show. Publishers can deduct those costs as business expenses, and many shows have a budget that includes provision for writers' travel and hotel accommodations. Very few writers can afford to pay airline fares and hotel bills, even though the trip is in their best interest.

If the television show has a limited budget or the publisher declines to cover expenses, the author must weigh the pros and cons of paying his own way. The travel expenses are a legitimate business deduction, and television exposure is an ideal method of advertising a book.

After financial arrangements are concluded, authors should query the producer about the number of minutes allotted for their segment. Whether you have three or fifteen minutes, prepare your remarks to fit the time frame. Accept their time allotments in a spirit of cooperation. Many other writers would love to take your place, and the hectic pace of producing a television show leaves little room for coddling unaccommodating or "difficult" writers.

Find out the hotel's name and address, the name, address and phone number of the show's producer or assistant, your expected arrival time at the studio, and advise your contact that you will confirm your arrival when reaching town. This professional consideration saves producers from worrying. Some people get so excited that they forget to make these simple plans and get lost, have no one's number to call on a Sunday night, and end up a wreck!

Watch the show beforehand if you have the opportunity. You will pick up the program's general tone, how the host conducts interviews, and whether or not there is a live audience. By reviewing the show, you'll feel like you've been there before when you walk onto the set. You will be more natural on the set if you are familiar with the furniture, the host's demeanor, and the overall atmosphere—some shows are lighthearted while others are serious.

Traveling and Clothing

Writers (thankfully) are not expected to be fashionable, so don't worry about wearing the latest style, but do take an outfit in which you feel comfortable. If you are a casual dresser, don't go out and buy a suit. Clothes should fit well and be clean. Be sure the colors match. The producer doesn't care about your clothes, but only about how well you can perform. White is the only color to be avoided because the technicians have difficulty adjusting the television lights to its brightness. Most of the shots will be of your face and upper torso, but pay attention (for men) that your socks cover your calves and (for women) that your hose are not baggy. Avoid heavy necklaces which clunk against attached microphones or jangling bracelets that rattle every time you move.

Carry-on luggage ensures that you will reach your destination with all your belongings and escape what might be a long wait for baggage at the air terminal. You want to reach the studio as relaxed as possible, so dress comfortably on your trip. Don't rush about the town sightseeing or trying out exotic, new foods.

Getting Ready

If you feel nervous about the impending show, meditate in your hotel room. Concentrate on a mental image of yourself handling the situation with grace and good humor. Take a soothing bath, wash and fix your hair, and dress comfortably. We always carry television appearance clothes to the studio to put on a few minutes before our segment. At a taped show you may have an hour's delay before your turn. It is more relaxing to wear jeans while you wait than to worry if your outfit will be wrinkled and sweaty by the time you are called to perform. The backstage staff is usually dressed informally and will not be surprised by your attire.

Take a copy of your book as insurance against a forgetful publisher or the book's becoming misplaced on a busy set. Don't ask if they have a copy of your book (a sure sign of an amateur). If the book is missing, a harried assistant will find you and use your copy.

If you are driven to the studio by a publicity person, let him do his job—reporting your name and the show to the studio gate guard, parking, finding the correct studio, and introducing you to the show's staff. If you are alone, the employees at studios are usually kind, considerate, and helpful. They want you to feel welcome so you will perform and entertain their audience. They're on your side. Arrive on time.

You will be appointed a dressing room with your name printed on a card on the door. It makes you feel wonderful! Sometimes a show's budget allows the inclusion of iced champagne in your dressing room—best left to enjoy after the show, even though it is tempting to have a celebrational drink beforehand.

Makeup

Next, someone will usher you to the make-up room. Make-up artists do wonders with facial flaws, so don't worry if you think your nose is too long or your wrinkles might show. These master craftsmen look upon your face as a canvas and paint you with the harsh television lights in mind. They enjoy chatting with their clients and will concentrate on making you look your best, giving you as much attention as any well-known celebrity.

Waiting To Perform

Depending on your personality—extrovert or introvert—you can join the other performers, publicity people, agents, and production staff in the Green Room or wait in your dressing room for your call. All television shows call the waiting area the Green Room. It is a comfortably furnished "holding area" for the entertainers before they appear. It has a closed circuit television for people to watch the show. The studio supplies food and drink and the atmosphere is usually friendly, people making comments about the show. Speak to everyone and don't hesitate to compliment a famous person—they always respond with delight when praised. Everyone you come in contact with is creative, whether on the crew, production staff, or other performers. They consider you a part of their creative family and enjoy exchanging stories. Refrain from munching too heartily on the snacks. You want to feel light and alert for the show. If you feel the atmosphere is too exciting and makes you nervous, retire to your dressing room and spend the time meditating or relaxing with deep breathing.

Assume the host or hostess will not have read your book, but will have questions prepared by the assistant producer. It is not an insult, just symptomatic of the fast-paced life of television talk show hosts. It is a pleasant surprise when an interviewer has actually read your work and asks personal questions related to the text.

Just before your appearance, someone will collect you and lead you onto the set. If it's a walk on—if you are introduced and come from behind the scene—you will be told where to stand and when to move. If you will be introduced in a sitting position, you will be led to a chair and a microphone will be clipped to your clothes. Now is the time to clear your throat and adjust your clothing. The technicians appreciate it if you acknowledge them, thanking the sound man for the mike, smiling at the cameraperson and other production assistants. Relating to these other creative people puts you more at ease.

When walking on the set, watch out for the ever-present cables. You don't want to stumble and fall into view for your first impression. Most importantly, don't touch anything that looks mechanical.

The Actual Show

After years of performing on television, our best advice to authors is for them to relate to the interviewer and forget about the unseen television audience. If there is a live audience, think of them as interested friends, but concentrate on your host or other guests taking part on the show. Forgetting about the camera is amazingly easy to do if you are looking at the person directing questions. Cameras can show you to your best advantage when you act natural and ignore them. (Don't try to catch a glimpse of yourself on the many monitors around the set because it makes you look sneaky. If it is a taped show, you will be informed of the air time and can look at yourself at leisure.) When you are not speaking, assume the camera is recording your actions and refrain from squirming, licking your lips, or looking bored.

Even if publishers nag you to continually say, "In my book, *The Road to Happiness . . .*" don't mention the title. It turns the viewers off and they think you only want to sell your book without giving them additional information. Most times when you speak, your name will be flashed on the screen, often with the title of your book. If you are an interesting guest who speaks with authority, people will remember your name and book title.

The segment will seem to flash by as if in seconds; the lights, cameras, audience, and your response to the interviewer merge into a few intense moments. You will perform the best when you act naturally.

Your female author, Veryl, is forever indebted to Jack Linkletter, who was hosting a live hour-long television program entitled, "America Alive!" Jean and I were slated for the entire show, sharing stepparenting experiences with Lucille Ball and her husband Gary Merton; a family with a new stepmother; as well as responding to the audience and Jack's questions and comments. We were introduced to Mr. Linkletter and led to a comfortable couch. Moments before the show began, Jack, an affable, unaffected man, strolled over to me and started teasing me, saying, "Just look at this mannequin, hands quietly folded, legs all arranged, and a proper, dignified posture. Do you actually sit so still when you see your patients? Don't you gesture when speaking? Are you going to hold a professional pose for a whole hour?" He was smiling and patting me while joshing about my stiffness. (I'm not a stuffy person in real life.) Jack started me laughing at myself and when the camera started grinding, I was completely at ease, sitting naturally and looking like I was in my own living room. Although we never saw the performance, friends and relatives reported I had never spoken with such verve and bounce, told more touching funny stories, or let my optimistic personality shine through.

Lucille Ball is quite a famous actress, experienced and full of savvy when it comes to upstaging other performers. Jack's method of relaxing me enabled me to enjoy competing for air time with the seasoned actress—all in good fun, but we didn't travel to New York to sit in silence. We did want to sell some books!

We discovered that when you share a program with several highly verbal, bright people, an author must speak up and sometimes pleasantly interrupt others when there is a valid contribution to be made. (Whoever is speaking will be featured on the screen, since the cameraman and, in this case, the boom microphone technician, follow the voice of the speaker.) Any reticence about performing disappeared after the "America Alive!" show. Even though I had appeared on many previous programs, I learned something extremely valuable about projecting my natural presence.

Another aid to an easygoing, informative interview is to keep in mind that you are not being investigated by the host—he or she wants you to be entertaining. Even the deadly serious Ralph Nader cracks an occasional joke to get across an important point. If you are asked an obtuse question or one which is unrelated to your book, respond with an anecdote or short explanation of something you find relevant. The show moves forward, and no one will stop the show to point out that you changed the subject. If you don't know the answer to a specific point, you can admit it and flow into conjecture. The host will not stop the show and insist on clarity, but will admire your adroit delivery. Don't fret over mispronunciations or a malapropism. No one notices and television's insistent rule is to move on uninterrupted.

We were taping *The John Davidson Show* and discussing teenagers when Jean, in response to a question about gradual adolescent maturity said, "Teenagers levitate [instead of gravitate] toward healthy companions. . . ." Both of us realized the mistake, and perhaps Mr. Davidson did too, but you would never know by our facial expressions that Veryl was thinking, (What?! Levitate?!) and Jean was inwardly wincing, imagining a group of teens slowly lifting into the air. We continued on and received no negative comments about the mistaken usage of the word when the show aired. A confident demeanor, a smile, and a smooth delivery can see you through errors—everyone makes them.

If you blunder into stuttering, have an uncontrolled coughing fit or spill coffee over everyone, the producer will stop the taping and begin again. This happened to us once. The host was upset because the show had been cancelled and this was the last program. He talked too fast and garbled his sentences, rushing us through the segment. He finally threw his cards up in the air and yelled, "I can't think straight. Let's start over!" Everyone took his feelings into consideration and we began again.

You may have an opportunity to appear on a live show in which at-home viewers and the live audience ask questions. Listen attentively and give sound, short answers. Be prepared for strange questions, often miles away from your area of expertise, and don't hesitate to remind the caller that you cannot give professional advice.

We were being interviewed on a live San Francisco talk show on the subject of loneliness. A woman called in and addressed a question to Veryl. Her life was profoundly sad, lonely, and despairing, and Veryl—featured on the screen—burst into tears in empathy for the caller's plight. This isn't very professional, but she had no idea the woman would touch her so deeply. Jean quickly began answering the woman as Veryl composed herself. After the show, the entire staff thanked her for being so human. They had never seen a psychoanalyst cry before and thought it perfectly acceptable, revealing that "experts" are not always objective or unfeeling. Being yourself certainly insures an authentic performance.

When the host or hostess concludes the interview, remain seated and continue chatting with the interviewer or other guests until you are told to stand up. Often, the camera pulls back for a long shot at the end of the program (when authors usually appear), and you don't want to be seen jumping up looking for the exit.

Sometimes the star will ask you to autograph the book—a sure sign you were a successful performer. After thanking the producer, leave the studio quickly, making room for the next performers. Your publicity person should give you an honest evaluation of your performance. Listen closely to the constructive advice. If you made mistakes, forgive yourself and plan to do better the next time.

Post-Show Appraisal

When viewing yourself on the air you will probably be surprised at your facial expressions, mannerisms, and tone of voice. Everyone thinks he could look better, that his voice sounds unfamiliar, or his wording peculiar. You won't remember hearing or responding to some of the questions because of the excitement generated during the actual show. Although it does feel strange to watch yourself on television, concentrate on your appraisal. Did you field and answer questions with confidence? Did you speak directly to the host? Did you sprinkle too many lazy phrases—"um," "you know," "well"—into your conversation? Did you appear to enjoy the experience, or were you nervous? These qualities may be overlooked by the audience, but are important considerations for your own evaluations.

Hopefully, you will appear on television and take pleasure in the broadening, exciting world of video.

Radio

Radio shows are less tense than television promotion work; because you don't have to worry about your visual impact, you can pay more attention to the subject. You are usually alone with an announcer in a broadcast booth, where you can smoke, drink coffee, and relax during commercials. Most radio personalities have loyal followers, and the announcers are keenly in tune with their interests. Let the broadcaster direct the questions. You will be speaking into a microphone, and the announcer will let you know with hand signals if you are leaning too close or drifting too far from the device.

Radio interviews are usually longer than television spots, giving you the opportunity to go into more elaborate subject detail. Try to be concise, and avoid long, rambling sentences that tend to put the audience to sleep.

Hostile questions on a call-in show can be handled politely. Allow room for the caller's right to disagree. Defend your position without abrasiveness, and thank the caller for his or her interest and viewpoint. If the language becomes too strident or shrill, the broadcaster will cut off the call, saving you from an extended, on-the-air argument.

Newspaper Interviews

A newspaper reporter usually comes for an interview equipped with a tape machine or notebook and will record or take notes while you talk. In our experience, most reporters have read the book and ask specific, intelligent questions. They are usually busy with deadlines to meet and appreciate your promptness, preparedness, hospitality (order some coffee from room service if you are in a hotel room on tour), and your ability to discuss issues clearly and surely. Sometimes a photographer will accompany a reporter. They will manage a better picture when you act naturally and don't freeze into a self-conscious pose. These professionals are a part of the creative family and hope for the best story and picture for their reading audience. Think of a newspaper interview as an elaborate book review with a personal touch.

Staying Sane

Traveling around the country on a promotional tour can be exhausting unless common sense precautions are taken to ward off fatigue, both physical and mental.

After several days of talking about your book, you will be bored with the subject. Interviewers, however, will continue to find it interesting, since they are only required to discuss the book a single time. To maintain a fresh attitude, try focusing attention on varied aspects of the book instead of duplicating anecdotes on every show. Many times an interviewer will have a personal interest in a particular chapter, which will give added richness to your discussion.

Few freelancers are able to concentrate on writing new material while traveling but a journal can be kept, recounting the impressions of shows, hosts, regional trends, and stimulating meetings with other guests which keeps you continually observing and writing. It is fun to share the journal's contents with friends when you return home and want to recount your experiences.

There will be stretches of time on any tour when you have leisure hours between shows. This is an excellent chance to relax, put your feet up, read, or watch television. Every city has local programming that reveals the area's interests, problems, and general atmosphere—all of which adds to your general knowledge.

The temptation to overeat while traveling should be curbed. A light diet will keep you mentally alert and in good physical condition to withstand the rigors and stresses of travel. Your exercise and meditation routines are essential to an overall sense of physical and psychological balance.

Treat yourself to frequent telephone calls with your family to feel connected and loved. You will miss home, bed, family, and friends, but most book tours are limited to a week or ten days. You'll soon be enjoying home cooking again.

The attention you receive on tour can color the experience with unreality—it's the opposite of a writer's normal isolated life. Most publicity people and interviewers hold writers in awe, treating them with great respect and often expressing amazement over their ability to write. Little do they know about the lengthy process of rewriting, editing, and evaluation involved before the book is printed.

The pleasure and gratification of media exposure goes far beyond book sales. You learn the survival arts of traveling, meet many unusual characters, and develop additional self-esteem from good performances.

We turned to each other in disbelief after having a delightful meeting with a fellow writer who followed our segment on a morning Los Angeles news program—Margaret Truman, a charming person, bubbling with compliments about our performance and pleased to share a magical moment between authors. Who would have dreamed from our beginnings as children without advantages that we would ever speak so easily to a President's daughter?

The possibilities of new experiences are endless when touring. Be open to conversation with everyone you encounter, from cab drivers to fellow guests, and you will surely become an enriched person and a greater writer.

Chapter Twelve

Expanding Your Frontiers

CREATIVE PEOPLE'S lives are filled with the same mundane daily events that are the fabric of everyone's day-to-day living—physical chores, working, relating to others, trying to pay the bills, and keeping oneself and one's family fed and clothed. We all must cope with the shocks caused by unexpected, traumatic events and continue to grow with the changes of life.

The difference between those born with the creative seed that blossoms into artistry with words and those who find satisfaction in other pursuits is that writers have the gnawing desire and the learned ability to comment and entertain.

A writer who is a houseperson rearing children can turn the often tedious, unending duties of family care into a touching or funny story, play, or novel to which other parents can relate. Inside the story, a character's reaction, a child's unique perception about his complicated life, or an exchange between adults can lighten the reader's spirits, lift a person's sense of isolation, or bring a chuckle up from a weary heart. The writer reveals the essence of an everyday situation and gives the reader a glimpse into another world.

An author who lives through the crisis of divorce, chronic illness, death of a loved one or sudden injury does not react by merely surviving the ordeal, but turns the maturing experience into a manuscript, sharing the emotional pains, and perhaps offering readers advice on expected depressions, guilts, and anger which result from loss. The author enlightens his readers and eases their fears of being thought strange or selfish when normal (so-called socially unacceptable) feelings emerge in the wake of sudden loss or grief.

Cartoonists and comedy writers are beloved by everyone, for they are able to make us laugh at our prejudices and small-minded concerns. Their secret is taking everyday situations and shining light on their absurdities, ultimately making readers more aware of themselves through the vehicle of humor.

The written word, in whatever form you use it, has the power to effect a change in others' viewpoints, add to their knowledge, entertain them, or cause them to pause and think about their lifestyles, goals, and behavior. Authors must take special delight in this opportunity to make a mark on the world—even if only one person is positively changed by your message, you will have made an impact on a stranger's way of thinking.

"My life was distinctly focused by the classic, *Black Beauty*," recounts Gilda, a novelist. "I was reared in a strange, unloving family where no one ever smiled or spoke kindly. I felt out of place because I had the joy of life in my spirit and I remember feeling it as a strong force even from the age of three. I was constantly admonished for being silly—finding happiness in flowers, giggling at my own jokes, and making up skits which had funny endings. No one I knew ever talked about love.

"An aunt came to take care of my brothers and sisters and me when I was five, because my parents had to attend a funeral out of town. She had the same glint in her eye as I did and we bonded immediately. I remember other relatives dourly whispering about her irreverent view of life, and figured I had met a kindred spirit. She read—and gave—me *Black Beauty*. I identified with the horse and the hope and love message in the book, and I knew from that day onward that love was the most important and sustaining force in the world. I probably couldn't have verbalized it back then, but I *knew*. I vowed to find and give love as soon as I could grow up and get away from my overly serious, unaffectionate parents.

"I saw every love story that came to the movie theater, read countless romances when I was a pre-teen, and as an adolescent and adult searched for authors who revealed the intricacies of love between the sexes, in friendships, and the love for the preciousness of life. I devoted myself to finding a romantic partner as if my life depended on it, and I truly believe that without mutual, sharing, caring love, I would wither away and die. I did find a soul-mate and, of course, learned how to nourish love and keep it as warm and wonderful as the first magical attraction.

"My life's driving force rests squarely on the truth I perceived in the novel *Black Beauty*. Perhaps another author could have reinforced my life, but I am filled with gratitude that there was *any* book which revealed the importance of love. I started writing my own love stories when I was an adolescent and the same thread is woven throughout my novels today."

George, a screenplay writer, forever was impressed when, as a young teenager, he read *The Fountainhead*. "I was marked with the message that a lone person can overcome enormous odds if he believes in himself. It has been a credo for my entire life."

Many of you have probably been changed by insights revealed in poetry, novels, plays, and movies. You now have the challenge to effect similar changes in the future generations.

Exploring

When the curious discover you are a writer, they usually want to know what *kind* of writing you do. People have an unspoken, programmed barometer of respect concerning the varieties of writers, usually related to how much money you make from your talents. This materialistic gauge is of little value, for all types of writing are creative and a unique expression.

You may have put your writing skills to work in one area and labeled yourself a novelist, poet, nonfiction, or technical writer. Once you have achieved some success in one area, try another. You may find intense pleasure in a new avenue or become frustrated within its confines, but you will have investigated a different potential. Your horizons expand when you consider that writing has endless possibilites and that you can investigate them all.

In the past your authors wrote mainly poetry and nonfiction, but we have learned to use our psychological knowledge for authentic character behavior and believable dialogue in screenplays. Screenplay writing was totally foreign to us but we accepted the challenge as a new frontier. It's extremely different from the outlining, chapter restrictions, and anecdotal style of nonfiction, but equally rewarding. We have also increased our creative pursuits to include novels. We have learned that you can write in all the rooms of your creative mansion.

The rules and skills of another writing form are easily acquired by reading specialized books, talking to fellow writers in different fields, and constantly reading current material that informs you of the public's interests.

Sheila, a journalist for many years, recently tried her hand at a novel. "I had some problems at first, because a newspaper story has to grab the audience's attention immediately and tell the complete story in the first sentence—the old who-what-when-where-and-why formula. The rest of the piece elaborates on that first sentence. I found myself beginning my novel with sentences like, 'This story is about. . . .' I realized I had plenty of time to describe my heroes and their motivations and that I could even be poetic. I find novel writing refreshing compared to the deadline-filled world of journalism."

Whenever you switch gears from one type of writing to another, you will be more likely to meet members from different sides of the writing family and add to your accumulation of knowledge and experience. We must continue to grow and learn to keep abreast of the times and to maintain a modern writing style. Everyone we encounter adds to the file we keep of future material.

"Whenever I begin to feel like a hermit, I follow a prescribed routine of re-entry into the hustle and bustle of life," reports Jennie, a novelist. "I spend a day at the library, reading all the current magazines. I watch the patrons, noting their dress and interests and making mental notes of their moods.

"Then I visit the hospital and follow a friend who is working as a volunteer, dispensing coffee and chit-chat. The varieties of patients eager to exchange conversation with a sympathetic visitor always stuns me. Each person's life contains the makings of a novel. I always end up on the maternity ward, where the magic of birth gives me a sense of the continuum of generations.

"My final stop for keeping in touch with the world is the neighborhood hamburger heaven where teenagers hang around attempting to overcome their shyness and impress each other. They are so filled with life and promise that I feel back in the mainstream, rejuvenated, and able to write again. I feel so lucky to be a writer, able to define and present the different stages of life and the ways in which each age group handles the complexities of living."

Passing It On

All writers have a creative responsibility which goes beyond personal dedication, assertive marketing approaches, and self-motivation. We have a duty to assist beginning authors by passing on our expertise learned from years of experiences, good and bad. Many would-be writers never move beyond dreaming about writing to taking the plunge because no one encourages their aspirations or takes time to explain the realities connected with the writing life.

You may feel uncomfortable when a young writer asks you to comment on material or seeks advice on how to begin submitting works. Some established writers fear hurting a beginner's feelings when works need extensive revisions or have glaring faults in style. Any serious artist will not be offended if you point out errors in an atmosphere of helpful, constructive advice, but will be grateful for the time and effort you extend on his behalf.

Discussing writing and submission policies with an inexperienced but talented newcomer will be a cherished gift from you and very often sparks new ideas for your future writing.

Jamie, the poet, says, "I still take time to explain to unpublished bards that most editors don't want to read a lengthy, personal letter when they review submissions. They want to see talent in a poem, not read letters about sensitive souls. My advice takes only a few minutes but saves amateurs from appearing foolish when they seek publication. I pass on my experiences whenever I am asked, because it feels good to give an aspiring writer some helpful hints."

Sharing adds to your self-esteem, because any selfless act increases our sense of worth and adds to our feelings of kinship with other artists. Generous writers, not believing that everyone should suffer as they did, gladly encourage and advise those climbing onto the creative ladder. We are all members of the same psychological family—the watchers, probers, and visionaries of our brief time on earth.

Louis L'Amour, a world-famous writer of Westerns, recently spoke during a celebration near our home, saying he believed a new and amazing frontier was beginning in our society—a frontier of creative expression unknown before. He has felt the vibrations in his travels around the world. He senses a rekindling spirit of originality in writers which will have a profound impact on mankind.

When we spoke with him, Mr. L'Amour had piercing questions about our book for writers. He received no encouragement as a beginning author and believes a writer should depend only on himself to keep motivation high and shine his own beam on a goal to write better every day. He said to forget what the critics say and write for your intended audiences, pleasing them and yourself with your best efforts.

An older gentleman, he still has the shining, twinkling eyes of a young person, enjoying his craft and entertaining millions. He maintains his creative delight, even though some of his works are still rejected by editors.

In order to keep an enthusiastic, optimistic attitude toward writing, we must always value our ability to perceive the ordinary or mundane and record it as new, finding innate satisfaction in the pursuit of writing.

A Final Note—Keeping Aware

As your career develops, remember that productivity will increase in proportion to the attention you pay to your inner psychological mechanisms.

Your ongoing awareness of the unconscious's efforts to drain energies from creativity will keep psychological undoings caged and controlled.

Only you can maintain the watch on your unconscious, negative forces. We have enjoyed describing the ammunition required to fight against the negatives and allow the positive creative flow to flourish.

All of us are fortunate to be gifted with special sensitivities and a burning drive to express our unique views about the mysteries of life.

Use your talent all your days and never let discouragement replace the joy of following your song.

INDEX

Other Writer's Digest Books

General Writing Books
    Writer's Market, $17.95
    Beginning Writer's Answer Book, edited by Polking, et al $9.95
    How to Get Started in Writing, by Peggy Teeters $10.95
    Law and the Writer, edited by Polking and Meranus (paper) $7.95
    Make Every Word Count, by Gary Provost (paper) $6.95
    Treasury of Tips for Writers, edited by Marvin Weisbord (paper) $6.95
    Writer's Resource Guide, 488 pp. $12.95

Magazine/News Writing
    Craft of Interviewing, by John Brady $9.95
    Magazine Writing: The Inside Angle, by Art Spikol $12.95
    Magazine Writing Today, by Jerome E. Kelley $10.95
    Newsthinking: The Secret of Great Newswriting, by Bob Baker $11.95
    Stalking the Feature Story, by William Ruehlman $9.95
    Write On Target, by Connie Emerson $12.95
    Writing and Selling Non-Fiction, by Hayes B. Jacobs $12.95

Fiction Writing
    Fiction Writer's Market, edited by Fredette and Brady $16.95
    Creating Short Fiction, by Damon Knight $11.95
    Handbook of Short Story Writing, edited by Dickson and Smythe (paper) $6.95
    How to Write Best-Selling Fiction, by Dean R. Koontz $13.95
    How to Write Short Stories that Sell, by Louise Boggess $9.95
    One Way to Write Your Novel, by Dick Perry (paper) $6.95
    Secrets of Successful Fiction, by Robert Newton Peck $8.95
    Writing the Novel: From Plot to Print, by Lawrence Block $10.95

Special Interest Writing Books
    Children's Picture Book: How to Write It, How to Sell It, by Ellen E.M. Roberts $17.95
    Complete Book of Scriptwriting, by J. Michael Straczynski $14.95
    Guide to Greeting Card Writing, edited by Larry Sandman $10.95
    How to Write and Sell Your Personal Experiences, by Lois Duncan $10.95
    How to Write "How-To" Books and Articles, by Raymond Hull (paper) $8.95
    Mystery Writer's Handbook, edited by Lawrence Treat (paper) $8.95
    The Poet and the Poem, Revised edition by Judson Jerome $13.95
    Poet's Handbook, by Judson Jerome $11.95
    Successful Outdoor Writing, by Jack Samson $11.95
    TV Scriptwriter's Handbook, by Alfred Brenner $13.95
    Travel Writer's Handbook, by Louise Purwin Zobel $13.95
    Writing and Selling Science Fiction, Compiled by The Science Fiction Writers of America (paper) $7.95
    Writing for Children & Teenagers, by Lee Wyndham. Revised edition by Arnold Madison $10.95
    Writing to Inspire, by Gentz, Roddy, et al $14.95

The Writing Business

Complete Handbook for Freelance Writers, by Kay Cassill $14.95
How to Be a Successful Housewife/Writer, by Elaine Fantle Shimberg $10.95
How You Can Make $20,000 a Year Writing, by Nancy Edmonds Hanson (paper) $6.95
Jobs For Writers, edited by Kirk Polking $11.95
Profitable Part-time/Full-time Freelancing, by Clair Rees $10.95
Writer's Survival Guide: How to Cope with Rejection, Success, and 99 Other Hang-Ups of the Writing Life, by Jean and Veryl Rosenbaum $12.95

To order directly from the publisher, include $1.50 postage and handling for 1 book and 50¢ for each additional book. Allow 30 days for delivery.

Writer's Digest Books, Department B
9933 Alliance Road, Cincinnati OH 45242
Prices subject to change without notice.

Writer's DIGEST

THE WORLD'S LEADING MAGAZINE FOR WRITERS

Would you like to:

● get up-to-the-minute reports on the writing markets?

● receive the advice of editors and professional writers about what to write and how to write it to maximize your opportunities for getting published?

● read interviews of leading authors that reveal their secrets of success?

● hear what experts have to say about writing and selling fiction, nonfiction, and poetry?

● get a $3 discount?

(See other side for details.)